Crispin Thurlow, Christa Dürscheid, Federica Diémoz (Eds.)
Visualizing Digital Discourse

Language and Social Life

Editors
David Britain
Crispin Thurlow

Volume 21

Visualizing Digital Discourse

Interactional, Institutional and Ideological Perspectives

Edited by
Crispin Thurlow
Christa Dürscheid
Federica Diémoz

DE GRUYTER
MOUTON

ISBN 978-1-5015-2713-5
e-ISBN (PDF) 978-1-5015-1011-3
e-ISBN (EPUB) 978-1-5015-1018-2
ISSN 2364-4303

Library of Congress Control Number: 2019951930

Bibliographic information published by the Deutsche Nationalbibliothek
The Deutsche Nationalbibliothek lists this publication in the Deutsche Nationalbibliografie;
detailed bibliographic data are available on the Internet at http://dnb.dnb.de.

© 2021 Walter de Gruyter, Inc., Berlin/Boston
This volume is text- and page-identical with the hardback published in 2020.
Typesetting: Integra Software Services Pvt. Ltd.
Printing and Binding: CPI books, GmbH, Leck

www.degruyter.com

Dedicated to the memory of Federica Diémoz

Crispin, Christa and Federica, Neuchâtel, November 2017
(photo courtesy of Christina Siever)

Contents

Author bios —— IX

Crispin Thurlow and Christa Dürscheid
Introduction: Turning to the visual in digital discourse studies —— 1

Rodney H. Jones
1   Towards an embodied visual semiotics:
    Negotiating the right to look —— 19

Part 1: Besides words and writing

Crispin Thurlow and Vanessa Jaroski
2   "Emoji invasion": The semiotic ideologies of *language endangerment* in multilingual news discourse —— 45

Georg Albert
3   Beyond the binary: Emoji as a challenge to the image-word distinction —— 65

Rachel Panckhurst and Francesca Frontini
4   Evolving interactional practices of emoji in text messages —— 81

Part 2: The social life of images

Sirpa Leppänen
5   Revisualization of classed motherhood in social media —— 107

Axel Schmidt and Konstanze Marx
6   Making Let's plays watchable: An interactional approach to gaming visualizations —— 131

Dorottya Cserző
7   Intimacy at a distance: Multimodal meaning making in video chat tours —— 151

Rebecca Venema and Katharina Lobinger
8 Visual bonding and intimacy: A repertoire-oriented study of photo-sharing in close personal relationships —— 171

Part 3: Designing multimodal texts

Hartmut Stöckl
9 Multimodality and mediality in an image-centric semiosphere – A rationale —— 189

Lara Portmann
10 Designing "good taste": A social semiotic analysis of corporate Instagram practices —— 203

Jana Pflaeging
11 Diachronic perspectives on viral online genres: From images to words, from lists to stories —— 227

Dorothee Meer and Katharina Staubach
12 Social media influencers' advertising targeted at teenagers: The multimodal constitution of credibility —— 245

Index —— 271

Author bios

Georg Albert is a tenured academic assistant for linguistics in the Department of German Language and Literature at the University of Koblenz-Landau, Germany. In 2012, he completed a PhD at the University of Mannheim with a thesis examining innovative writing and syntactic variation in online chats and discussion boards. His research interests include semiotics, multimodality and media theory, interactional linguistics, sociolinguistics, language change and variation.

Dorottya Cserző completed her PhD at the Centre for Language and Communication at Cardiff University, Wales, UK. Her research project explored the domestic use of videochat through the analysis of video recordings and interviews. She is co-editor of *Downscaling Culture: Revisiting Intercultural Communication* (2016, Cambridge Scholars).

Francesca Frontini is Associate Professor ("maître de conférences") in Computational Linguistics at the Paul-Valéry University of Montpellier in France where she is also a member of the Laboratoire Praxiling. She earned a PhD from the University of Pavia, Italy, with a thesis in corpus linguistics and later worked at the Institute for Computational Linguistics in Pisa. Her research interests lie in natural language processing, corpus linguistics, computational lexicography, digital humanities, as well as language resources, creation, standardisation and preservation.

Vanessa Jaroski completed her PhD in language and communication at the University of Bern, Switzerland. As part of a larger SNSF-funded project (*What's up, Switzerland?*), her thesis examined the representation of digital media in international news media discourse from a multimodal and multilingual perspective. In this work, she explored the intersection of language, media and semiotic ideologies with a particular view to women and girls. This project also centered on the development of an open-access, participatory archive, the *Digital Discourse Database* (www.digitaldiscoursedatabase.org).

Rodney H. Jones is Professor of Sociolinguistics and Head of the Department of English Language and Applied Linguistics at the University of Reading, England, UK. He has published widely in the areas of digital literacies, mediated discourse analysis and health communication.

Sirpa Leppänen is a Professor in the Department of Language and Communication Studies at the University of Jyväskylä, Finland. Drawing on insights provided by sociolinguistics, discourse studies, the study of multimodality and cultural studies, she has investigated a range of informal and interest-driven social media discourses. She has published widely on (1) semiotic (linguistic, discursive, visual, auditory) diversity as a resource for interaction and cultural production in translocal social media, (2) identifications and communality online, and (3) transgression as a means for cultural production, digital work and political activism.

Katharina Lobinger is Assistant Professor for Online Communication at the Institute of Digital Technologies for Communication at USI (Università della Svizzera italiana), Switzerland. Her main research interests include networked photography, online communication, digital (visual) culture, ethics for the digital age, and creative and visual research methods. She is principal investigator of the project "Visualized relationships – functions and problems" funded by the Swiss National Science Foundation. She is currently chair of the visual communication division of the German Communication Association.

Author bios

Konstanze Marx is Full Professor in German Linguistics at the Greifwald University, Germany. Before she was also Research Fellow in the Department of Pragmatics at the Leibniz Institute of German Language and the Technical University of Berlin. She studied German, Phonetics, Media Science and Educational Science at the University of Jena and completed her Habilitation on cyberbullying at the Technical University of Berlin. Her research focuses on internet linguistics, language and emotion, and medialinguistic prevention. She is co-founder of *Journal für Medienlinguistik/Journal for Media Linguistics*.

Dorothee Meer is academic counsellor in Applied Linguistics and German Linguistics and Didactics at the Ruhr-University Bochum, Germany. Her publications include monographs and chapters on discourse analysis and academic talk, as well as chapters on multimodality and digital media.

Rachel Panckhurst is Associate Professor in Computational Linguistics at Paul-Valéry University in Montpellier, France, where she is also member of the *Dipralang* laboratory. Her research interests include mediated digital discourse, mobile technology and innovative eLearning practices. She directed the *sud4science* project (sud4science.org); was director of Montpellier University's METICE Centre for open, distance and digital education; and has authored or edited over 190 publications, including three books.

Jana Pflaeging is a researcher in English and applied linguistics in the Department of English and American Studies at Salzburg University, Austria. She is currently pursuing a binational PhD at Salzburg University, Austria, and Halle-Wittenberg University, Germany. Her research interests are in multimodal genre studies and text/discourse linguistics. Trained in English linguistics and fine arts, she explores the synergies between both fields when creating visualizations of linguistic and multimodal theories, methods, and data.

Lara Portmann is a doctoral candidate at the University of Bern, Switzerland. Her current project focuses on UX writing as a site for studying audience design, 'digital pragmatics' and the language-ideological implications of wordsmiths. As with the chapter here, she is also interested in social semiotic approaches to digital media representations; this work has already appeared in major international venues such as *New Media & Society*.

Axel Schmidt is Research Fellow in the Department of Pragmatics at the Leibniz Institute of German Language and Professor in the Media and Communication Department at the University of Mannheim, Germany. He studied Sociology and Educational Science in Frankfurt am Main University, completed a PhD at Koblenz-Landau University on peer-group communication, and then a post-doctoral (Habilitation) project at the University of Basel (Switzerland) on staging in reality television. His research focuses on theatre, television, video games as well as on interaction analysis and multimodal video analysis. Currently he is investigating interactions in media productions.

Katharina Staubach is a postgraduate researcher at Ruhr-University Bochum, Germany. She is currently working on the GramKidSII project (Grammatische Kenntnisse in der Sekundarstufe II) directed by Professor Björn Rothstein. Her publications to date focus on issues of multimodality and digital media.

Hartmut Stöckl is Full Professor of English and Applied Linguistics in the Department of English and American Studies at Salzburg University, Austria. His main research areas are in semiotics, media/text linguistics/stylistics, pragmatics and linguistic multimodality research. He is particularly interested in the linkage of language and image in modern media, typography and an aesthetic appreciation of advertising. A volume on '*shifts towards image-centricity in contemporary multimodal practices*' with Routledge/New York (2019) is his most recent co-edited book.

Crispin Thurlow is Professor of language and communication based in the Department of English at the University of Bern, Switzerland. His research examines the social semiotics of difference and inequality in contemporary life, particularly in the contexts of global mobilities and digital media. His more recent publications include *Elite Discourse: The Rhetorics of Status, Privilege and Power* (2018, Routledge) and *The Business of Words: Wordsmiths, Linguists and Other Language Workers* (2020, Routledge).

Rebecca Venema is doctoral candidate and research/teaching assistant at the Institute of Digital Technologies for Communication at USI (Università della Svizzera italiana), Switzerland. From 2013 until 2017 she was a research associate at the Centre for Media, Communication and Information Research (ZeMKI) at the University of Bremen. Her research interests include (visual) networked everyday communication, norms and ethics of communication, ethics for the digital age, methods of repertoire-oriented cross-media research, and research ethics.

Crispin Thurlow and Christa Dürscheid
Introduction: Turning to the visual in digital discourse studies

1 Setting the scene

In a chapter titled 'New frontiers in interactive multimodal communication' for a handbook on *Language and Digital Communication*, internationally renowned scholar of language and digital media Susan Herring (Herring, 2015: 402) remarks on the need for scholars to develop more properly multimodal approaches to computer-mediated communication. This is what she says: "An approach needs to be developed that analyzes disparate modes in relation to one another, ideally with a common set of research questions, methods, and so forth, to permit meaningful comparisons across modes and across platforms." An approach such as this, Herring goes on to explain, requires attending to the way different modes interact (or not) in different digital texts and contexts.

It is precisely this understanding, indeed this empirical reality, which motivates our volume here. Although we do not claim to offer a monolithic approach or even a common set of research questions, we believe *Visualizing Digital Discourse* is the first dedicated volume of its kind which brings together the work of language and communication scholars committed to understanding the role of visuality (and multimodality) in the context of digital media. The volume showcases the work of leading scholars, established scholars and emerging scholars from across Europe, and addresses a diverse range of digital media platforms (e.g. messaging, video-chat, social media, gaming, video-sharing, photo-sharing), communicative settings (e.g. interpersonal, commercial, institutional), visual modalities (e.g. written language, typography, emojis, photography, video, layout) and methodologies (e.g. discourse analysis, corpus-based analysis, social semiotics, ethnography, conversation analysis) and languages (e.g. French, German, Italian, English, Finnish). Throughout, contributors are specifically focused on understanding the particular role of visual communication in (or about) these digital media platforms as a way to better understand how linguistic and communicative practices are multimodally accomplished. Sometimes visual resources (e.g. typography, photos, emojis, video) are central, at other times they are incidental; regardless, they are always integral to the servicing of people's interactional, institutional and/or ideological objectives.

Whether online or offline, digitally mediated or face-to-face, everyday communicators take up and combine different 'semiotic resources' (cf. van Leeuwen, 2005) in ways which are sometimes creative, sometimes strategic, but always purposeful and meaningful.

As its title suggests, *Visualizing Digital Discourse* is situated primarily within that field of research known as computer-mediated discourse analysis (e.g. Herring, 2007, 2013), new media sociolinguistics (e.g. Danesi, 2016) or just digital discourse studies (see Thurlow, 2018). We will not rehearse the literature here; suffice it to say, however, the study of linguistic and communicative practices in the context of digital media is now well established. This is also a field which has historically been driven by edited collections, starting with Susan Herring's (1996) ground-breaking *Computer-mediated Communication: Linguistic, Social and Cross-cultural Perspectives*. (Our volume's sub-title is styled partly to pay homage to her volume.) Other productive takes on the field include the volumes by Thurlow & Mroczek (2011), Jones, et al. (2015), Georgakopoulou & Spilioti (2015a), Squires (2018) and, most recently, Bou-Franch & Garcés-Conejos Blitvich (2019). Still within English-language scholarship, a number of important journal special issues have likewise helped drive the field; notably, for example, Androutsopoulos (2006) and Androutsopoulos & Beißwenger (2008). The range of perspectives represented in our volume responds either directly or indirectly to the kinds of issues and recommendations proposed over the years by these collections and special issues, as well as by prominent scholars like Susan Herring (ibid.), Jannis Androutsopoulos (e.g. 2011a), Naomi Baron (e.g. 2010), Lauren Squires (e.g. 2010), and so on. We certainly recognize from amongst this field, the scholarship of Rodney Jones (e.g. 2009), lead contributor to the current volume. We might even mention some of our own contributions over the years: Crispin Thurlow (e.g. 2006, 2014, 2018) and, especially in the German-language world, Christa Dürscheid (e.g. Dürscheid et al., 2010; Jucker & Dürscheid, 2012). While trying to keep up with the latest technological changes, digital discourse studies has constantly sought to stay current, undertaking a number of key theoretical and methodological 'turns'. One of the most notable of these was a turn towards more situated (e.g. ethnographic) studies of new-mediated linguistic and communicative practices. As indicated in the Herring quote above, we are beginning to witness rising scholarly interest in – a turn towards – the inherent, unavoidable multimodality of digital media.

In some ways, multimodality should always have been a taken-for-granted in new media sociolinguistics. It is certainly nowadays regarded as a core concept in sociocultural linguistics and discourse analysis more generally (e.g. Jewitt, 2004; Kress & van Leeuwen, 2001; Scollon, 2001; and, especially, Norris & Jones, 2005).

Often, however, a lot of digital discourse scholarship continues – perhaps not altogether surprisingly – to be structured by its disciplinary focus on language and linguistic phenomena. The increasingly multi-media and inherently multimodal nature of digital communication makes this single-track, and sometimes single-minded, approach more and more untenable (see Georgakopoulou & Spilioti, 2015b, for a similar point of view). As we say, this is especially germane given the growing complexity of the *multi-media* formats of newer new media, brought about by the inevitable *convergence* of old and new media (cf. Jenkins, 2006) and the *layering* of new media with other new media (cf. Androutsopoulos, 2011; Myers, 2010). Regardless, digital discourse studies is certainly in need of advanced analytical equipment if it is to keep track of the changing significance (in both common senses of the word) of language in the *synaesthetic* (cf. Kress, 2003) and *heteroglossic* (cf. Androutsopoulos, 2011b) spaces of digital media. A fully multimodal analysis will, of course, require an even wider scope than the one we offer here; nonetheless, we hope *Visualizing Digital Discourse*, with its special attention to visuality, begins to point the way.

There are certainly good reasons for opening up digital discourse studies to a broader multimodal perspective, as Thurlow (2017) has recently attested. The most obvious of which lies in simply paying more attention to visual communication per se. We know well, for example, that even word-based digital discourse is often as much visual as it is linguistic, concerned as much with the look of words as with their semantic or stylistic properties (e.g., Vaisman, 2014). In addition to research on issues like orthographic and typographic design, however, there is certainly some useful work being done on the communicative uses of visual resources such as emoji, video, GIFs, and non-moving images (see Highfield & Leaver, 2016, for a useful review). In this regard, we note two good examples of research in precisely this direction: Androutsopoulos and Tereick (2015) and Dürscheid and Siever (2017). Beyond these moves, there is also value in considering metadiscursive perspectives; in other words, research which examines how visuality in digital discourse is talked about by everyday users. By the same token, scholars might examine how digital media are visually represented in, for example, commercial advertising, print or broadcast news, cinema and television narratives and/or public policy and educational settings. Certainly, and as Thurlow and his colleagues have shown (Thurlow, 2017; Thurlow, Aiello & Portmann, 2019), visual discourse encodes and combines a range of influential media and semiotic ideologies. Again, *Visualizing Digital Discourse* addresses both these ways of approaching visuality from a metadiscursive angle.

2 Organization of the book

The current volume has its origins in a conference *Visualizing (in) the New Media* hosted by the co-editors in November 2017 as part of a four-year, multi-party research project funded by the Swiss National Science Foundation (see Acknowledgments). The co-editors lead two of the projects' constituent sub-projects. Definitely not a conference proceedings, our volume represents a carefully, competitively curated selection of papers initially presented at the conference. To start, the initial rejection rate for conference papers was about 20 to 25%. We started with chapters by the conference's three original keynote speakers (Jones, Leppänen and Stöckl), all internationally regarded scholars in their own right. We then solicited and accepted a further seven chapters based on work initially presented at the conference; these chapters reported novel research findings and/or cohered nicely around our three core perspectives on visuality in digitial media (see below). These seven chapters were also selected based on a review of full drafts submitted competitively, with a rejection rate of some 35%. Finally, two additional chapters were specially commissioned, including one co-authored by editor Crispin Thurlow.

Visualizing Digital Discourse is organized into three main sections. Following this short introduction, we open with a powerful framing chapter by Rodney Jones, one of the world's leading scholars working at the interface of sociolinguistics, digital media studies, and multimodal discourse studies. As a case-study examination of selfies and surveillance culture, Jones' chapter sets the scene perfectly with regards the volume's scholarly focus and critical stance. Each subsequent section of the book opens with a chapter by a prominent, established scholar of digital/visual discourse studies. We provide more detailed summaries of all the chapters below, but we first offer the following potted account of the book's organization.

In Part 1 (*Besides Words and Writing*), we have three chapters which center on micro-level communicative practices but also from macro-level perspectives. Focusing on the poster child of new-media visuality – emojis – the chapters offer, respectively, a metadiscursive, theoretical, and quantitative approach. In their chapter, Crispin Thurlow & Vanessa Jaroski take up the cultural politics introduced by Jones. Drawing on an archive of multilingual news stories, they consider the emergence of a discourse of 'language endangerment' whereby emjois are viewed as a threat to words. Specifically, they pinpoint three rhetorical tactics and then examine the kinds of semiotic ideologies this discourse reinscribes. In the next chapter, Georg Albert takes up issues of semiosis by asking what kind of communicative mode emojis are, whether they function like words or images or something in between. With illustrative examples, he attempts to answer the question by considering how emojis signify or make meaning in practice. In their chapter, Rachel Panckhurst and Francesca Frontini take things to the ground by looking at actual uses of emoticons/emojis in a very large corpus of SMS messages; they identify their three key functions and examine their grammatical significance. Together, these three chapters establish the inherent, complex multimodalities of digital discourse, while surfacing some of the cultural-political and theoretical challenges in making sense of digital life beyond or besides language.

In Part 2 (*The Social Life of Images*), we have four chapters which focus on the way visual resources are used for managing everyday, personal relations – or for personalizing digital discourse anew. In other words, these chapters demonstrate precisely why visual communication really matters to people. In her opening chapter, Sirpa Leppänen examines how different 'styles of visuality' are taken up by everyday social media users – specifically, blogging mothers. She too considers the ideological implications of these visual practices which offer opportunities for parody but which are also rooted in normative judgement. In their chapter, Axel Schmidt and Konstanze Marx provide an interesting link between personal practice and the kinds of institutional practices which are otherwise the focus of Part 3. They examine *Let's Plays* which are curated online videos of gamers sharing and commenting on their first-hand playing. The authors consider how participants draw on, and combine, linguistic and visual resources for making their videos not only comprehensible (i.e. easy to follow) but also entertaining and watchable. In the next chapter, Dorottya Cserző presents her research on videochat (e.g. Skype) and the way ordinary users take advantage of its distinctive visual affordance for sustaining long-distance contact and intimacy. The specific focus of her analysis are virtual tours (e.g. of a hotel room) conducted between two siblings separated while one of them is travelling away from home. Sticking with the theme of relational maintenance, and in the fourth and last chapter of Part 2, Rebecca Venema and Katharina Lobinger report the results of a 'repertoire-oriented' study in which they interview romantic partners and close friends about their sharing of photos. In effect, the authors offer an empirically-based retort to popular misconceptions about visuality in digital media; in their case, informants report how photos, as both symbolic and material objects, are a central part of their long-term relationships and friendships. In fact, from across the four chapters in Part 2, we have first-hand evidence of everyday visual literacies at work, where visuality is always meaningfully and sometimes skillfully or creatively taken up.

In Part 3 (*Designing Multimodal Texts*), we have four chapters which examine digital visuality in more obviously institutional or commercial contexts (as opposed to personal or interpersonal ones). The section opens with a chapter by Hartmut Stöckl, a leading scholar known for his work on the intersection of media theory and multimodality. In his chapter, he too takes a more theoretical-cum-methodological tack and, like Jones, considers how broader cultural landscapes are being changed by the rise of visuality (cf. Kress & van Leuween, 2001). Specifically, he demonstrates the role of 'image-centricity' in both old/print media and new/social media, asking how and what has changed, if anything. In many ways, the remaining chapters all respond to this polemic. In her chapter, Lara Portmann presents a social semiotic analysis of Instagram used for the strategic purposes of corporate marketing; her specific, topical focus is the visualization (and aestheticization) of food by two major grocery chains in Switzerland. Often heralded for their egalitarian, participatory potential, social media here are again implicated in the production of social hierarchies of taste and, thus, of privilege. In a similar vein, the chapter by Jana Pflaeging takes up social networking and, specifically, a viral genre known as the 'listicle'. She presents a diachronic analysis for tracking the shifting multimodal composition of this particular genre, and finds a counter-intuitive (given Stöckl's position) move from images to words. In the final chapter of Part 3, Dorothee Meer and Katharina Staubach examine how credibility is multimodally produced by social media influencers in so-called haul videos on YouTube. As a case-study, they consider the 'osmotic advertising' of one a well-known German influencer targeting young (female) people. Thanks to the four chapters in Part 3, we have evidence for the way images, video and visuality more generally are shifting institutional practice. We also see the role of visual communication plays in blurring boundaries between the personal and the commercial. As such, the book ends how it started, with a view to larger-scale cultural and ideological shifts happening through the visualization of/in digital discourse.

3 Detailed chapter summaries

In his 'flagship' chapter, **Rodney Jones** explores issues around the *embodied* nature of visual semiotics in the age of the smartphone, in particular, the ways in which people use everyday practices of making images of themselves and others to negotiate both 'being-in-the-world' (*Dasein*) and 'being-with' (and for) other social actors (*Mitsein*) (Heidegger, 2008) within various networks of power, status and social control. The rise of the world-wide web, digital imaging and graphic user interfaces in the late 1990s precipitated an intense interest in the fields of sociolinguistics and discourse analysis in multimodal communication, resulting in a range approaches to visual semiotics, including some that focused on the impact of image making on issues of power and social identity. The more recent rise of mobile digital communication, supported by digital video cameras and social media platforms such as Instagram and Snapchat, which compel users to constantly produce themselves and their experiences visually and to construe meaning from the visual representations of other people's experiences, presents significant challenges to the 'grammars' of visual communication developed at the turn of the century, forcing analysts to engage more fully with the ways multimodal meaning emerges not from 'signs' per se, but from *techno-somatic entanglements* in which the most important communicative resource is not what is visible, but communicators' embodied experiences of seeing it. 'Seeing' and 'being seen', in this regard, are never neutral, uninvolved acts: seeing is always entangled with the mediational means through which it is accomplished, with what is seen and what is happening to it, with what seeing *does* to the watcher and the watched, and with sets of rules and expectations associated with particular contexts, and particular societies, about who has the right to look, and who has the right to be seen. Jones argues that mobile digital photography has opened up possibilities for a more post-representational perspectives on visual semiotics – digital media have forced us to see not just images, but texts in general, along with 'bodies' and 'media' not as objects but as relational categories that intersect in complex moments of action that can only be understood by engaging with how they are *lived*. Rodney Jones calls for an approach to digital visual communication which combines social semiotics with phenomenology, particularly the post-phenomenological approaches of scholars like Ihde (2001), with the aim of helping us to understand how people use the embodied and affective dimensions of visual communication to negotiate their physical experiences in the world and their relationships with others. In order to illustrate this approach, he applies it to two current practices of digital imaging making: the embodied act of taking selfies, and the practice of using smartphones to record encounters with law enforcement officers. He shows how both 'selfies' and videos of police stops involve social actors performing the experience of seeing and being seen, and argue that this performance can have profound consequences on people's ability to articulate particular versions of the world and their place in it. Central to this ability is the use of technology to negotiate what Mirzoeff (2011) calls 'the right to look'. Claiming the right to look doesn't just mean claiming the right to look at the other. It's also about claiming the right to turn the camera around – to make oneself visible – to say 'look at me. I'm here'. As Mirzoeff (2011, p. 1) puts it: 'the right to look means requiring the recognition of the other in order to have a place from which to claim rights and to determine what is right'. This, Rodney Jones argues, should be the key focus of a new semiotics of the visual, not just how people look or what they see, but how they claim the right to look, and the right to be seen.

To open their chapter, **Crispin Thurlow and Vanessa Jaroski** start by nothing how news-makers commonly maintain an unduly negative perspective on the impact of digital technologies vis-à-vis people's linguistic and communicative practices. With their particular institutional and cultural investment as professional language workers, journalists consistently reproduce language-ideological depictions of digital discourse which exaggerate its newness and distinctiveness, and which erase individual variation, reflexivity and creativity. Against this backdrop, Thurlow & Jaroski examine an emerging but closely allied metadiscursive framing of digital discourse: the perceived threat to language posed by visual communication and, specifically, emojis. In this case, as they demonstrate, long-standing narratives of linguistic decline or ruin usually attributed to technology are redirected to the deleterious impact of visuality. They refer to this as a discourse of *language endangerment* (cf. Duchêne & Heller, 2007). Instead of a concern to defend (minority) languages from other (majority) languages, however, they find language itself being construed as autonomous and superior, and, more importantly, in need of protection from visual communication. Their study draws on in an in-house archive of news stories related to language, communication and digital media and, specifically, a sample of stories from January 2014 to September 2017 imported into *AntConc* for generating two corpora (French and English). Ultimately, Thurlow & Jaroski argue that the discourse of language endangerment is one rooted in, and constitutive of, not only language ideologies but also deep-seated *semiotic ideologies* (cf. Keane, 2003). In other words, as Thurlow (2017) has elsewhere argued, popular beliefs about digital media fundamentally misrecognize meaning-making in language, in visual communication, and in the inherently multimodal interplay of the two. In an otherwise visual age and at a time when visual literacies are so key (see Kress & van Leeuwen, 1996), it is especially problematic (or, at least, unhelpful), they argue, when journalists promote such contradictory, specious ideas about visual communication and about human communicative action more generally.

Quite apparently – as Thurlow & Jaroski prove – emojis are widely considered to be quintessential examples of visual communication in digital media. However, because any element of a writing system is clearly also a visual sign, **Georg Albert** argues that a more detailed, nuanced look at the semiotic qualities of signs is important. To this end, in his theoretical rather than empirical chapter he explains why emojis should not be simplistically identified with images; nor, he argues, are they graphemes either. Even though emojis are often thought to compensate for the lack of mimic signs in written discourse, their communicative uses are far more complex. Using as illustrative examples of private messages sent by acquaintances or drawn from his previous studies (e.g. Albert, 2015), Albert maps a better way to understand the diversity of visual signs with a semiotically informed focus on the functional dimensions of emojis, and by comparing them to various writing systems. For this, he orients to scholarship on symbols and writing from, for example, Nelson Goodman, Catherine Elgin and Christian Stetter as well as to Rudi Keller's reinterpretation of Charles S. Peirce's typology of signs. Ultimately, he argues, emojis should be understood in terms of the ways they are actually used rather than their origin or outward appearance. As an effect of their usage, for example, emojis have become conventionalized and are frequent features of written discourse. The more conventionalized a sign becomes, the less it resembles a prototypical image; as such, they end up sharing important features with certain customary elements of the writing system. By the same token, emojis are not straightforwardly equivalent to images either. Ultimately, therefore, argues Albert, emojis need to be treated as a phenomenon sui generis.

In their chapter, **Rachel Panckhurst and Francesca Frontini** examine actual uses of emojis by drawing on a large corpus of French-language text-messages. In their analysis, they pin-point three main usage situations: (a) *redundant addition* where an emoji is used in addition to written text, but it is not required in order to understand the text; (b) *necessary addition* where an emoji is also used but its inclusion is necessary in order to avoid misinterpretation; and (c) *lexical replacement* where an emoji is used instead of a word. Along these lines, Panckhurst & Frontini find that emojis are used more often redundantly (66%) or necessarily (28%), and sometimes as 'softeners' for lexical replacement (7%). Syntactically speaking, the positioning of emojis appears in descending order: final closure positions of text-messages and at the end of sentences (87%), the middle of messages (8%), and at the start of messages (1%). Then, by using automatic part-of-speech tagging, the authors also examine the immediate grammatical environment of emojis for a more in-depth analysis of linguistic functions which is also cross-compared with sociolinguistic variables (e.g. age, gender). In this regard, for example, they find that emojis are located most often at sentence/message closure (87%), and serve as boundary markers rather than as referential elements. However, in a comparison of these results with a 2017 questionnaire on French social media usage (Rascol, 2017), the authors note a slight increase of lexical replacement usage (14%). The chapter concludes by outlining areas for future research such as the need for diachronic comparisons with more recent data coming, for example, from the *What's up, Switzerland?* (see Ueberwasser & Stark, 2017), a project of which this volume's editors have been a part. By the same token, Panckhurst & Frontini also point to the value of exploring, amongst other things, intercultural variation and cross-platform differences.

In opening Part 2, **Sirpa Leppänen** focuses on what she calls 'revisualization' in social media practices. Focusing on Finland-based social media, she discusses how particular 'styles of visuality' are reanimated and subverted in constructions of, and interactions around, the shifting and contested social category of *motherhood*. Drawing on discourse studies, the study of multimodality and critical sociolinguistics, she examines how social media users/producers revisualize motherhood in often parodic ways. Accordingly, Leppänen argues that these revisualizations end up challenging neo-conservative ideological assumptions concerning the nuclear family and notions of good mothering. They also challenge the aesthetics of home purported in such popular social media genres as the 'homing blogs' of young women who have created highly aestheticized life journals of their home-based lives and lifestyles (see Jäntti et al., 2017). Ultimately, and following the work of Thurlow & Jaworski (2017) on elite discourse, Leppänen argues that social media parodies of motherhood nonetheless remain ambivalent and elitist in the way they orient to motherhood as a classed category. On the one hand, they can be seen as a form of transgressive political critique highlighting a representational style Hatherley (2018) refers to as a working class anti-Pygmalion aesthetics. On the other hand, however, and from a Bourdieusean perspective, they can be interpreted as disparaging the tastes of low class women, bringing class distinctions into even sharper focus.

In the next chapter, **Axel Schmidt and Konstanze Marx** turn to so-called *Let's Plays*; these are videos hosted on, say, YouTube where gamers present and comment on their first-hand games. The communicative setting is highly complex with the gaming presented for an absent audience but, for example, with a so-called facecam where the gamer is made visible as well as with sidebars for chatting about the game. All of which makes the matter of participation framework (Goffman, 1981) particularly interesting. For the audiences of *Let's Plays*, the games are obviously not playable, but they do need to be rendered entertaining or watchable. Indeed, as the authors note, these are one of the fastest-growing and least-studied kinds of fan production and one of the most successful genres on YouTube. It is for this reason that Schmidt & Marx seek to establish how precisely players make the games so watchable for viewers. To this end, they document how players use a combination of verbal and visual means to reintegrate interactivity and make the product immersive again. One pervasive practice is the formulation by players of their own actions, much of which is accomplished visually although ultimately multimodally. In fact, it cannot be conveyed solely through the visuals; verbal resources are needed for transforming the stream of visual events into a comprehensible trajectory of action.

In her chapter, **Dorottya Cserző** analyses virtual tours, a new practice made possible by the development and popularity of videochat. Today, videochat is available through a variety of platforms – most notably Skype and FaceTime – on a range of devices such as laptops, tablets and smartphones. In fact, the devices used make it increasingly easy to move around during a videochat session; as such, users can give each other virtual tours by moving the camera around to show off their environment. Through a systematic analysis of the structure of a virtual tour, Cserző documents the resources available to videochat users and the interactional functions of virtual tours. The main theoretical framework she uses is multimodal interaction analysis informed by nexus analysis – also sometimes referred to as mediated discourse analysis (Norris & Jones, 2005). This kind of approach combines the micro-analysis of speech, camera movement, gesture, posture, and gaze with a broader consideration for the materiality of devices, locations and bodies. Specifically, her analysis focuses on a recorded videochat session between Kate and Charlie, during which Charlie gives a virtual tour to his sister Kate. Cserző presents the virtual tour using a multimodal transcript combining conversation analysis and screenshots from the video. She shows how the camera movement is co-ordinated with Charlie's commentary and Kate's responses to create a coherent virtual tour. As the various features of the room are shown and framed, each one is jointly evaluated. It is in this way that Charlie and Kate align with each other by forming a shared stance. Amongst other things, Cserző shows how pointing the camera is a powerful interactional resource for directing attention in a way that is not possible in face to face interaction. Inevitably, however, the 'shower' must frame what is shown with verbal commentary, making the tours fully multimodal accomplishments.

In their chapter, **Rebecca Venema and Katharina Lobinger** examine the role and relevance of visual communication in these close social relationships. The taking and sharing of photos has, of course, become a highly routine part of people's lives and is fully integrated into their everyday interactions. Indeed, this is nowadays one of the key ways many social relationships are created and maintained. In this regard, Venema & Lobinger present a qualitative study of the way photos are used, both symbolically and as material objects, in couples' and friends' relationships. They take a cross-media approach which is grounded in the notions of 'polymedia' and repertoire-oriented media. A repertoire-oriented approach surfaces the role of visuals/visual interactions in the context of respondents' general communicative routines. Empirically speaking, they draw on 34 problem-focused, semi-structured single- and pair-interviews, applying qualitative thematic coding. Their findings confirm how pictures are essential resources for both couples and friends, but with differences in the way images are shared and integrated into everyday interactions. In fact, their findings run somewhat contrary to public debates about the negative implications of changing visual practices for social relationships. Photo-sharing is clearly used for the purposes of self-expression and self-representation. Photos also serve as materialized memories and thus another important emotional resource for couples/friends. Ultimately, as Venema & Lobinger show, this kind of visual communication is key for upholding relationships, not least because photo-sharing facilitates the maintenance of proximity, shared experiences and mutual bonds.

Opening Part 3 of the volume, **Hartmut Stöckl** proposes an explanation of *image-centricity* as a vital concept in multimodality research and reflects on its implications for media and genre. The central argument is that image-centric practices are crucially shaped by the technological and social affordances of media. Consequently, for example, Twitter or Instagram are likely to promote different multimodal genres and types of image-centricity as compared with magazine or newspaper articles. Based on widely accepted mediated and situational factors (see Herring, 2007), Stöckl sketches the central differences between old/print media and new/social media. These differences are used in a second step to develop general hypotheses about how the design of image-centric genres and practices are likely to differ – observations that may guide empirical research with large data sets. He concludes by offering some brief, rough-and-ready suggestions for studying image-centric media and communication. The chapter starts with a critical examination of image-centricity as re-developed from Caple's (2008) earlier notion of image-nuclearity. The centricity of images involves their compositional and perceptual dominance on the one hand, and their semantic and conceptual centrality on the other hand. He then teases out key mediational differences between print and social media, noting how both show signs of an increasing variety of image-centric genres. In this regard, Stöckl observes some of the typical features of social media which strongly affect image-centric practices and differ greatly from old-style print media: collaborative sharing of co-constructed messages, modal richness, a strong social indexicality of semiotic choices, and flexible/fast-paced message formats. Ultimately, he argues that image-centricity is not a newly 'emergent' trait in social media but one that is very 'familiar' from old media and that may be 'reconfigured' (Herring, 2013) through shareability, heightened media convergence and resignification in what Jucker & Dürscheid (2012) have previously labelled communicative act sequences.

In the next chapter, **Lara Portmann** examines the way food and foodways are visualized in social media; eating is of course a well-known site where judgements about taste are employed for boundary-marking and class status maintenance. As Bourdieu (1984: 5) famously notes, 'good taste' are matters of social distinction. With its strong emphasis on images, the photo-sharing platform Instagram is a perfect example of this practice. To this end, her chapter presents a social semiotic analysis of the corporate uses of Instagram by Switzerland's two major grocery chains, Coop and Migros. Combining visual content analysis and social semiotics, she offers first a quantitative-descriptive perspective on their posts and then a more qualitative-interpretive one, highlighting in particular the design and compositional meanings of photos. The quantitative results show how the foods depicted are largely mundane, unmarked, and decontextualized, which leads me to argue that in order to understand how these posts work; for this reason it becomes useful to look beyond what is shown and consider also *how* it is shown. In this regard, Portmann then discusses two visual-discursive tactics: materiality and modality. By deploying material attributes (e.g. marble surfaces or fabric napkins) and by using colour and texture, Coop and Migros aestheticize otherwise quite ordinary foods. By emphasising form over function in this way, these corporations construct privileged eating practices. For all their claims to participatory democracy or egalitarianism, these strategic uses of social media effectively reinforce social hierarchies of taste. Portmann argues that 'intangible' semiotic strategies like visual materiality and modality, when positioned vis-à-vis supposedly unambiguous representational resources like written language, can be used to 'fashion' banal goods in ways which both construct and obfuscate privilege.

In her chapter, **Jana Pflaeging** turns our attention to the world of so-called viral content providers (or aggregators) on Facebook – in particular, one called Distractify. Her specific interest lies in the genre known as the 'listicle' which Wikipedia hurriedly defines as short-form writing which uses a list as its thematic structure. Pflaeging's data comprise two sets of 50 exemplars of listicles elicited from Distractify in 2014 and 2017. She examines these materials through a diachronic approach to viral online genres, implemented through a multi-layer analysis of the genre's communicative situation, textual function, and (structural/rhetorical) multimodal composition. On this basis she identifies some general but revealing communicative trends. In 2014, for example, Distractify published articles such as *The 16 Greatest Battles Fought By The Most Courageous Cats Of Our Time* in list form. These multimodal documents were composed of $\bar{x}$ = 19.2 list-items typically employing a structurally and rhetorically central photograph, video, or GIF. Listicles show only few traces of a narrative discourse structure; instead, they present – often in no particular order – a spectrum of visual associations that Facebook users can enjoy. By 2017, however, the page space of listicles had been significantly reorganized with a noticeable decrease in visualization intensity and a list-logic that was no longer structurally or rhetorically maintained. Instead, in the 2017 subset (e.g. *A Guy Ordered One Slice Of Cheese From*

McDonald's And Twitter Lost It) were typically organized around long stretches of running text with an abundant embedding of topically-related Tweets used for narrating a single social occurrence. In effect, therefore, Distractify had turned to story-telling and this entailed a shift from image-centricity (see Stöckl, this volume) to word-centricity. It is in this way that Pflaeging documents an 'evolution' in viral online genres, one which shows how the design of their textual surfaces can change swiftly. This, she argues, also evidences a continual oscillation between commercial and interpersonal interests.

As the final chapter, **Dorothee Meer and Katharina Staubach** consider hugely popular 'haul' videos (or just hauls) posted on YouTube by so called social media influencers. Here, a person (usually young and female) presents their latest purchases to an audience of young, mainly female people. The authors present hauls as a digitally mediated form of *osmotic* advertising (after Katheder, 2008); unlike conventional print or TV advertising, young followers come to trust social media influencers as experts but also as peers or friends. Meer and Staubach's analysis focuses on the multimodal production of credibility in a case-study haul posted by the very successful German social media influencer Dagi Bee. In doing so, they attend closely to the *parasocial* (Horton and Wohl, 1956) strategies Dagi Bee uses for connecting with viewers. For example, they consider how she creates a tangibly shared living (i.e. bedroom) space, thereby staging herself as an older sister or friend. All of which makes her product recommendations more credible: friendly advice given by an older, more competent friend. Having said which, the authors also argue that Dagi Bee bears the hallmarks of a trickster (in Lévi-Strauss's, 1955, terms) as she leaves the amateur frame of the bedroom for an altogether more professional frame (e.g. posing like a model). Ultimately, though, her teenage fans/viewers are inclined to believe her recommendations because they experience her, on the one hand, as the trustworthy peer of roughly the same age, and on the other hand, as an expert in the field of fashion.

Acknowledgements: We take this opportunity to offer some important words of thanks which we do also on behalf of our esteemed colleague Federica who died in August 2019 after a serious illness. First and foremost, we are indebted to the Swiss National Science Foundation (SNSF Sinergia: CRSII1_160714) whose funding made possible the 2017 conference in Neuchâtel which was the impetus for the current volume. In this regard, we are enormously grateful to Etienne Morel, Christina Siever and Vanessa Jaroski who, as (post-)doctoral researchers on the SNSF project, oversaw so much of the conference organization. We offer special thanks to Crispin's student assistant Nicolas Rötlisberger for his meticulous, patient help with preparing the manuscript. Thanks are likewise due to Gwynne

Mapes, also at the University of Bern, for her last-minute editorial assistance with some of the chapters. We also thank Kirstin Börgen and Lukas Lehmann at De Gruyter for their patient, hands-on support. Finally, we are pleased to have the chance to acknowledge the indispensable, constant support of Elisabeth Stark and Simone Ueberwasser as, respectively, principal investigator and coordinator of the *What's up, Switzerland?* project – thank you, dear colleagues.

References

Albert, Georg. 2015. Semiotik und Syntax von Emoticons. *Zeitschrift für angewandte Linguistik* 62(1). 3–22.

Androutsopoulos, Jannis (ed.). 2006. Sociolinguistics and computer-mediated communication. Special Issue of *Journal of Sociolinguistics* 10(4).

Androutsopoulos, Jannis. 2011a. Language change and digital media: A review of conceptions and evidence. In Tore Kristiansen & Nik Coupland (eds.), *Standard Languages and Language Standards in a Changing Europe*, 145–161. Oslo: Novus.

Androutsopoulos, Jannis. 2011b. From variation to heteroglossia in the study of computer-mediated discourse. In Crispin Thurlow & Kristine Mroczek (eds.), *Digital Discourse: Language in the New Media*, 277–298. New York: Oxford University Press.

Androutsopoulos, Jannis & Michael Beißwenger (eds.). 2008. Data and methods in computer-mediated discourse analysis. Special Issue of *Language@Internet* 5.

Androutsopoulos, Jannis & Jana Tereick. 2015. Youtube: Language and discourse practices in participatory culture. In Alexandra Georgakopoulou & Teresa Spilioti (eds.), *The Routledge Handbook of Language and Communication*, 354–370. Abingdon: Routledge.

Baron, Naomi. (2010). *Always on: Language in an online and digital world*. New York: Oxford University Press.

Bou-Franch, Patricia & Pilar Garcés-Conejos Blitvich (eds.). 2019. *Analyzing Digital Discourse. New Insights and Future Directions*. London: Palgrave Macmillan.

Bourdieu, Pierre. (1984). *Distinction: A Social Critique of the Judgement of Taste* (trans. R Nice). Cambridge, MA: Harvard University Press.

Caple, Helen. 2008. Intermodal relations in image-nuclear news stories. In Len Unsworth (ed.), *Multimodal Semiotics. Functional Analysis in the Contexts of Education*, 125–138. London: Continuum.

Danesi, Marcel. 2016. *Language, society and new media sociolinguistics today*. New York: Routledge.

Duchêne, Alexandre & Monica Heller. 2007. Discourses of endangerment: Sociolinguistics, globalization and social order. In Alexandre Duchêne & Monica Heller (eds.), *Discourses of Endangerment: Interest and Ideology in the Defense of Languages*, 1–13. London: Continuum.

Dürscheid, Christa & Christina M. Siever. 2017. Jenseits des Alphabets – Kommunikation mit Emojis. *Zeitschrift für Germanistische Linguistik* 45(2),256–285.

Dürscheid, Christa, Franc Wagner & Sarah Brommer. 2010. *Wie Jugendliche schreiben. Schreibkompetenz und neue Medien*. Berlin: De Gruyter.

Georgakopoulou, Alexandra & Tereza Spilioti (eds). 2015a. *The Routledge Handbook of Language and Digital Communication*. London: Routledge.

Georgakopoulou, Alexandra & Tereza Spilioti (eds). 2015b. Introduction. In Alexandra Georgakopoulou & Tereza Spilioti (eds), *Handbook of Language and Digital Communication*, 1–16. London: Routledge.

Goffman, Erving. 1981. Footing. In Ervin Goffman (ed.), *Forms of talk*, 124–159. Philadelphia: University of Pennsylvania Press.

Hatherley, Frances. 2018. A working-class anti-Pygmalion aesthetics of the female grotesque in the photographs of Richard Billingham. *European Journal of Women's Studies* 25(3), 355–370.

Heidegger, Martin. 2008. *Being and Time*, Reprint edn. New York: Harper Perennial Modern Classics.

Herring, Susan C. 2007. A Faceted Classification Scheme for Computer-Mediated Discourse. *language@internet* 4.

Herring, Susan C. 2013. Discourse in Web 2.0: Familiar, reconfigured, and emergent. In Deborah Tannen & Anna Marie Trester (eds.), *Georgetown University Round Table on Languages and Linguistics 2011: Discourse 2.0: Language and New Media*, 1–25. Washington, DC: Georgetown University Press.

Herring, Susan C. 2015. New frontiers in interactive multimodal communication. In Alexandra Georgakopoulou & Tereza Spilioti (eds), *Handbook of Language and Digital Communication*, 398–402. London: Routledge.

Horton, Donald & Richard R. Wohl. 1956. Mass communication and para-social interaction: Observations on intimacy at a distance. *Psychiatry* 19, 215–229.

Ihde, Don. 2001. *Bodies in Technology*, 1st edn. Minneapolis: University of Minnesota Press.

Jäntti, Saara, Tuija Saresma, Sirpa Leppänen, Suvi Järvinen & Piia Varis. 2017. Homing blogs as ambivalent spaces for feminine agency. *Feminist Media Studies* 18(5), 888–904.

Jenkins, Henry. 2006. *Convergence Culture: When Old and New Media Collide*. New York NYU Press.

Jewitt, Carey. 2004. Multimodality and new communication technologies. In Philip Levine & Ron Scollon (eds.), *Discourse and Technology: Multimodal Discourse Analysis*, 198–195. Washington, DC: Georgetown

Jones, Rodney H. 2009. Dancing, skating and sex: Action and text in the digital age. *Journal of Applied Linguistics and Professional Practice* 6(3), 283–302.

Jones, Rodney H., Alice Chik & Christoph A. Hafner. 2015. *Discourse and Digital Practices: Doing Discourse Analysis in the Digital Age*. London: Routledge.

Jucker, Andreas H. & Christa Dürscheid. 2012. The linguistics of keyboard-to-screen communication: A new terminological framework. *Linguistik Online* 56(6/12), 39–64.

Keane, Webb. 2003. Semiotics and the social analysis of material things. *Language and Communication* 23, 409–425.

Kress, Gunther. 2003. *Literacy in the New Media Age*. London: Routledge.

Kress, Gunther & Theo van Leeuwen. 1996. *Reading Images: The Grammar of Visual Design*. London: Routledge.

Kress, Gunther & Theo van Leeuwen. 2001. *Multimodal Discourse – The Modes and Media of Contemporary Communication*. London: Arnold.

Lévi-Strauss, Claude. (1955). The structural study of myth. *Journal of American Folklore* 68, 428–444.

Mirzoeff, Nicholas. 2011. *The Right to Look: A Counterhistory of Visuality*. Durham, NC: Duke University Press Books.
Myers, Greg. 2010. *The Discourse of Blogs and Wikis*. London: Continuum.
Norris, Sigrid & Rodney H. Jones (eds.). 2005. *Discourse in Action: Introducing Mediated Discourse Analysis*. London & New York: Routledge.
Rascol, Stephanie. 2017. L'évolution de l'utilisation des emojis de la sphere privée à la sphere publique. Université Paul-Valéry Montpellier 3.
Scollon, Ron. 2001. *Mediated Discourse: The Nexus of Practice*. Routledge.
Squires, Lauren. 2010. Enregistering internet language. *Language in Society* 39(4), 457–492.
Squires, Lauren (ed.). 2018. *English in Computer-Mediated Communication: Variation, Representation, and Change*. Berlin: De Gruyter.
Thurlow, Crispin. 2006. From statistical panic to moral panic: The metadiscursive construction and popular exaggeration of new media language in the print media. *Journal of Computer-Mediated Communication* 11(3).
Thurlow, Crispin. 2014. Disciplining youth: Language ideologies and new technologies. In Adam Jaworski & Nikolas Coupland (eds.), *The Discourse Reader*. 3rd edn., 481–496. London: Routledge.
Thurlow, Crispin. 2017. "Forget about the words"? Tracking the language, media and semiotic ideologies of digital discourse: The case of sexting. *Discourse, Context & Media* 20, 10–19.
Thurlow, Crispin. 2018. Digital discourse: Locating language in new/social media. In Jean Burgess, Thomas Poell & Alice Marwick (eds.), *The Sage Handbook of Social Media*, 135–145. New York, NY: Sage.
Thurlow, Crispin, Giorgia Aiello and Lara Portmann. 2019. Visualizing teens and technology: A social semiotic analysis stock photography and news media imagery. *New Media & Society*. doi.org/10.1177/1461444819867318
Thurlow, Crispin & Adam Jaworski. 2017. Introducing elite discourse: The rhetorics of status, privilege, and power. *Social Semiotics* 27(3), 243–254.
Thurlow, Crispin & Kristine Mroczek. 2011. *Digital Discourse: Language in the New Media*. New York: Oxford University Press.
Ueberwasser, Simone & Elisabeth Stark. 2017. What's up, Switzerland? A corpus-based research project in a multilingual country. *Linguistik Online* 84(5).
Vaisman, Carmel L. 2014. Beautiful script, cute spelling and glamorous words: Doing girlhood through language playfulness on Israeli blogs. *Language & Communication* 34, 69–80.

Rodney H. Jones
1 Towards an embodied visual semiotics: Negotiating the right to look

1 Introduction

On July 6, 2016, Philando-Castile, a 32 year-old African American man was shot after being pulled over, ostensibly for a broken tail-light, in the town of Falcon Heights, Minnesota. While her boyfriend lay bleeding, Diamond Reynolds videoed the scene from the passenger seat, livestreaming her video to Facebook.[1] "Stay with me," she said into the screen, and then tilted her hand to reveal Castile, still strapped into his seatbelt, his head tilted back, his while shirt stained with blood. "We got pulled over for a busted taillight in the back", she continued, "and the police just, he's ... he's ... he's ... covered." Here she pulled the camera back to her own face, revealing a jerky close-up of her mouth and her eerily composed eyes. Then she turned her head towards the window on the other side of the car, and pointed her phone in the same direction, saying, "He ... they ah killed my boyfriend." At that moment, the disembodied voice of the officer could be heard through the window. "Fuck!" it said.

The aim of this chapter is to explore issues around the *embodied* nature of the visual in the age of the smartphone, in particular, the ways in which people use everyday practices of making images of themselves and others to negotiate how they are looked at and the rights and responsibilities they have to look at others. In it I will take a post-phenomenological approach, framing looking and being looked at as a matter of what Heidegger (2008) calls "being-in-the-world" (*Dasein*) and "being-with" (and for) other social actors (*Mitsein*).

The rise of the web, digital imaging and graphic user interfaces in the late 1990s precipitated an intense interest in the fields of sociolinguistics and discourse analysis in multimodal communication, resulting in a range of approaches to the ways people make and construe meaning with visual signs (see for example Baldry & Thibault 2006; Bateman 2008; Forceville 1996; Kress 2009; Kress & van Leeuwen 1996; O'Halloran 2004), including some approaches that focused on the impact of image making on issues of power and social identity (Machin & Mayr 2012; Machin & Van Leeuwen 2007). The more recent rise of mobile digital communication via social media platforms such as YouTube, Instagram and Snapchat, which invite users to produce themselves

---

[1] https://www.youtube.com/watch?v=K_J3sYIgvUE

https://doi.org/10.1515/9781501510113-002

and their experiences visually and construe meaning from the visual representations of other people's experiences, however, presents significant challenges to the "semiotics" and "grammars" of visual communication developed at the turn of the century, forcing analysts to engage more fully with the ways multimodal meaning emerges not from "signs" *per se*, but from *techno-somatic entanglements* in which the most important communicative resource is not what is visible but communicators' *embodied experiences* of seeing it. "Seeing" and "being seen", in this regard, are never neutral, uninvolved acts: seeing is always entangled with the mediational means through which it is accomplished, with what is seen and what is happening to it, with what seeing *does* to the watcher and the watched, and with sets of rules and expectations associated with particular contexts and particular societies about who has the *right to look* and who has the *right to be seen* (Mirzoeff 2011).

2 The hegemony of vision

The fact that we are living in a "visual age" has become somewhat of a cliché. We are reminded of it constantly in the discourse that circulates in our halls of learning, in the media that we consume, and the products that we buy. In our daily lives, we are constantly compelled not just to confront the visual, but to produce ourselves visually through technologies such as smartphones and social media sites. It seems we have finally arrived at what Guy Debord (2000) called "the society of the spectacle", a society totally dominated by images, commodities, and images of commodities, or that we have finally become captive to what David Levin (Levin 1993) calls "the hegemony of vision". In her book *Nonhuman Photography*, Joanna Zylinska (2017) argues that we live in an age in which being human has become defined through the representations we make of ourselves, and are made of us, through photography. She writes (pp. 2–3):

> All-encompassing in the workings of traffic control cameras, smart phones, and Google Earth, photography can therefore be described as a technology of life: it not only represents life but also shapes and regulates it – while also documenting or even envisioning its demise. Thanks to the proliferation of digital and portable media as well as broadband connectivity, photography has become pervasive and ubiquitous: we could go so far as to say that our very sense of existence is now shaped by it. In the words of Susan Sontag (2004), "To live is to be photographed, to have a record of one's life, and therefore to go on with one's life oblivious, or claiming to be oblivious, to the camera's nonstop attentions."

This ascendance of the visual, of course, is not something that began in the digital age, or even with the invention of photography. In his essay "The Age of the World Picture," Heidegger (1977) argues that the hegemony of vision had its beginnings in the philosophies of ancient Greece, but came to fruition in the work of Descartes, who, in his 1644 *Principles of Philosophy* (1985) formulated a model of vision that came to dominate enlightenment thinking, a model which involved the implicit separation of subject and object, the seer and the seen, in which all that is seen in essentially *representation* within the mind of the seer.

Of course, the invention of photography helped to naturalize this model. By the mid-20th century, photographs had come to take on a "truth value" that exceeded even human experience and memory (Sekula 1982), and the physical act of photographing someone materially instantiated the separation between the seer and the seen, mediated through the technology of the camera lens. Taking a photograph of someone, as Ron Scollon (1998) points out, invariably transforms the unit or participation from a "with" (Goffman 1966), a group of people perceived to be together, to a "watch", which Scollon defines as "any person or group of people who are perceived to have attention to some spectacle as the central focus of their (social) activity. The spectacle together with its watchers constitutes the watch" (p. 283). What characterizes this type of participation unit, of course, is its *asymmetry*, the fact that the watcher can invariably claim the right to pass judgement on the spectacle (R. H. Jones 2012).

By the time Heidegger got around to writing about it, there was a sense that we had entered a "new epoch", one in which "the ocular subject [had] become the ultimate source of all being and the reference point for all measurements of *value* of being" One in which "the very being of the world is equated with our images and representations" (Levin 1993, p. 6 summarizing Heidegger). To put it in Scollon's terms, the state of "being in the world" (*Dasein*), which for Heidegger was crucially a matter of relating to people in the context of *withs* (*Mitsein*), has become more a matter of relating to people in the context of *watches*.

Most approaches to visual semiotics that dominate discourse analysis today, rather than getting us beyond the Cartesian ocular centrism that Heidegger so worried about, have tended to more firmly reinforce it. The empirical frame of most scholars of the visual in social semiotic and discourse analytical traditions, with some notable exceptions (see for example Thurlow 2016), has been to take "bodies", "images" and "media", as objects that exist separately and have relative ontological stability. The preoccupation of the analysis has been mostly on *representation*, what pictures (or bodies or gestures) "mean", rather than with the more fundamental ways *image-making* has come to transform the very nature of meaning and the very nature of being.

3 Bodies in technology

Ironically, mobile digital photography, especially since late 2003 when Sony Ericsson and Motorola introduced front-facing cameras, rather than perpetuating this hegemony of the representational, has actually acted to destabilize it, opening up possibilities for a more post-representational perspective. Digital media have not only compromised the "truth value" of photographs (Mitchell 1994), but have also forced us to see "images", "bodies" and "media" not as separate objects but as relational categories that intersect in complex moments of action, categories that can only be understood by engaging not just with what they mean but with *how they are lived* (Barad 2007). They have opened up space for a new form of visual semiotics that focuses less on "meaning" and "representation" and more on how people use the embodied and affective dimensions of visual communication to negotiate their physical experiences in the world and their relationships with others.

By the "embodied" dimension of meaning I do not just mean the tricks of perspective that scholars like Kress and van Leeuwen talk about by which image makers employ technical devices to make viewers feel like they are "part of the picture". What I'm trying to get at is more complicated than that, something that we see – or rather, feel – in pictures such as Figure 1.1 below taken from Areej Albawardi's (2017) corpus of Snapchat images of female Saudi university students, an image in which what is communicated is not the just perspective of the photographer but her embodied experience of vision as it is entangled with the materiality of spaces and objects and friendships and relationships of power. Understanding this photo the way those who received it through Snapchat requires an understanding of what a body taking a picture like this feels like, what the surface of the desk feels like, as well as what the danger involved in taking a picture like this feels like in a class in which the translation teacher is famous for confiscating students' phones.

These quotidian windows on experience have a way of short-circuiting the subject/object detour derived from Descartes and pointing much more directly to something akin to what Wittgenstein (1973) referred to as "the experience of meaning". It is not so much "visual communication" as it is communicating the embodied experience of the visual made possible by the "equipment" of the mobile phone. When I use the word "equipment", I do not just mean it in the conventional sense, but also in the Heideggerian sense: For Heidegger, objects in the world become "equipment" when they are connected in some meaningful way to the activities in which "Being" is absorbed. Tools are not simply objects that have certain qualities. Rather, what a tool is is dependent upon its use, its relationship to its user and to other tools, and the degree to which it is

Figure 1.1: Snapchat image (from Albawardi 2017, p. 186).

"ready at hand" to use (*zuhandenheit*). To be "ready at hand" does not just mean "present" – it is about how things are interconnected with other things within webs of social practices and social identities, involvements and interests.

Beyond Heidegger's phenomenology another place we can look for ideas about the relationship of "equipment" to how we experience ourselves in the world is in what has been called "post-phenomenology", which is a way of studying bodily relations to technology from both a phenomenological and a pragmatic perspective. The most prominent proponent of this approach is Don Ihde (2001, 2012). Ihde is interested not just in how technologies mediate our experience, but also in how technologies themselves become embodied, thereby transforming human perception and subjectivity. He traces the ways different kinds of technologies, like bows and arrows, have shifted ontologically through history becoming embodied differently in different cultural contexts in different ways. Key to Ihde's theory of embodiment and technology is his argument that there are always two bodies involved. *Body one* is the phenomenological body of the human person. It is the body according to which we experience up and down, left and right, the speed of movement or falling through the air, the body which feels the smooth glass case of our iPhones when we stretch our arms out to take selfies. The second body, *body two*, is the one reflected back at us through our technologies, constituted by our cultural practices of using these technologies and the ideologies these entail. *Body one*, Ihde writes, (2001, p. 17) is "Merleau-Ponty's body," the body that experiences technology, and *body two* is "Foucault's body," the body that technology experiences.

It is my argument that an "embodied" visual semiotics, one which can explain how people communicate their experiences of meaning though digital technologies like mobile phones, must take into account both of these bodies, the body that experiences technology and the body that technology experiences, as well as the ways these two bodies interact. In order to do this, scholars of the visual need to get away from thinking about the visual and start thinking about *visuality* – by which I mean the *physical experience* of being visible, as well as the practices and relationships and discourses through which visibility is socially accomplished and negotiated.

4 Visuality

The term visuality is an attempt to reconfigure Ihde's post-phenomenology of being into a post-phenomenology of *seeing*, an attempt to get beyond the ocular dimension of seeing to the embodied and affective dimensions of seeing and being seen. I take the term *visuality* from Chis Otter, who, in his book *The Victorian Eye: A political history of light and vision in Britain, 1800 to 1910* (2008) talks about how human subjectivity was transformed by the introduction of gaslights, and later, electric lights, into British urban life, facilitating both the independence of citizens (though practices like private reading) and their subjugation (though the increased surveillance of public spaces). "The term *visuality*," writes Otter (p. 25), "captures the simultaneously physiological, practical, discursive, and technospatial nature of the visual." In other words, visuality is how, through the visual we are able to communicate *both* the meaning of experience and the experience of meaning.

In order to illustrate the application of this idea to visual analysis, I will consider two rather different examples of the "handiness" of digital cameras: the embodied act of taking "selfies", and the practice of using cell phone cameras to document and negotiate encounters with law enforcement offices. In exploring these examples, I will focus on the three most important aspects of visuality for the kind of embodied semiotics that I am proposing. They are:
1. *looking*, which has to do with the way technologies enable us to channel our attention and that of others to certain aspects of experience;
2. *seeing*, which has to do with the ways technologies and their embodied ideologies enable or constrain our perception;

3. *being*, which has to do with the kinds of people technologies allow us to be, both phenomenologically and socially.

All three of these components, however, depend upon and help to constitute a fourth component: our *right to look*: What we look at, what we see and who we are able to be are inevitably tied up with the ethical dimension of visuality, the relationships of power and histories of oppression in the societies in which we live.

4.1 Looking

Perhaps the most powerful affordance of photography is to direct the gaze, to say, "Look at that!" The most conspicuous feature of digital photography, however, at least since the introduction of front-facing cameras a decade ago, has been to reverse the direction of the gaze. More and more, photography became less about "Look at that" and more about "Look at me," to the consternation of many, who take this new detour of the photographic gaze as evidence of the rise of a pathological form of narcissism and/or the general corruption of civilisation (see for example "Addicted to selfies?" 2015; Kale 2018; McCain et al. 2016). But the affordances that front facing cameras give for looking at the self are about more than narcissism. The camera has become a complex instrument of visual communication, of self-presentation and self-reflection with which people negotiate their embodied experiences of the visual (Warfield 2017). Selfies are not just a way of showing myself to you, but of communicating to you *my experience* of being looked at. As Paul Frosh (2015, p. 1610) puts it, "[the selfie] says not only "see this, here, now," but also "see me showing you me." It points to the performance of a communicative action rather than to an object, and is a trace of that performance." It is impossible for a selfie not to engage in what Goffman (1987, p. 6) called "social portraiture," which he defined as practices by which social actors "arrange themselves microecologically to depict what is taken as their place in the wider social frame, allowing them, in turn, to celebrate what has been depicted."

Looking at the self, of course is about checking the self out, assessing it, operating within the countours of the very self-consciousness we have created. Figure 1.2 is another example from Areej Albawadi's Snapchat corpus; in this example, the photographer has pointed her camera deliberately at "what's wrong" with her appearance, even using the affordances of Snapchat to circle her unravelling braids and scrawl the word "why?". At the same time, she also assures us of what is "right" – "eyeliner on fleek thou" along with a sassy girl emoji. According to Warfield (2017, p. 83), one function of the camera in the

Figure 1.2: Snapchat image (from Albawardi and Jones 2019, p. 2).

production of selfies is to act as a device of self-reflection where "corporal glitches like misplaced hair and imperfect makeup" are managed. The goal, Warfield argues, is not always to communicate corporal perfection, but rather to portray what she calls the *"affective authenticity"* of the body, which sometimes involves calling attention to rather than concealing imperfections. "A good selfie" she writes (p. 85) is "a combination of representationally gendered tropes and affective relationality – it [has] to look good but also *feel authentic*." Quoting Russell (2012, p. 3), she argues that such glitches can help to reveal "messy moments in gender, which simultaneously [reveal] the ghostly conventionality of gender norms and ideals, and the potentiality of a break with such conventions." "It is in these moments," Warfield continues, "where gender norms embedded in the technology of the camera are, via the glitch, shaped by the historical gendered invariants of the technology, performed by the body, and negotiated alongside the momentary and changing affectively felt sense of self which is also the result of a whole genealogy of material and discursive entanglements." So in this example, it is not just a matter of the photographer inviting us to look at her, or communicating the embodied experience of being looked at. Here, with the affordances of snapchat, the body itself has become for this young woman a *canvas* upon to which to write her experiences with it, to reflect upon norms governing appearance and to subtly challenge them – using the body to communicate the "glitch" while at the same time using the "sassy girl" emoji and the expression "eyebrows on fleek" to invoke gendered norms of perfection without actually having to display them. The dynamic of revealing and concealing the self, however, plays an even more subversive role in the culture in which this photo was produced, a point I will take up in the following section.

There is probably nothing more different than the presentation of the self in selfies like this, which involve the self managing its own visibility, and the presentation of the self in videos of encounters with police like that taken by Diamond Reynolds after her boyfriend was shot, which reveal a self under inspection from the outside, subject to the gaze of authority, but which, at the same time, seek to use images of the self to turn that gaze around, to call attention to possible moral "glitches" in police behaviour. Much has been written about the potential of citizen "sousveillance" (Mann & Ferenbok 2013) via cell phones to call attention to police abuses and empower oppressed communities (see for example Brucato 2015; Wall & Linnemann 2014). The assumption in most of these studies is that the main affordance of the camera is to be "at hand" as a kind of "auditor" in order to prevent police from engaging in bad behaviour and to capture evidence of such behaviour in cases where it occurs. The reality of such encounters is, of course, far more complicated, involving not just producing for the non-present audience a particular version of events, but also producing for the police officers the *experience of being watched*. The degree to which citizens are able to pull off these two tasks, depends on more than just the technology "at hand", but also how that technology is entangled with bodies and discourses and the histories of how certain kinds of citizens are treated by the police.

Figures 1.3 to 1.6 are stills from a video of a police encounter that was very different from the encounter experienced by Philando Castile and Diamond Reynolds which I sketched at the start of the chapter. In this encounter, a white Uber driver named Jesse Bright, who also happens to be an attorney, argues with police officers about their right to search his car, and his right to film the encounter.[2] What is striking about such encounters are the complex ways citizens manipulate their cameras to communicate the act of looking and negotiate its boundaries.

There are at least four ways citizens involved in police stops can use the camera as a tool to communicate their embodied experiences of looking and

---

[2] https://www.youtube.com/watch?v=-UQKkYWDUQ4

Figure 1.3: Camera as 'witness'.   **Figure 1.4:** Verbal commentary.

being looked at. One of the most obvious ways is pointing the camera outward to monitor what officers are doing (Figure 1.3), an act of looking designed not just to communicate to the non-present audience "Look at this," but also to communicate to officers the fact that they are being looked at, saying to them "Look at "us" looking at you." In such cases, while the camera is constructed as a more or less "objective" witness to events, what is being witnessed is co-constructed by the driver, who decides where to point the camera, and the officer, who decides how to respond to the camera's gaze.

Interestingly, however, for the majority of the time in this video (as well as in Diamond Reynold's video), the camera is turned towards the citizen, who sometimes narrates to the camera what is happening to him (Figure 1.4), saying things like "I'm driving an Uber and my passenger is being arrested", turning the camera into a participant in a conversation designed to be overheard by the officer, and sometimes producing non-verbal commentary on the situation through the use of ostentatious poses or facial expressions that rehearse the same kind of social portraiture that we see in selfies (Figure 1.5). Here what is communicated is "Look at me being looked at by this police officer". Finally, citizens can situate the camera to capture "performed conversations" between

1 Towards an embodied visual semiotics: Negotiating the right to look — 29

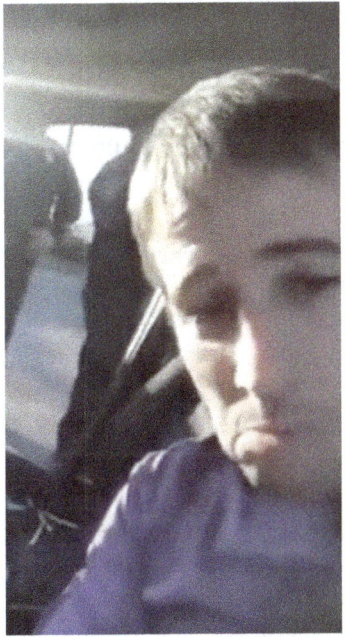

Figure 1.5: Non-verbal commentary.   **Figure 1.6:** 'Performed' conversation.

themselves and authority figures, so that both the citizen and the officer are put into the position of watching themselves being watched and simultaneously accounting for their actions both to each other and to the non-present audience. Such conversations are frequently meta-discursive in nature, with participants explicitly negotiating the boundaries and meanings of looking. Below is an example from the video pictured above:

> Officer: hey bud (.2) turn that off \
> Driver: no I'll keep recording thank you (.2) it's my [right
> Officer: [don't record me=
> Driver: =I will (.) look \ (.3) you're a police officer on duty...
>
> Driver: I'm sitting in my car (.3) I'm just recording in case anything happens (.) I'm surrounded by five police (.) officers^
> Officer: you're being a jerk \

Looking, then, is not just about directing one's attention to particular visual stimuli. It is about being able to articulate a particular version of events, about, in the words of Mirzoeff "matching the seeable to the sayable." A similar dynamic can be seen in the video produced by Diamond Reynolds in which "looking" involved not just Reynolds pointing the camera at her dying boyfriend or using it to audit the actions of Jeronimo Yanez, the officer who shot him, but also verbally articulating what is being looked at, saying "Look at what you have done." The conversation she performs with the officer is designed to make explicit *what* she witnessed. "You just shot four bullets into him, Sir," she says. "He was just getting his license and registration, Sir ... " At the same time, the officer is compelled to use this same strategy of performing both for her and for the non-present audience *his* version of events: "I told him not to reach for it ... I told him to get his hand out ... "

4.2 Seeing

The main debate in the Philando Castile shooting, at least from the point of view of the jury who had to rule on Officer Yanez's culpability, was not just about what he did, but about what he *saw* that might have caused him to shoot. While looking is about directing the gaze, seeing is about how different tactics, discourses and technologies enable and constrain what can be seen. What can be seen is never straightforward. Visibilities, in the words of Halpern (2014, p. 24), consist of: "accumulations of a density of multiple strategies, discourses, and bodies in particular assemblages at specific moments ... constituted through a range of tactics from the organization of space – both haptic and aural – to the use of statistics." While most people might assume that the whole point of selfies is making the self visible, closer examination of people's actual practices show that selfies sometimes entail concealing as much as revealing, simultaneously communicating the seen and the unseen. Selfies allow people to play with what Grant Bollmer and Katherine Guinness (2017, p. 156) call "a dialectic of aesthetic and anaesthetic relations that either unveil or close off the body towards another, relations [that] may have different political valances depending on context."

One context where the political valances governing the relations between the seen and the unseen are particularly complex is Areej Albawadi's collection of selfies from young Saudi women in which that which is pointed to – for example, "eyeliner on fleek" – is at the same time *not seen*. The main reason for this is, of course, the social and religious conventions of Saudi society against women circulating pictures of their faces over social media. But these "faceless selfies" also highlight how these women subtly defy these prohibitions by making the unseen *seeable*, by creating a perceptual gap, a "slot" that the viewer cannot help but fill in with "fleekness". Albawardi's corpus is full of instances in which her participants use the affordances of image and text to avoid unveiling their faces while at the same time communicating the experience of self-reflection (see Figure 1.7 and Figure 1.8). By creatively appropriating different affordances of the medium to both conceal and reveal, they are able to simultaneously address the demands of communicating with their friends – enacting membership in particular peer communities such as fashionistas and university students, and the broader demands and constraints of being Saudi women.

Figure 1.7: Snapchat image (from Albawardi 2017, p. 189).

Figure 1.8: Snapchat image (from Albawardi' corpus, previously unpublished).

Visibility is about negotiating these political valances through managing what is seen and what is not. But often, the access to the tools for negotiating such valances is unequally distributed, with the powerful determining what gets seen, or determining how the "gaps" created by the unseen get filled. The video that Diamond Reynolds took of the shooting of Philando Castile is not the only video of that incident. Another version of events comes from the dash cam of the officer's car. Importantly, this video reveals those moments that led up to the shooting before Diamond Reynolds began her live stream. They also provide a different perspective, making what occurred outside of the car – the actions of Officer Yanez – visible, while not showing what occurred inside the car: the actions of Philando Castile. Despite the poor audio quality of the video, the following conversation can be heard:

> Castile: Sir I have to tell you I have a firearm on me.
> Yanez: Don't reach for it though, don't pull it out.
> Castile: I'm not pulling it out.
> Yanez: Don't pull it out.
>
> →
>
> (Gunshots)
> Reynolds: You just killed my boyfriend.
> Yanez: Don't move, Don't move, don't move.

Of course, the question of Yanez's culpability in the shooting hinges on that which we cannot see, what Philando Castile did at the moment in this exchange marked with an →. As viewers, we are compelled to populate this gap – to fill it with some image, to ask "what did the officer see – and what did it mean to him?". According to Yanez, what he saw was Castile reaching for his firearm. What Reynolds saw was her boyfriend reaching for his wallet in order to provide the officer with his license and registration. Here, of course, what was seen cannot be separated from the bodies that saw it: it might be that the association between black men reaching into their pockets and danger was made by the officer long before he approached Philando Castile's car – it might have been an association deeply sedimented in his "historical body" (Nishida 1966; Scollon 2001). Indeed, Philando Castile certainly is not the first black man who was deemed a threat for putting his hands in his pockets, or for being killed for it (see for example Mandero 2014; Morley 2016).

In the end of the day, what was seen by the officer and what was seen by the girlfriend is unknowable, and, as is often the case in such situations, the ultimate determination is made by "experts" – lawyers, forensic scientists, journalists and other commentators equipped with what Goodwin (1994) calls "professional vision", which is in essence, the art of reading visual phenomena through the lens of a particular profession, with its particular practices of seeing and particular ideological agenda. The example Goodwin gives is the way the lawyers in the trial of the police officers who brutally beat Rodney King in Los Angeles in 1991 while a bystander surreptitiously videotaped it interpreted the incident for the jury. By transforming the video into a series of still images and assigning meaning to micro aspects of these images, they were able to make it seem as if King constituted a threat and the four officers that beat him were merely trying to defend themselves.

After the Philando Castile shooting and the release of the dash-cam video, the media was awash with such experts called upon to explain what had happened, to make the unseeable "sayable". These media reports involved not just the "professional vision" of the experts that journalists had interviewed, but also the journalists themselves, who had their own practiced way of seeing and ways of explaining what could not be seen (R. H. Jones & Li 2016). Below is an example from KARE, a local television station in Minneapolis:

> Presenter: Mylan Mason was a 12 year veteran of the Minneapolis Police Department and former director of the law enforcement program at Hennepin Technical College.
> Expert: I don't see anything I could change...
> Presenter: We watched parts of the video with her, and she points out Officer Yanez's calm demeanour before the shooting until something provokes his response
> Expert: Something in the car made him realize there was danger...
> Presenter: Mason says, to her, training is the single most important part of this encounter, in that Castile identified that he had a firearm and to Yanez it appeared he was reaching for it shortly after.
> Expert: I believe it happened so quickly. He was not tense. He reacted to his training, of the years of experience he's had, and the years of training he's had with his firearm.[3]

Interestingly the way this expert fills in the gap for us is by appealing to the officer's embodied experience of vision – by talking about his "bodily hexis" (Bourdieu 1977) and the training that has been sedimented into his "historical body" (Scollon 2001) – "He must have seen something that triggered that training" she says – his body tells me so. What the officer saw is constructed as part of his embodied experience – a function of his historical body. At the same time, what viewers of the television station KARE see of the expert's reading is itself filtered through the interpretation of the journalist/presenter, who strategically selects snippets of what the expert says and fills in the gap with her own "summary", delivered in the form of a voiceover while the body of the expert, intently staring at a computer, fills the screen.

At this point, representations of what happened begin to get quite far away from the actual incident, from the words people said and actions they took. They become representations of "practices" (training, protocols, professional conduct) rather than actions, representations of "historical bodies" rather than the actual

---

[3] https://www.kare11.com/video/news/local/philando-castile/yanez-dash-cam-video/89-2637744

bodies of Officer Yanz screaming "Fuck!" and of Philando Castile bleeding to death.

So seeing is not just about what is seen. It is really more about what is unseen – and who gets to fill in the gap– whose version – or rather vision – of events takes precedence and is given authority. How the gap gets filled is never neutral. Visibilities, as Deleuze (1988) (channelling Foucault) argues, are not sites of perception so much as sites of *production*, "constituting an assemblage of relationships, enunciations, epistemologies, and properties that render agents into objects of intervention for power ... historically stipulated apparatuses for producing evidence about bodies" (Halpern 2014, p. 24).

Visuality, then, is not just a matter of what we see or what we make visible to others – it is a matter of who we *are*, and who we are *able to be* within the constraints of our embodied relationships with the technologies we have access to – our phenomenological selves – and the constraints of our relationships with larger sociotechnical assemblages – our social selves, which brings me to the third key aspect of visuality: *being*.

4.3 Being

There has been plenty written about the *disciplinary* function of selfies, particularly when it comes to expressions of gender, how they re-inscribe the narrow stereotyped parameters of women's visual selves and take part, in the words of Anne Burns (2015:1727), "in a wider process by which subjects are encouraged to adhere to a specific framework of behaviour laid out by experts". These experts, however, are rather different from the lawyers, journalists and criminologists I discussed above – they are instead celebrities and supermodels and YouTube make up consultants who teach young girls how to put their "eyeliner on fleek" (see Figure 1.2) and, more fundamentally, that "fleekness" is an attribute for young women to aspire to. In this regard, selfies become not just a way of seeing the self, but a way of being the kind of person deserving to be seen. At the same time, however, the disciplinary apparatus of the selfie is used to denigrate those who have been disciplined, to construct these gendered performances as symptoms of narcissism. "By devaluing selfies and by identifying them as feminine," Burns argues, "popular discourse serves to direct disdain at young women openly – and largely without challenge. As such, the low value of women's cultural practices is used to enforce a social hierarchy." What Burns calls "selfie discipline", in other words, puts women into a new kind of "double bind", asking them to choose between the risk of "promiscuous" visibility and the risk of "social death" associated with invisibility (Bucher 2012).

An example of how this double bind played out on the political stage can be seen in the public reaction to a viral photograph from the Hillary Clinton's presidential campaign in which the candidate's audience of millennial women are shown with their backs turned to her, their cell phones raised, taking simultaneous selfies with Clinton in the background. This is how the photo was described in the *Guardian*:

> It is a curiously grotesque image. While a tightly packed crowd all took selfies with the Democratic party's US presidential candidate, a sly photographer slipped around the side. The resulting view is unflattering – not only to Hillary Rodham Clinton but the crowd. They all have their backs turned to her while they hold up phones to take pictures of ... themselves, with the blue-suited HRC in the background. No one seems to want a picture just of the candidate. It's a selfie or nothing. Meanwhile, waving and smiling, Clinton cuts an eerily isolated figure on her little stage, up against the wall, separated from the selfie-shooters by a railing, like a Francis Bacon Pope in his glass booth. (J. Jones, 2016)

What images like this remind us of is that often taking selfies is not just about "being", but about "being with", both in the conventional sense of "Look at whom I am with!", and in the Heideggerian sense (*Mitsein*), in which how we think about ourselves is inextricably tied up with our ability to recognize and engage with others. It was this latter sense that people seemed most concerned about in comments on social media: "The photo says it all," tweeted one critic. "Our society is selfie-centred". Another tweeted: "Hillary Clinton waves to the "look at me" selfie generation."

Of course, there are other ways to read this image that do not necessarily rehearse cultural narratives of female narcissism. One way would be to interpret it as these young women collectively identifying with the first female major party presidential nominee in US history and performing a dramatic gesture of inserting themselves into that history. Another would see it as a calculated attempt at social media marketing by the candidate who, according the comments from her staffers, initiated the moment with the words: "Okay everybody, turn around and we'll do a group selfie" (Kircher 2016). In her book *The Selfie Generation*, Alicia Eler points out the double standard that dominated news coverage of the campaign, in which Trump was valorised for his (albeit dark) social media genius while Hillary Clinton's attempts to exploit social media were portrayed as just another example of feminine narcissism.

The concepts of "being" and "being with" were also front and centre in media narratives of Diamond Reynolds's live streaming of her boyfriend's shooting, mostly in the form of praise for her courage in the face of extraordinary circumstances, the way she was simultaneously able to "be with" her boyfriend, her young daughter (who was sitting in the backseat of the car) and her internet audience, all the while remaining so calm, so composed. Appearing on the talk show *The View*, Reynolds attributed her demeanour to her desire to authentically bear witness: "I really wanted to make sure that no matter what, my side, his side, our side of the story could be viewed by the people," she explained (Hope 2016).

It wasn't long, however, before experts, armed with their "professional vision" offered an alternate explanation of Diamond Reynolds's "being". In an article provocatively entitled "This is the brain on horror", *The Washington Post* quoted psychologists from Harvard Medical School attributing Reynolds's behaviour to the fact that her "brain" had "shut down": In circumstances like this, people are "literally not feeling in their body what's going on" (Paquette 2016). At the same time, even in the face of tragedy, Reynolds was not able to escape accusations of narcissism. In a gesture typical of right wing media's strategy of demonizing victims of police violence, the *Conservative Tribune* "reported" that Reynolds's own mother had accused her of "being a narcissist" for persistently posting unflattering videos of herself online (Zeal 2016).

5 Conclusion: *The Right to Look*

Questions about "being" inevitably lead back to questions about "looking", or rather, what Nicholas Mirzoeff (2011) calls "the right to look", the right that some social actors are able to claim to aim their gaze at other social actors. The right to look is both granted by society, deeply tied up with privilege and power, and a product of moment by moment embodied negotiations. It is both a medium for the transmission and dissemination of authority, and for radical acts of emancipation in which the gaze of the powerful is turned back on itself.

It is this latter function that people invoke when speaking of the emancipatory potential of digital technologies (Wall & Linnemann 2014). Digital video cameras, they argue, have allowed ordinary citizens a way to exercise their right to monitor authority figures and expose abuses. The reality, of course, as the examples I have discussed in this chapter make clear, is much more complicated. Technologies themselves are not enough; the right to look comes from the way technologies are deployed in particular situations from particular embodied positions – the way technologies operate together with bodies and discourses and other aspects of the material world. So, the white Uber driver in Figures 1.3–1.6 can claim the right to look by invoking the visibility of the other, by saying "You're a police officer on duty … I'll keep recording thank you … it's my right", whereas Diamond Reynolds, whose boyfriend has just been shot, must claim her right to look by verbalizing her own visibility, assuring the officer whom she is filming: "I will keep my hands where you can see them, Sir."

But claiming the right to look does not just mean claiming the right to look at the other. It is also about claiming the right to turn the camera around – to make oneself visible – to say "Look at me. I'm here. I am claiming the right to be *recognized*." "The right to look" says Mirzoeff (2011, p. 1) "means requiring the recognition of the other in order to have a place from which to claim rights and to determine what is right." At the same time, it is about reclaiming control over the terms of such recognition and the purposes to which it is put.

In April of 2018, twenty-one months after the shooting of Philando Castile, Luke Willis Thompson, a 30-year-old Fijian-New Zealand artist was nominated for the Turner Prize, Britain's most prestigious art award, for his short film "Autoportrait". The piece was a silent black and white portrait of Diamond Reynolds, elegantly dressed and looking peaceful and meditative, meant to act as a "sister image" to the cellphone video she had taken nearly two years before. It came about as a result of Thompson reaching out to to Reynolds and her lawyer with an invitation to work together to create for her a form of visibility that would allow people to see her in a different light, to get beyond the blurred, pixelated image of her negotiating her right to look while Officer Yanz stared at her down the barrel of his gun. Thompson's own claim to the right to look at Reynolds, however, was not without controversy. At the opening of the exhibition at the Tate Britain a group of activists and artists of color silently protested Thompson's nomination wearing identical tee-shirts that said: BLACK PAIN IS NOT FOR PROFIT (Cascone 2018). In response the Tate issued the following carefully worded statement:

> Luke Willis Thompson does not identify as white, he is originally from New Zealand, of Polynesian heritage and is mixed race. This trilogy of work by Luke Willis Thompson reflects his ongoing enquiry into questions of race, class and social inequality, which is informed by his own experience growing up as a mixed-race person in New Zealand. These films were made in the shadow of the Black Lives Matter movement and the artist sees his works as acts of solidarity with his subjects. He links his own position as a New Zealander of Fijian descent, treated as a person of colour in his home country, to that of other marginalised and disempowered communities. He finds ways of suggesting connections while also acknowledging the limits of what we can know of another's pain, and how it can be represented.

The point of raising this controversy is not to pass judgement on whether or not Luke Willis Thompson had the racial "credentials" to make Reynolds the object of his (and our) gaze, but to highlight that the right to look is *always* problematic, always a matter of the positionality of those who do the looking, those who offer themselves to be looked at, and those who might somehow profit from all of this looking. That includes my own (embodied) re-presentations of other people's experiences of looking, seeing and being in this chapter. The point is not to highlight the limitations of representing another's pain as much as to highlight the limitations of representation itself, the limits of any semiotics that aims to separate meaning from the bodies that produce it and the bodies that interpret it.

The right to look, then, is perhaps the most important component of visuality, because it is what makes *looking* and *seeing*, and even, to some degree, *being* possible. It is through negotiating our right to look at others and at ourselves that we stake out our positions in the world, laying claim both to our autonomy and to our connectedness to our social worlds.

The questions that digital technologies pose to those of us who fancy ourselves scholars of the visual, therefore, are not just questions about meaning. They are questions about how people use visuality to claim the right to look. They are questions about how we ourselves claim the right to look. They are questions about how we fill in the gaps between the seen and the unseen, between the seeable and the sayable.

Mirzoeff takes the idea of the right to look from Jacques Derrida's collaboration with the photographer Marie-Françoise Plissart which goes by the English title *Rights of Inspection* (1998), a collection of photographs portraying the intimate and mundane moments of a lesbian relationship, photographs which position the viewer in the thrilling and uncomfortable role of a voyeur. In the postscript, Derrida offers a compelling confession of one allowed the privilege of inspection. "One becomes adept at enlarging or magnifying the minute and discrete element," he writes. "Thus, whether deliberately or not, it necessarily becomes possible to idealize it, to dematerialize or spiritualize it, to charge it with significance." What is striking about these images, however, as Jorge Amado (1999) puts it in a review of the volume, is not the way Derrida makes sense of the figures in them, but the way these figures seem to be striving to make sense of themselves.

It is precisely this urge to magnify, to chase "significance", that we, as scholars of the visual must endeavour to interrogate. Scholarship is not just a matter of looking harder or more closely, but of uncovering the ontological assumptions that frame our seeing (Lather 1993), of confronting the spaces of power/knowledge that are part of all practices of visuality, of asking ourselves not just "what are we looking at", but "who are we to look?"

References

Addicted to selfies? Why you could be a psychopath. 2015, January 9. Available: https://www.telegraph.co.uk/news/newstopics/howaboutthat/11330225/Take-too-many-selfies-You-could-be-a-psychopath.html (28 March, 2019)

Albawardi, Areej. 2017. *Digital literacy practices of Saudi female university students*. University of Reading, Reading, UK.

Albawardi, Areej & Rodney H. Jones. 2019. Vernacular mobile literacies: Multimodality, creativity and cultural identity. *Applied Linguistics Review*. Advance online publication. doi.org/10.1515/applirev-2019-0006

Baldry, Anthony & Paul J. Thibault. 2006. *Multimodal transcription and text analysis*. London; Oakville, CT: Equinox Publishing.

Barad, Karen. 2007. *Meeting the universe halfway: Quantum physics and the entanglement of matter and meaning*. Durham: Duke University Press.

Bateman, John. 2008. *Multimodality and genre: A foundation for the systematic analysis of multimodal documents*, 2008 edn. Basingstoke, Hampshire: Palgrave Macmillan.

Bollmer, Grant & Katherine Guinness. 2017. Phenomenology for the selfie. *Cultural Politics*, 13(2), 156–176.

Bourdieu, Pierre. 1977. *Outline of a theory of practice*. R. Nice, Trans. Cambridge, U.K.; New York: Cambridge University Press.

Brucato, Ben. 2015. The new transparency: Police violence in the context of ubiquitous surveillance. *Media and Communication*, 3(3), 39.

Bucher, Taina. 2012. Want to be on the top? Algorithmic power and the threat of invisibility on Facebook. *New Media & Society*, 14(7), 1164–1180.

Burns, Anne. 2015. Selfies| Self(ie)-Discipline: Social regulation as enacted through the discussion of photographic practice. *International Journal of Communication*, 9(0), 18.

Cascone, Sarah. 2018, September 25. "Black Pain Is Not for Profit": An activist collective protests Luke Willis Thompson's Turner Prize nomination. Available: https://news.artnet.com/exhibitions/luke-willis-thompson-turner-prize-1356151 (28 March, 2019)

Debord, Guy. 2000. *Society of the spectacle*. Detroit, Mich. Black & Red.

Deleuze, Guy. 1988. *Foucault*. P. Bove (ed.), S. Hand, Trans. 1st edn. Minneapolis: University of Minnesota Press.

Derrida, Jaques & Marie-Françoise Plissart. 1998. *Right of inspection*. D. Wills, Trans. First American Edition edn. New York, N.Y.: Monacelli Press.

Descartes, René. 1985. In Robert Stoothoff & Dugald Murdoch (eds.), *The philosophical writings of Descartes*. John Cottingham, Trans. Cambridge: Cambridge University Press.

Forceville, Charles. 1996. *Pictorial metaphor in advertising*. London: Routledge.

Frosh, Paul. 2015. The gestural image: The selfie, photography theory, and kinesthetic sociability. *International Journal of Communication*, 9, 1607–1628.

Goffman, Erving. 1966. *Behavior in public places: Notes on the social organization of gatherings*. New York: The Free Press.

Goffman, Erving. 1987. *Gender advertisements*. New York: Harper and Collins.

Goodwin, Charles. 1994. Professional vision. *American Anthropologist*, 96(3), 606–633.

Halpern, Orit. 2014. *Beautiful data: A history of vision and reason since 1945*. Duke University Press Books.

Heidegger, Martin. 1977. The age of the world picture. In *Science and the Quest for Reality*, 70–88. Palgrave Macmillan, London.

Heidegger, Martin. 2008. *Being and time*, Reprint edn. New York: Harper Perennial Modern Classics.

Hope, Clover. 2016, July 11. Diamond Reynolds talks to The View about staying "calm" while filming boyfriend's death. Available: https://jezebel.com/diamond-reynolds-talks-to-the-view-about-staying-calm-w-1783460089 (28 March, 2019)

Ihde, Don. 2001. *Bodies in technology*, 1st edn. Minneapolis: Univ of Minnesota Press.

Ihde, Don. 2012. *Experimental phenomenology, second edition: Multistabilities*, 2nd edn. Albany: SUNY Press.

Jones, Jonathan. 2016, September 26. Those taking selfies with Hillary Clinton aren't narcissists – but our best hope. *The Guardian*. Avaialble: https://www.theguardian.com/commentisfree/2016/sep/26/taking-selfies-hillary-clinton-not-narcissists (28 March, 2019)

Jones, Rodney H. 2012. Constructing and consuming "displays" in online environments. In Sigrid Norris (ed.), *Multimodality in practice: Investigating theory-in-practice-through-methodology*, 82–96. New York: Routledge.

Jones, Rodney H. & Neville C. H. Li. 2016. Evidentiary video and "professional vision" in the Hong Kong Umbrella Movement. *Journal of Language & Politics*, 15(5), 567–588.

Kale, Sirin. 2018, January 8. Narcissists love liking other narcissists' selfies on Instagram. Available: https://broadly.vice.com/en_us/article/mbp9db/narcissists-love-liking-other-narcissists-selfies-on-instagram (28 March, 2019)

Kircher, Madison M. 2016, September 26. The truth behind that viral Hillary Clinton selfie photo. Available: http://nymag.com/intelligencer/2016/09/hillary-clinton-selfie-photo-explained.html (28 March, 2019)

Kress, Gunther. 2009. *Multimodality: A social semiotic approach to contemporary communication*, 1st edn. London: New York: Routledge.

Kress, Gunther & Theo van Leeuwen. 1996. *Reading images: The grammar of visual design*. London: Routledge.

Lather, Patti. 1993. Fertile obsession: Validity after poststructuralism. *The Sociological Quarterly*, 34(4), 673–693.

Levin, David M. (ed.). 1993. *Modernity and the hegemony of vision*, 1st edn. Berkeley: University of California Press.

Machin, David & Andrea Mayr. 2012. *How to do critical discourse analysis: A multimodal introduction*. Los Angeles: Sage Publications Ltd.

Machin, David & Theo van Leeuwen. 2007. *Global media discourse: A critical introduction*, 1st new edn. London; New York: Routledge.

Mandero, Laura. 2014, December 3. Man, cop film stop for walking with hands in pockets. *USA Today*. Available: https://www.usatoday.com/story/news/2014/12/03/police-man-hands-in-pockets-michigan/19799199/ (28 March, 2019)

Mann, Steve & Joseph Ferenbok. 2013. New Media and the power politics of sousveillance in a surveillance-dominated world. *Surveillance & Society*, 11(1/2), 18–34.

McCain, Jessica L., Zachary G. Borg, Ariel H. Rothenberg, Kristina M. Churillo, Paul Weiler & W. Keith Campbell. 2016. Personality and selfies: Narcissism and the Dark Triad. *Computers in Human Behavior*, 64, 126–133.

Merleau-Ponty, Maurice. 1968. *The visible and the invisible*. C. Lefort, (ed.), A. Lingis, Trans. 1st edn. Evanston: Northwestern University Press.

Mirzoeff, Nicholas. 2011. *The right to look: A counterhistory of visuality*. Durham, NC: Duke University Press Books.

Mitchell, William J. 1994. *The reconfigured eye: Visual truth in the post-photographic era*. Cambridge MA: MIT Press.

Morley, Nicole. 2016, September 29. Unarmed black man killed by police after pulling vape from his pocket. Available: https://metro.co.uk/2016/09/29/unarmed-black-man-killed-by-california-police-after-pulling-vape-from-his-pocket-6159235/ (28 March, 2019)

Nishida, Kitaro. 1966. *Intelligibility and the philosophy of nothingness: Three philosophical essays*. Honolulu: East-West Center Press.

O'Halloran, Kay. (ed.). 2004. *Multimodal discourse analysis: Systemic functional perspectives*. London; New York: Continuum.

Otter, Chris. 2008. *The Victorian eye: A political history of light and vision in Britain, 1800–1910*. Chicago: University of Chicago Press.

Paquette, Danielle. 2016, July 7. "This is the brain on horror": The incredible calm of Diamond "Lavish" Reynolds. *Washington Post*. Available: https://www.washingtonpost.com/news/wonk/wp/2016/07/07/the-incredible-calm-of-diamond-lavish-reynolds/ (28 March, 2019)

Russell, Legacy. 2012, December 10. Digital dualism and the glitch feminism manifesto. Available: https://thesocietypages.org/cyborgology/2012/12/10/digital-dualism-and-the-glitch-feminism-manifesto/ (28 March, 2019)

Scollon, Ron. 2001. *Mediated discourse: The nexus of practice*. Routledge.

Sekula, Allan. 1982. On the invention of photographic meaning. In Victor Burgin (ed.), *Thinking Photography*, 84–109. London: Macmillan Education UK.

Sontag, Susan. 2004, May 23. Regarding the torture of others. *The New York Times*. Available: https://www.nytimes.com/2004/05/23/magazine/regarding-the-torture-of-others.html (28 March 2019)

Thurlow, Crispin. 2016. Queering critical discourse studies or/and Performing "post-class" ideologies. *Critical Discourse Studies*, 13(5), 485–514.

Wall, Tyler & Travis Linnemann. 2014. Staring down the state: Police power, visual economies, and the "war on cameras". *Crime, Media, Culture*, 10(2), 133–149.

Warfield, Katie. 2017. MirrorCameraRoom: the gendered multi-(in)stabilities of the selfie. *Feminist Media Studies*, 17(1), 77–92.

Wittgenstein, Ludwig. 1973. *Philosophical Investigations*. G. E. M. Anscombe, Trans. 3rd edn. New York: Pearson.

Zeal, Cillian. 2016, July 14. BREAKING: Mom of girlfriend who says Castile was innocent drops BOMBSHELL claim. No longer available.

Zylinska, Joanna. 2017. *Nonhuman photography*. Cambridge, MA: MIT Press.

Part 1: **Besides words and writing**

Crispin Thurlow and Vanessa Jaroski
2 "Emoji invasion": The semiotic ideologies of *language endangerment* in multilingual news discourse

1 Introduction: Setting the scene

In digital discourse studies, it is well established that newsmakers often maintain an unduly negative perspective on the impact of digital technologies especially vis-à-vis young people's linguistic and communicative practices (Thurlow 2006, 2007; also Tagliamonte & Denis 2008). With their particular institutional and cultural investment as elite language workers or wordsmiths, journalists consistently reproduce language-ideological depictions of digital discourse which exaggerate its newness and distinctiveness, and which erase individual variation, reflexivity and creativity. In this chapter, we examine an emerging but closely allied metadiscursive framing of digital discourse: the perceived threat to language posed by visual communication and, specifically, emojis. In this case, we witness how long-standing narratives of linguistic degradation or ruin usually attributed to technology are redirected to the deleterious impact of visual communication. We refer to this as a discourse of *language endangerment* (cf. Duchêne & Heller 2007). Instead of a concern to defend (minority) languages from other (majority) languages, however, we find language itself being construed as autonomous and superior, and, more importantly, in need of protection from visual communication. As we will argue, this perceived threat to language is underwritten by deep-seated beliefs and/or misconceptions about how communication works, how meaning is made, and how different communicative modes (e.g. words, images) intersect; all of which are quintessential matters of semiotic ideology (cf. Keane 2003; also Thurlow 2017). As a case in point – and as a good starting point – we offer a typical story from the UK's Guardian newspaper extracted in Figure 2.1 here.

Under the headline "Emoji invasion: the end of language as we know it:/", we have a story explicitly and ostensibly concerned with words being threatened by images. As the by-line explains, "Emojis are the fastest growing language in the UK – what does this mean for the future of communication?" The doom-and-gloom stance of the article is cued further by the use of an emoticon in the headline for expressing dismay or despair. No less importantly, the accompanying image also does some important framing work (see Thurlow, Aiello & Portmann, 2019); here, we have a stock photograph of an old-fashioned typewriter with the

https://doi.org/10.1515/9781501510113-003

Emoji invasion: the end of language as we know it :/

Emojis are the fastest growing language in the UK – what does this mean for the future of communication?

Figure 2.1: Extract from The Guardian newspaper (see and Acknowledgements).
The full Guardian story in Figure 1 is available at: https://www.theguardian.com/media-network/2015/jun/25/emoji-invasion-the-end-of-language-as-we-know-it- (21 February, 2019)

letter keys replaced by emojis. The image is itself framed and anchored with the following tagline: "Emojis are merely a depiction of the body language signals that humans have been reading for centuries."

In the short, opening space of this one news-media story, we have a quintessential encapsulation of the language endangerment discourse and the various ways it is rhetorically accomplished. In a nutshell, we find emojis being framed explicitly as a bona fide language and as an external, unwanted and destructive assault on not only language but human communication altogether. Meanwhile, in the above quote, we have language itself being restricted to written language, and in a way which is patently anachronistic – perhaps specially for journalists, a nostalgic, self-referential appeal to the typewriter. Finally, we see how emojis are dismissively and erroneously (see "merely a depiction") rendered equivalent to so-called body language. As it happens this short story, for all of its dubious views on language and communication, turns out to be fairly measured, answering its own "end of language as we know it" provocation with an emphatic "no", and with a clear understanding that human communicative practice is always changing over time. Nonetheless, such is the power of the headline, the influence of subeditors and picture editors, that the story as a whole presents readers with an overarchingly negative view.[1]

2 Theoretical context: Visualizing digital discourse

Our chapter here locates itself in digital discourse studies (see Thurlow 2018, for a recent overview), a field which typically focuses on sociolinguistic and discursive phenomena in and around "new" media. More specifically, the chapter examines commentary *about* digital discourse. As such, we are less concerned with the way people are actually using digital media and more with the ways their real or putative practices are publically represented and talked about. We find ourselves therefore looking at language about language or discourse about discourse – hence *metadiscourse*. And this is particularly important when it comes to high-stakes, high-authority spaces like the news media.

Studies of metadiscourse orient heavily to – or are allied with – the notion of language ideologies which, as Woolard and Schieffelin (1994: 55–56) explain, "envision and enact links of language to group and personal identity, to aesthetics, to morality, and to epistemology." In other words, when people get to talking about other people's ways of speaking or communicating, they are invariably (more) invested in wider acts of social categorization and judgement. Metadiscursive commentary, like language ideologies, is almost always organized by the same three discursive features or actions: iconization, erasure and recursivity (Irvine & Gal 2000). Respectively, what this means is that certain stereotypical linguistic features or practices are singled out for critique or ridicule; individual variation, creativity and other benefits are meanwhile overlooked; and the ostensibly linguistic "facts" are extrapolated to other aspects of speakers, such as their intellectual capacity, social behavior, or moral rectitude. When it comes to digital discourse, and following Gershon (2010), we also find metadiscursive commentary bound up in tightly related media ideologies, which is to say beliefs about, for example, the material affordances of technology, the nature of authorship, and the apparent newness of everything.

---

[1] We treat newspaper headlines as a distinctive sub-genre of the news stories (cf. Bell 1991) but also as an especially influential one in terms of the dominant framing work headlines do (see Ecker et al. 2014).

Increasingly, scholars of digital discourse have considered the ways language intersects with other modes of communication, thereby addressing the inherently multimodal nature of discursive practice. There are certainly good reasons for opening up digital discourse studies to a broader multimodal perspective; the most obvious of which lies in simply paying more attention to visual communication. We know well, for example, that even text-based digital discourse is often as much visual as it is verbal, concerned as much with the look of words as with their semantic or stylistic properties (e.g., Vaisman 2014). In addition to research on issues like orthographic and typographic design, however, there is also more and more work being done on the communicative uses of visual resources such as emoji, video, GIFs, and non-moving images (e.g., Androutsopoulos & Tereick 2015; Dürscheid & Siever 2017). There is also value in considering how visuality in digital discourse is depicted in, for example, commercial advertising, print or broadcast news, cinema and television narratives and/or public policy and educational settings. Certainly, and as Thurlow (2017; also Thurlow, Aiello & Portmann, 2019) has shown, visual discourse encodes and combines a range of language and media ideologies.

Finally, as in Thurlow's (2017) study of mediatized representations of sexting, we too are keen to consider how metadiscursive framings of digital discourse are also structured by *semiotic ideologies* (after Keane 2003). In this case, we find speakers expressing their beliefs about meaning-making and the relative value of different semiotic modes. This is very evident in the ways people – journalists and others – discuss the interplay between language and visual communication, and the ways they understand (or not) the particular affordances of different semiotic modes; for example, in ideas about the separateness of modes, the realism of pictures or the intellectual, "civilizational" importance of words. We will return with more detail about semiotic ideologies later, but we turn now to the empirical heart of the chapter.

3 Our study: "Emojis versus words" in the news

As part of a larger research project (see Jaroski, forthcoming), we are focusing here on a convenience sample of English-language and, for an indicative multilingual comparison, French-language news articles. The articles are all drawn from our online news-media archive the *Digital Discourse Database*, an open-access archive populated with newspaper stories addressing language and communication in various digital-media contexts.² The archive covers Swiss, European and international news sources publishing in a range of languages but primarily German and French, two of the major national languages of Switzerland, and English.

For the current dataset, we selected all stories from the period January 2014 to September 2017. All 910 articles from our sample were then imported into *AntConc*, a freeware concordancer intended for corpus-linguistic analysis (see Baker et al. 2008). In this way, we started with two corpora – one in French, one in English – and used the in-built concordance tool for focusing on keywords and their semantic clusters. We selected out all uses of *language* (in English) and *langue* and *langage* (in French) as a way to focus on instances where journalists were specifically and explicitly referring to language. We were left with 715 occurrences of *language* and 393 of *langue/langage*. Given our specific interest in emojis, we then sub-sampled further by attending only to stories about language *and* emojis, manually discarding cases addressing, for example, foreign languages, language skills in general or language in artificial intelligence. In this way, our final dataset comprised 62 French-language instances and 106 English-language instances of stories which, much like the Guardian article above, focused specifically on the relation between language and emojis – altogether a total of 168 distinctive lines of data.³

As a device for presenting our analysis, we organize ourselves below into two steps: one more quantitative and descriptive, one more qualitative and interpretative and critical (cf. Fairclough 1989: 20–21; Thurlow & Aiello 2007: 313). In the first step, we rely mostly on our concordance analysis for revealing basic numerical trends and for identifying the most common rhetorical *tactics* used in the news media's framing of the emoji-and-language relationship. On this basis, we arrived at the larger metadiscursive *strategy* of language endangerment which becomes the focus of the second step in our analysis where we look more closely at examples from our dataset with a specific view to semiotic ideologies. The distinction we draw between rhetorical tactics and discursive strategies is borrowed from De Certeau (1984), although in a less political, more analytical sense; strategies refer to larger-scale formations and tactics to the specific actions by which formations are achieved.

---

2 All the news media stories at the heart of our analysis are archived the *Digital Discourse Database*: http://www.digitaldiscoursedatabase.org. (21 February, 2019)
3 A list of the original source newspapers from which our extracts are taken is available online here: http://crispinthurlow.net/endangerment.pdf

3.1 Step 1 – Pinpointing "language endangerment"

As we say, following a loosely organized content analysis, we identified three rhetorical tactics across our French- and English-language data. These were not the only tactics or tropes at work but they were the three most common ones (see the indicative percentages given below). To be clear, a single line or instance generated by AntConc could be coded more than once if it indexed any two or all three of the rhetorical tactics. As far as possible we have tried to draw examples from different papers and stories; we have also tried to give examples in both languages, indicating (underlining) the parts of the extract under consideration. This is not to say that the rhetorical tactics were equally represented across the two languages; such a comparative analysis is beyond the scope of the current chapter. In the initial descriptive step, we offer just two examples of each rhetorical tactic; other examples follow in Step 2 where we consider the third tactic in more detail along with a few German- and Spanish-language examples for good measure.

3.1.1 First rhetorical tactic: Emojis as a (new) language

By far the most common trope to appear in our dataset (57.5%), emojis are commonly treated as equivalent to language/s. Take, for example, Extract 2.1 with its use of "langage emoji" (emoji language) or Extract 2.2 which refers to the "UK's fastest growing language" – a simultaneous appeal to its alarming rise and spread (see next section).

> **Extract 2.1** (Le Figaro, France)
> Les participants doivent décoder des messages en <u>langage emoji</u>.
> *Participants need to decode messages in emoji language.*
>
> **Extract 2.2** (Mirror, UK)
> As <u>the UK's fastest growing language</u>, emoji characters need to represent of a broad range of people.

As with texting style, emojis are framed explicitly or implicitly as foreign or cryptic and therefore in need of translation or decoding ('décoder'). Emojis may be indirectly rendered a language when set in comparison or contrast with references to real or proper language – or, from Extract 2.4 below, so-called traditional languages ('langues traditionelles'). (Nor does it help when academics themselves speak in similarly problematic, reductionistic terms; see Ge & Herring 2018.) Indeed, the driving objective in defining emojis as a language is to call attention to the negative impact this is having on language per se, as we see in the third rhetorical tactic. But the rhetorical stepping-stone for this is the depiction of "emoji language" as rapidly expanding and pervasive.

3.1.2 Second rhetorical tactic: The rise and spread of emojis

Emerging in 21.5% of our dataset, we find evidence for the same kind of "revolutionary" rhetoric Thurlow (2006) identified in relation to mediatized representations of text-messaging; in this case, we find dramatic appeals to the alarming rise and spread of emojis (See Extract 2.8 below for an explicit reference to 'révolutionné' (revolutionized).) This revolutionary framing of emojis is produced also through their apparent or relative newness – sometimes with comical effect, as in Extract 2.3 with its invocation of "the fastest growing language in history".

> **Extract 2.3** (Telegraph, UK)
> Emojis, a popular way to replicate non-verbal communication, are used <u>six billion times a day</u> and have been described as <u>the fastest growing language in history</u>.

> **Extract 2.4** (La Tribune de Genève, Switzerland)
> Mais face à <u>la déferlante de symboles</u>, faut-il craindre un appauvrissement des langues traditionnelles
> *But facing the <u>surge of symbols</u>, should we fear an impoverishment of traditional languages?*

As Thurlow (2006: 676) also noted, statements like "six billion times a day" (seldom given a source) are perfect examples of the kinds of "statistical panic" favoured by journalists and, following Tannen (1989), their function is largely to authenticate the narrative and to legitimate its central claims. In our French-language example from Switzerland (Extract 2.4), we find another well-established conceit: the clichéd metaphor of emojis as an inundation (i.e. 'la déferlante', surge). Through these patently negative allusions, journalists move a step closer to their idée fixe: the deleterious impact of emojis on language, cultural and intelligent life.

3.1.3 Third rhetorical tactic: Linguistic, cultural, and intellectual degradation

In just over a fifth (20.9%) of our dataset we found explicit reference to the deleterious impact of emojis, most specifically with regards cultural, intellectual and especially linguistic decline. In Extract 2.4, we have already seen a negatively loaded reference to 'appauvrissement' (impoverishment) as well as the invocation of tradition; this same sense of degradation is carried more explicitly in the following extracts:

> **Extract 2.5** (Le Figaro, France)
> Les emoticônes sont parfois perçus comme un danger pour la langue. Certains voient dans leur usage une régression de la langue.
> *Emoticons are sometimes perceived as a danger for language. Some people notice in their usage a regression of language.*
>
> **Extract 2.6** (Huffington Post, USA)
> But a number of us older folks, including academics, are more than a little worried about what the popularity of communicating with pictographs is doing to our language and literature.

In Extract 2.5, we see explicit reference to the danger posed by emojis for language ('un danger pour la langue') and, specifically, the decline of language standards or a so-called linguistic regression ('une régression de la langue') as possible outcomes of this threat. In the same extract, we also witness how journalists often serve as echo chambers for other people's anxieties, even if these are largely anecdotal or made-up sources. Extract 2.6 does much the same thing with its somewhat disingenuous blending of "a number of us older folks" and "academics" (presumably not all of them?). Notably here, we have a repeated concern about the impact of emojis ('pictographs') on language and, specifically, literature. We will take this particular point up again shortly.

It is across these three rhetorical tactics that we sense the broader discursive strategy of "language endangerment" emerging. Things culminate most clearly in the third tactic (i.e. linguistic degradation), but the idea of emojis' language-like qualities and the supposedly unprecedented rise and spread serve to compound the imagined threat. Unlike Thurlow's (2006, 2007) study, therefore, we have a case not of standard language under threat from digital discourse; instead, we find language *in toto* under threat from visual discourse. (Of course, the added moral panic about the impact of digital media continues to undergird everything.) Although the word *language* (in either English or French) is used, it typically collapses speech and writing which we otherwise know to be two very different modes of communicating. This is a matter to which we also return later. With this chapter, we are hoping to offer a useful extension of earlier work by offering not only an up-to-date perspective but also a multilingual one. More importantly, and in keeping with recent discussions by Thurlow (2017), our contribution lies also in the necessary shift from language ideologies to semiotic ideologies. This is where we turn next.

3.2 Step 2 – Semiotic ideologies in action

Initially coined by Parmentier (1994: 142), the notion of semiotic ideologies has been made more prominent for language scholars by Keane (2003). It is Keane's lead that we are following here, borrowing also from Thurlow (2017). Put simply, semiotic ideologies are concerned with people's beliefs about signification or meaning-making, and, specifically, issues such as intentionality, agency and arbitrariness. A key point that must also be made about semiotic ideologies is that, like language and media ideologies, they point to wider systems of social differentiation and symbolic authority – what Keane calls "representational economies" – and people's beliefs about meaning-making are always "enmeshed with the dynamics of social value and authority" (p. 415). In other words, the way we talk about meaning-making says a lot about whose ways of making meaning are considered better and whose beliefs about meaning-making are most powerful or influential. This, needless to say, is why it matters what journalists have to say about emojis and their relation to language.

One of Keane's specific concerns is the prevailing notion (in Western cultures) that language is often treated as meaningful, while other ways of communicating (e.g. material culture) are treated as more practical and less sophisticated. In this sense, it is possible to view semiotic ideologies as being essentially related to questions of multimodality, prompting the following types of questions: What is the relative importance or value of language vis-à-vis other modes of communication? Which modes are thought to "carry" meaning better or more reliably? Which modes of communication – which resources – are given status/authority? What social values (negative or positive) are attached to different modes of communication? Closely related to ideologies of language and media, these other sorts of ideological processes direct us to another way digital discourse can be metadiscursively framed. We see this clearly in the way emojis are depicted in our dataset. We thus return to the third of our rhetorical tactics from above (i.e. linguistic regression) together with some additional examples. In fact, for the sake of demonstrating the multilingual production and circulation of "language endangerment" we will also draw on a convenience sample of illustrative German- and Spanish-language examples from our larger archive.

> **Extract 2.7** (Le Figaro, France)
> Le Smiley a <u>révolutionné</u> les premières années du numérique. Jusqu'au <u>règne de l'émoji</u> sur le téléphone portable. Son créateur, Nicolas Loufrani, revient sur <u>l'incroyable histoire de ce langage</u> qui a conquis la planète.

> The Smiley <u>revolutionized</u> the early years of digital technology. Until the <u>reign of emoji</u> on the mobile phone. Its creator, Nicolas Loufrani, looks back at <u>the incredible history of this language</u> that has conquered the planet.

Extract 2.8 (Zeit, Germany)
Beherrschen Sie Emoji, die am schnellsten wachsende Sprache der Welt?
Can you master Emoji, the fastest growing language in the world?

Extract 2.9 (La Vanguardia, Spain)
Emojis, un nuevo lenguaje universal
Emojis, a new universal language

In order to make the claim that emojis are replacing words (see below), different modes of communication must also be rendered somehow equivalent so that one mode (emojis) can substitute for another (words). It is for this reason that emojis are so often depicted as being a distinctive language in and of themselves. In academic, theoretical terms, none of this is technically correct. At the very least, language requires three core features: modality, meaning, and grammar (Cohn 2013, 2016; Jackendoff 2002). All other modes must follow suit. As Cohn (2013:3) suggests, when modes such as sounds, gestures, or images follow "a *structured sequence* [emphasis added] governed by rules that constrain the output – i.e. a grammar – it yields a type of language". For instance, the sequential images of comics form a (type of) language. Although emojis express meaning using visual graphic signs as a modality, research by our colleagues Dürscheid & Siever (2017) show that they lack a grammar. Unlike the visual graphic signs of comics, emojis do not form structured sequences of visual signs, for example. None of which, of course, seems to bother newsmakers who, like many people, tend to use language in its more metaphorical sense – as in "body language" (as we saw above) or "the language of flowers".

Having settled on the distinctiveness and putative validity of emojis as a language, newsmakers are better positioned to pursue its antagonistic, colonizing relationship to language. As we say, one of the other common ways language endangerment is produced is through the tactical framing of emojis' dramatic rise and spread. This, in turn, lays the groundwork for the overall framing of threat and, eventually, decline which we want to discuss in more detail. To start, though, we want to note how the rise-and-spread rhetorical tactic is organized most obviously through various forms of lexical exaggeration: numerical claim ('six billion times a day'); superlatives ('fastest'), and metaphors of disaster ('la déferlante'). We also find a somewhat warped sense of history; recall "fastest growing language in history" in Extract 2.1 to which we now have 'die am schnellsten wachsende Sprache der Welt' (the fastest growing language in the world) in Extract 2. In Extract 2.7, meanwhile, talk of the 'l'incroyable histoire' (the incredible history) of emojis is clearly a type of scalar excess. Elsewhere, we also find metaphors of war (e.g. 'invasion') and references to the ubiquitous nature of emojis. In Extract 2.7, we have the same kind of lexical excess ('massivement' – massively) as well as telling evidence for the spread of emojis: their appearance in dictionaries even. Note also the kind of agency given to emojis – their rudely having invited themselves into the dictionaries!

Extract 2.10 (Le Monde, France)
Massivement utilisés, ils s'invitent jusque dans le dictionnaire
Used massively, they are even inviting themselves into dictionaries

Extract 2.11 (Tagblatt, Switzerland)
Schreiben Sie noch oder emojisieren Sie schon? Über die Bilder, welche die Handysprache erobert haben.
Are you still writing or are you already emojing? On the images that have conquered mobile language.

Extract 2.12 (La Prensa, Honduras)
Es el nuevo lenguaje de las emociones. Los emoticones se apoderan de la propuesta juvenil.
It's the new language of emotions. Emoticons have taken control of youth-oriented marketing.

Extract 2.10 is revealing in some key ways. Emojis are not only presented as a powerful – potentially destructive – phenomenon, but also as an agentive process somehow bringing about changes by itself. It is not the users of emojis who are at fault but instead it is emojis that are shown to be spreading, growing and generally infiltrating our lives. All of which is a typical expression of technological determinism – the belief that technology drives cultural change rather than vice-versa, and that technology dictates communicative or social practice as opposed to being shaped by communicative and social needs or uses. But this way of thinking about – and depicting – emojis also encodes a semiotic-ideological belief in the exteriority and thingness of language. It is akin to what Cameron (1990; also 1995: 5) characterizes as the "organic fallacy" – the mistaken belief that language, like a tree, just grows somehow willy-nilly beyond human control. This sense of (visual) communication gone wild – rampantly spreading – certainly serves the overarching preoccupation with the decline and even replacement of language.

Extract 2.13
With emojis you can send virtual flowers and kisses, so perhaps the question now is, will real language be lost to this new virtual one? (The Guardian, UK, 25 June 2015)

Extract 2.14
Assiste-t-on alors à un appauvrissement de la langue? La chercheuse observe en tout cas un phénomène nouveau par rapport aux premieres emoticônes: aujourd'hui, des emoji

remplacent des mots et ne font plus que venir en complément. (Le Matin, Switzerland, 24 April 2015)
Are we thus witnessing an impoverishment of language? The researcher observes in any case a new phenomenon compared to the first emoticons: today, some emojis are replacing words and are not only used as a complement.

Extract 2.15 (Tages-Anzeiger, Switzerland)
'Verhunzen die Smileys unsere Sprache?' fragte die Schweiz am Sonntag. Inflationär und gedankenlos eingesetzt, erschweren diese modernen Hieroglyphen bei SMS oder Whatsapp-Mitteilungen das Verständnis, statt die Kommunikation zu vereinfachen.
'*Are smileys ruining our language?' asks Schweiz am Sonntag. Used excessively and thoughtlessly, these modern hieroglyphics make it hard to understand SMS or Whatsapp messages rather than simplifying communication.*

Extract 2.16 (Infobae, Argentina)
Abusar de los 'Emojis': ¿El nuevo enemigo del lenguaje?
Emoji abuse: The new enemy of language?

Perhaps not surprisingly, Extract 2.13 comes from the same article featured in our title (see also Figure 2.1); with its headlined framing of invasion, the stance of the article is quite unambiguously pessimistic: words are being over-run and "real language" will be overtaken. In other words, language is being replaced. (In effect, we have a circular argument: if there is the possibility of emojis replacing words, then they must be capable of functioning like a fully-fledged language.) In the same way, Extract 2.14 moves swiftly from the potential impoverishment of language by emojis ('un appauvrissement de la langue') to the concern that words are to some extent being replaced ('des emojis remplacent des mots'). Our Spanish-language example makes the case most clearly by invoking the notion of an enemy of language ('enemigo del language) – another agentful misattribution – and by laying the blame, in principle, with emojis or, at least, their uncontrolled use ('abusar de los Emojis' – emoji abuse). As with our German-language example (Extract 2.15), the issues are framed as questions (e.g. 'Verhunzen die Smileys unsere Sprache?' – Are smileys ruining our language?), but even asking the question raises the possibility, especially when it is flagged in the main headline.

These comments point not only to a simplistic relationship of cause and effect, but also to the belief that emojis and words cannot function together, that they are inherently and/or inevitably incompatible. Indeed, the cause and effect structure (more emojis leads to fewer words) negates the possibility that while the use of emojis might well rise this does not mean that people will stop writing – or stop knowing how to write. These kinds of comments underscore the deeper concern that emojis (actually the use of emojis) will lead not only to linguistic degradation but also to intellectual and cultural regression. We see this most clearly expressed in the following English-language extracts which refer, respectively, to backwards evolution, a return to ancient hieroglyphics and the end of civilization.

Extract 2.17 (The Guardian, UK)
We are evolving backwards. Emoji, the visual system of communication that is incredibly popular online, is Britain's fastest-growing language according to Professor Vyv Evans, a linguist at Bangor University.

Extract 2.18 (CNBC, USA)
If these classes need to incorporate the language and symbols used in the mobile/digital world, aren't we just regressing back to the age of hieroglyphs?

Extract 2.19 (Telegraph, UK)
Some have questioned whether they represent the end of civilisation as we know it. Would Shakespeare turn in his grave if he could see what has become of our language?

These are, of course, all too familiar ways in which digital discourse practices are metadiscursively framed, although for slightly different ends. In his work on the news media's depiction of texting style, Thurlow (2006: 680) also picked up on references to hieroglyphics; in this case, however, journalists used the term for exaggerating the distinctiveness and unintelligibility of digital discourse. In this case, hieroglyphics is being invoked for its supposed "primitiveness" in terms of both its being non-modern and pictographic rather than alphabetic. (Recall from Extract 2.15 the ironic reference to 'moderne Hieroglyphen' – modern hieroglyphs.)

As something of an aside, we note that, in the same article extracted in 2.17, Professor Evans is actually reported as being a lot more circumspect: "People get hot and bothered about good language use, but emoji is not a language,' he says. 'Its job isn't to replace language; it's enhancing our communications." As Thurlow (2006: 683) has noted before, these otherwise rare moments of nuance are often undermined anyway by the driving narrative and/or concluding remarks of the article.

The over-riding tone or stance of Extracts 2.17, 2.18 and 2.19 is one of pessimism – or what Thurlow (2006) might characterize as moral panic. Emojis are depicted unforgivingly and one-dimensionally as a backward form of communication leading not only to the demise of language but, as a consequence, to intellectual and cultural stultification. It is a perfect example of recursivity which, with reference to language ideologies, Irvine & Gal (2000) identify as the often unfounded extrapolation of isolated (iconized) linguistic features or practices to whole new domains of life. The idea here is that any putative linguistic regression is equivalent to intellectual and cultural regression. This, too, is all a matter of semiotic ideology insofar as language is evidently upheld as the only and/or ideal bearer of culture and vehicle for intelligent expression. Of course, and as we have already seen in Extract 2.7, it is not all language which is regarded in this way. Implicitly or not, we are reminded that written language and particularly literary language are the true markers of culture, intellectual life and civilization. It is for this reason alone that, in true form, the British press turns worriedly to Shakespeare (Extract 2.19) as the ultimate arbiter of good, proper or real language. In his study, Thurlow (2006: 679) cites the following 2003 example from his data: "And to think this happened in the land of Shakespeare. If the bard were alive today, he'd probably write, '2B or not 2B'." Over fifteen years later, one could well imagine a journalist somewhere bemoaning the use of something like this:

The kinds of metadiscursive framing we have looked at so far clearly hinge on – and reproduce – a range of well-worn language ideologies (e.g. about standard language) which, in turn, are organized through the usual processes of iconization and erasure – selectively singling out some aspects and ignoring others. (We come to recursivity in a moment.) But our main focus here continues to be on the semiotic ideologies at play; in particular, the apparently irremovable divide or irresolvable contest between words and images, between language and visual communication. Everything it seems boils down to the issue of mode/modality. Indeed, this is a particular semiotic ideology which Riley (2011) actually chooses to label as a distinctive "modal ideology". (Riley is herself concerned with how cultural beliefs about language acquisition affect language socialization.) It seems that conflicting beliefs about the superiority/inferiority of images and writing are something which play out across the lifespan. In this regard, Kress and van Leeuwen (2006: 16) comment on the status of images at school; for instance, although pupils are encouraged to draw at school, their illustrations are rarely seen as a means to communicate, unlike words. And as they become older, students focus more and more on writing at the expense of images. Similarly, Cohn (2013: 3) explains how drawing is usually only viewed as a "skill" compared to writing which is seen as a "rule-governed system". Writing is thus commonly and widely regarded as a sign of progress and culture. This helps to explain the emergence of *language endangerment* and perhaps some of the fierceness with which it is expressed.

There is one other point of theory which we would like to offer in the way of explanation. While writing is itself inherently visual (Cohn 2013; Kress & van Leeuwen 2006), it is different from other types of visual discourse because, argues Cohn (2013: 6), for alphabetic scripts at least it is "based on the correspondence that graphic signs have with sound". This makes it more difficult – in theory and practice – to draw a neat distinction between the written mode and the visual mode, although one might reasonably distinguish between the written mode and the *image* mode. With regards the emojis-and-language relationship, moral panic arises when emojis are perceived to be substituting for words; as such, we do not see a rejection of visual communication in toto. This is how Kress & van Leeuwen (2006: 17) put it: "the opposition to the emergence of the visual as a full means of representation is not based on an opposition to the visual as such, but on an opposition in situations where it forms an alternative to writing and can therefore be seen as a potential threat to the present dominance of verbal literacy among elite groups". We might argue, therefore, that newsmakers and others are not rejecting image-based communication because it is visual, but because they give more importance to words and writing – and without recognizing that it, too, is a form of visual communication. The relationship between words and images is ultimately constructed as a necessarily competitive one.

4 Conclusion: Misrecognizing communication

> This kind of visual literacy (the "old" visual literacy) has, for centuries now, been one of the most essential achievements and values of Western culture [...] No wonder that the move towards a new literacy, based on images and visual design, can come to be seen as a threat, a sign of the decline of culture.   (Kress & van Leeuwen 1996: 15)

More than twenty years ago, Kress & van Leeuwen (quoted above) commented on the rise of visuality and design as powerful – perhaps even dominant – communicative modes in contemporary life. There was, they argued, an ever-growing importance attached to visual literacy but that this shift from conventional, logocentric notions of literacy would inevitably be met with resistance and anxiety. In many ways, it is precisely this kind of cultural reaction or public back-lash that we have been documenting in our chapter. The *language endangerment* is certainly a discourse being played out across the multilingual news-media data. Arguably for the reasons we have just discussed, this seems to be something which has captured the public imagination, fed in no small part by newsmakers. In this regard, and as a way to start wrapping up, we offer the following headlines from more recent data (also archived in the Digital Discourse Database), two stories from more conservative newspapers in the UK.[4]

> Emoji 'are ruining the English language because young people use them to communicate and don't bother with words'

> Emoji 'ruining people's grasp of English' because young rely on them to communicate

The study being cited in these two stories is, it transpires, concerned with popular perceptions, as the first article explains: "Of the two thousand adults, aged 16 to 65, who were asked their views, 94 per cent reckoned English was in a state of decline, with 80 per cent citing youngsters as the worst offenders." (It is perhaps all the more ironic that the use of "reckoned" in this sentence might well be considered "bad English" by many. For that matter, another pet peeve of grammar police appears with "regressing back" in Extract 2.18.) More to the point, and quite contrary to the driving argument of the headlines and the body of the articles, we also learn the following about the survey's results: "around three-quarters of adults rely on emoji to communicate". It seems that popular beliefs and feelings about emojis are generally quite confused; in the UK at least there certainly seems to be a double-standard about who is to blame for the demise of language. Regardless, the biggest nonsense in this story is the persistent suggestion – by survey participants and the journalists – that people (young or otherwise) no longer "bother with words" or must now rely exclusively on emojis for communicating.

As wordsmiths, journalists not surprisingly take a very logocentric view of emojis, assuming that words are necessarily superior. Theirs is an inherently ingrained belief that words are likely to be more sophisticated, more reliable bearers of meaning than images. But theirs is also an especially powerful, privileged position from which to reproduce and promote these beliefs. Even in the apparently innocuous act of valuing one mode of communication over another, journalists "have the potential to re-scale social, cultural, and symbolic capital, and thereby 're-shuffle' authority and expertise on particular issues" (Milani & Johnson 2010: 6). They are also able to shore up their own authority, using their position as workers-cum-arbiters of language "in the service of the struggle to maintain or acquire power" (Woolard 1998: 6). They do so by trying to fix certain semiotic ideologies, making them seem obvious and commonsensical. The media does not merely attempt to mirror reality but circulates a naturalized, but often distorted version of reality in which certain voices are privileged

---

4 The two stories come from *The Daily Mail* (18 April 2018) and *The Telegraph* (17 April, 2018).

over others and in ways which often contradict or erase what people are actually doing in their everyday communicative practices.

Emojis are everywhere and consistently portrayed by journalists as inherently simplistic and limited – in Bernstein's (1971) famous terms, this is a seriously "restricted" code – with the implication that they cannot possibly be as meaningful or sensible as words. It is not that we regard newsmakers as necessarily wrong, although they are sometimes clearly making things up. (Note the oddly inconsistent quotations in the two headlines above.) As Cameron (1995: 9) remarks, everyone is a prescriptivist or "verbal hygienist" of one kind or another – even academic linguists. We are less interested therefore in the inaccuracy and/or normativity of journalists' comments which are sometimes to the point of discriminatory when it comes to young people (again, cf. Thurlow 2014). It is not for us to confirm or deny the central premise of the language endangerment discourse, even though we may disagree or even disapprove. Rather, we are interested in tracking how "popular" discussions of putatively good or bad modes *misrecognize* communication in ways which expose underlying semiotic ideologies – that is, dominant cultural discourses about signification and meaning-making. By "misrecognition", we refer to Bourdieu's (1984) sense that something is misattributed to a different, inappropriate or inaccurate realm of meaning (cf. James 2015: 100). Things are not recognized for what they are because of naturalized assumptions that are deeply ingrained through a set of cultural, social, political processes. Consequently, people are not fully aware of – or willing to entertain – the complex nature of emojis, of language or the functioning of different semiotic modes. Of course, even experts like academics spend a great deal of time trying to figure these things out and arguing between themselves about the nature and relative merits of semiotic actions.

The "language endangerment" discourse we have pointed to here reveals a troubling but not altogether surprising misrecognition of language, visual communication and the inherently multimodal nature of all communication. In short, journalists appear simply unwilling to address the significant difference between semiotic modes – or to challenge the simplistic ways other people speak of these issues. The bottom line, as Kress and van Leeuwen (2006: 19) observe, is that not "everything that can be realized in language can also be realized by means of images, or vice versa". It all depends on the particular affordances of different mode or semiotic resources. More to the point, it seems that most ordinary speakers invariably find ways to express meaning using a combination of different modes; they also understand – intuitively or not – when meaning might be "lost in translation" if the "wrong" mode is used. It is not just emojis which come off poorly from the news media reporting, therefore, but also everyday speakers themselves who are effectively treated as unwitting or incapable dupes. Perhaps this is how journalists see the rest of us. Perhaps this is how they keep themselves gainfully employed as the great defenders of words.

Acknowledgements: This chapter reports research conducted as part of "The Cultural Discourses and Social Meanings of Mobile Communication", a sub-project of *What's up, Switzerland?* funded by the Swiss National Science Foundation (Jan 2016–Dec 2019; CRSII1-160714). It is also closely allied with Vanessa's doctoral thesis being conducted under the auspices of the same SNF sub-project. We take this chance to thank our research assistant Sabrina Subašić for her archival and data-entry support, and also Eva Rau for her help in identifying some German-language data as part of her BA thesis. We are grateful also to Christa Dürscheid for her close read, her insights and her help with polishing things.

We paid for permission to use the headline and byline in the Guardian newspaper extract (Figure 2.1). We are grateful also to Otto Yamamoto at All-Nite Images (Flickr) for permission to use the image in this extract.

References

Androutsopoulos, Jannis & Jana Tereick. 2015. Youtube: Language and discourse practices in participatory culture. In Alexandra Georgakopoulou & Teresa Spilioti (eds.), *The routledge handbook of language and communication*, 354–370. Abingdon: Routledge.
Baker, Paul, Costas Gabrielatos, Majid KhosraviNik, Michał Krzyzanowski, Tony McEnery & Ruth Wodak. 2008. A useful methodological synergy? Combining critical discourse analysis and corpus linguistics to examine discourses of refugees and asylum seekers in the UK press. *Discourse & Society* 19(3), 273–306.
Bell, Allan. 1991. *The Language of the News Media*. Oxford: Blackwell.
Bernstein, Basil. 1971. *Class, codes and control: Theoretical studies towards a sociology of language*. London: Routledge & Kegan Paul.
Bourdieu, Pierre. 1984. *Distinction: A social critique of the judgement of taste*. Cambridge, MA: Harvard University Press.
Cameron, Deborah. 1990. In John E. Joseph & Talbot J. Taylor (eds.), *Ideologies of Language*, 79–93. London: Routledge.
Cameron, Deborah. 1995. *Verbal hygiene*. London, UK: Routledge.
Cohn, Neil. 2013. *The visual language of comics: Introduction to the structure and cognition of sequential images*. London, UK: Bloomsbury.
Cohn, Neil. 2016. *The visual narrative reader*. London, UK: Bloomsbury.
De Certeau, Michel. 1984. The practice of everyday life. [S. Rendall, Trans.]. Berkeley, CA: University of California Press.
Duchêne, Alexandre & Monica Heller. 2007. Discourses of endangerment: Sociolinguistics, globalization and social order. In Alexandre Duchêne & Monica Heller (eds.), *Discourses*

of endangerment: Interest and ideology in the defense of languages, 1–13. London: Continuum.

Dürscheid, Christa & Christina M. Siever. 2017. Jenseits des Alphabets – Kommunikation mit Emojis. *Zeitschrift für Germanistische Linguistik* 45(2),256–285.

Ecker, Ullrich K. H., Stephan Lewandowsky, Ee Pin Chang & Rekha B. Pillai. 2014. The effects of subtle misinformation in news headlines. *Journal of Experimental Psychology: Applied* 20(4),323–335.

Fairclough, Norman. 1989. *Language and power*. London: Longman.

Ge, Jing & Susan C. Herring. 2018. Communicative functions of emoji sequences on Sina Weibo. *First Monday* 23(11). Available: https://firstmonday.org/ojs/index.php/fm/article/view/9413 (21 February, 2019)

Gershon, Ilana. 2010. Media ideologies: An introduction. *Journal of Linguistic Anthropology* 20(2),283–293.

Irvine, Judith T. & Susan Gal. 2000. Language ideology and linguistic differentiation. In Paul V. Kroskrity (ed.), *Regimes of Language: Ideologies, Polities, and Identities*, 35–84. Santa Fe: School of American Research Press.

Jackendoff, Ray. 2002. *Foundations of language: Brain, meaning, grammar, evolution*. Oxford: Oxford University Press.

James, David. 2015. How Bourdieu bites back: recognising misrecognition in education and educational research. *Cambridge Journal of Education* 45(1),97–112.

Jaroski, Vanessa. Forthcoming. *The affective regimes of digital discourse: A multimodal, multilingual study of language, media and gender ideologies*. PhD thesis, University of Bern, Switzerland.

Keane, Webb. 2003. Semiotics and the social analysis of material things. *Language and Communication* 23, 409–425.

Kress, Gunther & Theo van Leeuwen. 1996. *Reading Images: The Grammar of Visual Design*. New York, NY: Routledge.

Kress, Gunther & Theo van Leeuwen. 2006. *Reading images: The Grammar of Visual Design*. 2nd edn. New York, NY: Routledge.

Milani, Tommaso M. & Sally Johnson. 2010. Critical intersections: Language ideologies and media discourse. In Sally Johnson and Tommaso M. Milani (eds.), *Language ideologies and media discourse: Texts, practices, politics*, 3–14. London: Continuum.

Parmentier, Richard J. 1994. *Signs and society*. Bloomington, IN: Indiana University Press.

Riley, Kathleen C. 2011. Language socialization and language ideologies. In Alessandro Duranti, Elinor Ochs & Bambi Schieffelin (eds.), *The handbook of language socialization*, 493–514. Chichester, UK: Wiley.

Tagliamonte, Sali A. & Derek Denis. 2008. Linguistic ruin? LOL! Instant messaging and teen language. *American Speech* 83(1),3–34.

Tannen, Deborah. 1989. *Talking voices: Repetition, dialogue, and imagery in conversational discourse*. Cambridge: Cambridge University Press.

Thurlow, Crispin. 2006. From statistical panic to moral panic: The metadiscursive construction and popular exaggeration of new media language in the print media. *Journal of Computer-Mediated Communication* 11(3).

Thurlow, Crispin. 2007. Fabricating youth: New-media discourse and the technologization of young people. In Sally Johnson & Astrid Ensslin (eds.), *Language in the media: Representations, identities, ideologies*, 213–233. London: Continuum.

Thurlow, Crispin. 2014. Disciplining youth: Language ideologies and new technologies. In Adam Jaworski & Nikolas Coupland (eds.), *The Discourse reader*. 3rd edn., 481–496. London: Routledge.

Thurlow, Crispin. 2017. "Forget about the words"? Tracking the language, media and semiotic ideologies of digital discourse: The case of sexting. *Discourse, Context & Media* 20, 10–19.

Thurlow, Crispin. 2018. Digital discourse: Locating language in new/social media. In Jean Burgess, Thomas Poell & Alice Marwick, (eds.), *The sage handbook of social media*, 135–145. New York, NY: Sage

Thurlow, Crispin & Giorgia Aiello. 2007. National pride, global capital: A social semiotic analysis of transnational visual branding in the airline industry. *Visual Communication* 6(3),305–344.

Thurlow, Crispin, Giorgia Aiello & Lara Portmann. (2019). Visualizing teens and technology: A social semiotic analysis of stock photography and news media imagery. *New Media & Society*. doi.org/10.1177%2F1461444819867318

Vaisman, Carmel L. 2014. Beautiful script, cute spelling and glamorous words: Doing girlhood through language playfulness on Israeli blogs. *Language & Communication* 34, 69–80.

Woolard, Kathryn & Bambi Schieffelin. 1994. Language ideology. *Annual Review of Anthropology* 23, 55–82.

Woolard, Kathryn. 1998. Introduction: Language ideology as a field of inquiry. In Bambi Schieffelin, Kathryn Woolard, & Paul V. Kroskrity (eds.), *Language Ideology: Practice and Theory*, 3–50. Oxford, UK: Oxford University Press.

Georg Albert
3 Beyond the binary: Emoji as a challenge to the image-word distinction

1 Introduction

Emoticons and emoji are undoubtedly a major phenomenon of contemporary writing practices. Although the "smiley" existed well before the internet (cf. Bieswanger 2013: 470; Veszelszki 2017: 131), only the written interaction via internet services and mobile phones caused the enormous diffusion and formal differentiation of emoji. In our everyday lives we clearly link them to messengers and chats, they are indeed considered a prototypical feature of these written forms of interaction. Emoticons and emoji are not commonly accepted elements of the standard language, and their stylistic value is regarded very different by different social groups. While some users consider emoji usage infantile or inappropriate, others perceive emoji as indispensable for avoiding misunderstandings in written messages (cf. Albert 2015: 4; Veszelszki 2017: 185) and for enhancing communication.

Much like in the early days of the internet, which were times of experimentation and a pioneer spirit, the first linguistic works on internet phenomena could not rely on clear-cut categories or time-tested methods. Prior to the turn of the millennium, the term *smiley* was commonly used, but gradually *emoticon* became the preferred name (cf. Runkehl, Schlobinski & Siever 1998: 96). Both terms, however, remained vague, and analyses of emoticon usage within chats or email were somewhat cursory (cf. Thome 2001: 46; Imo 2015: 137). Many authors simply mentioned emoticons as a typical feature of computer-mediated communication and presented data samples without deeper theoretical reflection. Rarely were relations between emoticons and their verbal context discussed in depth.

Attempts to separate smileys, emoticons, emoji and kaomoji from each other are also worth mentioning. As Siever (2015: 289) notes, the various terminological differentiations are inconsistent because they are partly based on formal criteria and partly on functional differences. For the sake of convenience, I endorse Siever's approach which subsumes emoticons and kaomoji as special kinds of emoji. In this chapter, I therefore use *emoji* as an umbrella term also covering earlier ASCII emoticons. My focus here is specifically on those emoji which resemble faces; alongside hearts and very few others, these are the most frequently used but also the ones most relevant to my argument.

https://doi.org/10.1515/9781501510113-004

From the functional perspective which will be pursued here, there are no categorical differences drawn between smileys, emoticons, kaomoji and other kinds of emoji. Instead, and more importantly, they all need to be distinguished from photographs, videos and memes.

2 Functions of emoji

Many early works on emoji or rather emoticons presume that their (sole) function was to express emotions (cf. Runkehl, Schlobinski, & Siever 1998: 96). Some recent works also support such a view, as with Veszelszki (2017: 129): "The main function of emoticons is to express emotions and to substitute suprasegmental and extralinguistic means. The importance of their expressive function has been evidenced by examinations in the field of non-verbal communication." Unquestionably, emoji are valuable for emulating paralinguistic and nonverbal signs such as facial expressions and gestures, which occur in face-to-face conversations but not in written forms of communication (cf. Bieswanger 2013: 469; Arens & Nösler 2014: 52; Veszelszki 2017: 129). As some authors note, however, computer-mediated communication is also possible and successful without using emoji; this means that emoji might actually be used for purposes other than merely expressing moods and attitudes (cf. Höflich 2003: 187).

Some authors have described traditional emoticons as devices for increasing the impression of immediacy between participants of a written conversation by compensating for the missing mimic and gestural signs. This compensation model of emoticon usage, however, neglects other important functions, which are not related to emotive facial expressions. After all, the possible functions of emoji certainly cannot be reduced to just a single aspect. Dresner and Herring (2012: 61) point out: "[T]he conception of emoticons as expressing affect is incomplete at best ... many facial emoticons do not seem to express a single emotion, or indeed any emotion at all. Is a face with the tongue sticking out – e.g.,;- p – a sign of a specific emotion?"

The formal analogy between emoji faces in general and the corresponding facial expressions provokes the misleading inference that there must also be a functional analogy. Emoji faces, however, are not similar to immediately perceivable expressions on a person's face (cf. Christian 2017: 224). They are intentionally produced signs within or following a verbal message. Many authors underestimate the difference between automatic expressions of emotional states and conventional signs for emotions. A lot of confusion is also caused by not considering the nature of emotions and feelings. In fact, it is worthwhile pursuing terminological

3 Beyond the binary: Emoji as a challenge to the image-word distinction — 67

precision instead of treating *emotion, feeling* or other terms as more or less synonymous. Neuroscientific descriptions turn out to be helpful. Antonio Damasio proposes to distinguish various nonconscious states from a state of feeling made conscious (cf. Damasio 2000: 36).

In Damasio's terms, emotions are physiological conditions resulting in different brain representations. Only feelings, however, have the potential to become conscious (cf. Damasio 2000: 279). Feelings, consequently, but not emotions, may or may not be expressed verbally, evaluated, or interpreted. The potential stimuli for emotions are "not biologically prescribed to be emotionally laden" (Damasio 2000: 58) but correspond with individual or cultural factors. Even more so, the expression of feelings is largely governed by social and cultural factors. Gerhards (1988) points out that every cultural group develops both feeling norms and expression norms to regulate what feelings are expected in certain situations and how they can and should be expressed towards others (cf. also Christian 2017: 239, who refers to the psychologist Paul Ekman and mentions "display rules"). An example of when people make a startled face when realizing that they have let something slip which should not have been mentioned. Such "accidental" statements are facilitated by the ephemeral and irreversible nature of spoken language. The message in Figure 3.1, however, was sent despite the "inept" statement; the "flushed face" emoji therefore is not a reaction but part of a complex and ironic teasing:

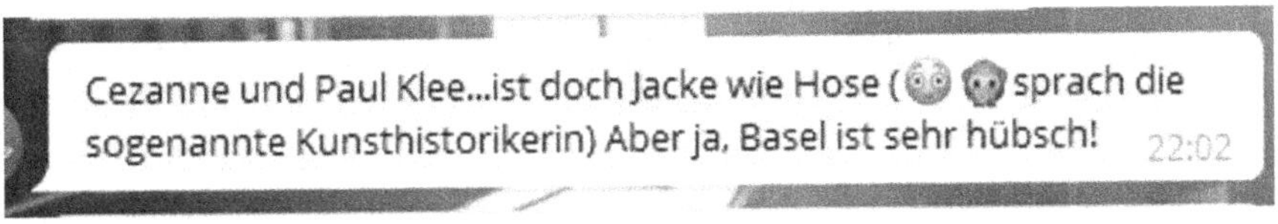

> Cezanne und Paul Klee…ist doch Jacke wie Hose (😳 🙊 sprach die sogenannte Kunsthistorikerin) Aber ja, Basel ist sehr hübsch! 22:02

Figure 3.1: Cézanne and Klee. Message stating that Paul Cezanne and Paul Klee are like six of one and half a dozen of another, followed by a "flushed face" emoji and a "speak-no-evil monkey". (Private source).

Put simply, it is highly unlikely that an emoji spontaneously or accidentally would indicate a specific emotional state. The neuro-physiological processes which are triggered by a state of emotion lead to the conscious perception of a feeling and may result in the decision to send an emoji. Yet these processes are not observable in the written data. The emoji's contribution to a communicative act, however, is undoubtedly an issue for linguistics. Fiehler (1990: 99) emphasizes that the expression of feelings in face-to-face-conversations are social phenomena. Even more in written conversations, expressions of feelings need to be analyzed within their social and interactional context. Whenever a person's feelings have a part in a conversation, manifestation rules (cf. Fiehler 1990: 100) apply. No smiling face – even less so a smiling emoji – enables a person to draw a certain conclusion about someone else's emotional state.

Initially, the use of emoticons was clearly guided by their resemblance to facial expressions. The most frequently used emoji, which have substituted the ASCII-emoticons in many contexts, are predominantly depictions of facial expressions, too. Various facial expressions are used conventionally as symbolic signs (i.e., not indexical or iconic signs) for specific feelings. These fundamental features of emoji, however, do not necessarily determine their possible functions and usage in written interaction.

The medial differences between face-to-face-communication and written messages suggest a comparison of emoticons (cf. Imo 2015: 137) and facial emoji with verbal elements rather than with gestural signs, mimic signs or prosody. Previous research has been able to describe metalinguistic and pragmatic functions of emoji, which differ very much from the non-verbal signs occurring during face-to-face-conversation. According to these studies, emoji prototypically fulfill at least one of four main functions: They can serve to (1) indicate an utterance's intended illocutionary force, (2) to structure and partition complex utterances, (3) to add information about the mode of an utterance, and (4) to indicate social styles or registers (cf. Dresner & Herring 2012: 60; Imo 2015; Albert 2015; Danesi 2017: 97–98; Pappert 2017). A fifth function can sometimes be observed in playful contexts, when (5) single letters, words, or entire phrases are substituted by an emoji (cf. Dürscheid & Siever 2017: 268–273). When indicating illocutionary force, emoji often mark utterances as ironic or diminish the face-threatening potential of an utterance. The structuring effect of emoticon usage is described in Imo (2015); emoticons as well as many of the newer emoji can be used like punctuation marks to separate sentential units, or they separate different communicative acts from each other, such as responses from topic changes. It must be mentioned that a single emoji usually serves more than one function and may also functionally overlap with other linguistic means.

The stylistic potentials of emoji have been neglected in many works. In a recent paper, however, Pappert (2017) proposes to apply principles of Interactional Stylistics to the analysis of emoji usage. From an interactional perspective, emoji are means of contextualization (cf. Pappert 2017: 180). The following example from a chat corpus demonstrates the stylistic use of an ASCII emoticon. Other possible functions do not play a role in this simple expression of joy:

freu mich schon so :)   English gloss: *i'm really excited* :)

In such cases, the emoticon or likewise the "grinning face" emoji adds nothing to the propositional content, nor does it affect the illocutionary force. It does mark the end of the utterance and thus – regarding only the distributional aspect – operates just like a full stop or an exclamation mark would do. The choice between these standard punctuation marks and the emoticon is therefore a matter of style (cf. Busch 2017). The emoticon conveys informality and social proximity, which is to say that it contextualizes the entire utterance (cf. Arens & Nösler 2014: 51). The message is straightforward, and the absence of mimic signs is not a problem at all; the emoticon is not required to compensate for that.

3 The image-word binary

The dualistic distinction between images (considered as natural signs) and words (considered as conventional signs) is common and seemingly straightforward. Due to their formal qualities, emoji are usually categorized as images. According to Goodman & Elgin (1988: 101), however, things in the world of symbols are not quite as clear-cut: "A number of symbols, including star charts, hieroglyphics, and Chinese pictographs, seem intermediate cases. It is not clear whether they should be considered natural or conventional signs".[1]

Previous research on emoticons and emoji has offered different kinds of categorizations and descriptions but not a consistent semiotic terminology (cf. for example Arens & Nösler 2014; Graßl 2014). A striking example for the ambiguous perception of the phenomenon is its localization "between the extremes of non-language and language" by Dresner & Herring (2012: 62). (See also Thurlow & Jaroski, current volume, for a popular version of this ideology.) In my chapter here, I want to demonstrate that any definite categorization of emoji as either linguistic or non-linguistic signs needs to highlight some aspects while neglecting others.

Many everyday digitally mediated conversations consist only of one or more emoji. Such non-verbal contributions are enabled by the context as well as the highly conventionalized meaning of some emoji. Kissing faces or heart-shaped emoji, for example, may be sufficient for partners in a close or romantic relationship to run a phatic conversation with each other. Nevertheless, emoji usage is ordinarily embedded in written verbal communication and combined

---

[1] From the perspective of a linguistic theory of writing, Goodman and Elgin are obviously referring to logograms but not pictographs. The development of the Chinese writing system, however, is an excellent example for the porous border between images and words.

with some verbal content. Therefore, when treating "the contribution of emoticons to computer-mediated interaction as independent of language" (Dresner & Herring 2012: 61), one might indeed miss important interdependencies.

Their entanglement with the verbal elements distinguishes the emoji from illustrative artwork. Unlike other visual elements within chats and messenger dialogues, emoji may be inserted into sentence structures or even replace single lexemes and graphemes (cf. Dürscheid & Frick 2014: 174; Siever 2015: 286). The bulk of emoji, however, appears at the end of conversational turns or to separate different speech acts from each other. In such cases, they indeed function as punctuation marks (cf. Thome 2001: 54; Dresner & Herring 2012: 62; Albert 2015: 18). The standard repertoire of punctuation marks, of course, consists of elements with well-defined functions but no explicable meaning of their own. Emoji do have a much richer semantic content and are not functionally restricted like "normal" punctuation marks. Therefore, they also share some of the features of established logograms such as <$>, <&> or <%>. Logograms in alphabetic systems do not belong to the graphemic repertoire, because they are not combined with graphemes to build meaningful morphemes but have a meaning of their own. A conventional meaning is a feature of words and not of images. In 2015, the frequently used "crying tears of joy" emoji was actually declared "word of the year" by Oxford Dictionaries. Although an emoji language is not likely to develop, the similarities between emoji and words are worth considering.

3.1 The meaning of emoji

Some scholars have tried to distinguish emoji from verbal signs on semantic grounds; these attempts are obviously based on the kind of dualism described by Goodman & Elgin (1988: 101):

> Pictorial representation is thought to be natural – a matter of resemblance between image and object. This resemblance, moreover, is taken to be an objective matter, visible to the human eye and evident to all who look. Linguistic representation, on the other hand, is considered conventional – working by rules and stipulations that secure the connection between words and the world.

An example of this dualistic reasoning can be found in Miller et al. (2016): "Emoji are used alongside text in digital communication, but their visual nature leaves them open to interpretation" (10). In the same vein, Veszelszki (2017) states that "emoticons are incomprehensible without context (or have only very general meaning)" but "help to avoid misunderstandings in written texts" (129). Essentially, these descriptions assume that words have clear and definite meanings, whereas images are semantically diffused. Miller et al. (2016) explicitly make this assumption: "Words have a dictionary definition, but emoji are nuanced, visually-detailed graphics that may be more open to interpretation" (1). Both claims, however, imply a double misconception: first, words themselves do not have a fixed or context-independent meaning; second, images are never completely open to interpretation. When Veszelszki (2017) says that emoji "have no meaning in themselves, they only gain it when used" (129), the same holds true for words (i.e., lexemes) according to major theories of natural language semantics. Siever (2015: 296) shows that emoji can indeed invoke frames just like words do.

The basic form of the emoticon <:-) > is said to have been first used by the computer scientist Scott Fahlman in 1982 to tag jokes (cf. Veszelszki 2017: 131). Since then, however, the number of emoji has increased enormously. The meaning of numerous emoji is subject of many online discussion boards, and usage differs between communities of practice (cf. Thome 2001: 54–55). Explaining emoji, therefore, must reach beyond the characteristics derivable from their resemblance to faces or objects, which is, after all, only relevant for their genesis. To understand emoji, one must consider the context of their appearance in the same way one would with verbal expressions. Following Giovannelli (2017: 5), a symbol can only be described in relation to a symbol system.

Unlike prototypical images such as photographs or paintings, emoji are enlisted and annotated. By now, they are not only presented in lists and collections compiled by users but standardized in Unicode (cf. Siever 2015: 284; Christian 2017: 222). Aside from the vagueness of individual utterances containing emoji, the very existence of a code and of explanatory lists reveals a key feature of emoji as Goodman & Elgin (1988: 110) explain: "Lexicons and grammars are possible only for systems whose symbols are determinate and discriminable. For lexicons and grammars consist of generalizations that apply to symbols because they are tokens of specific syntactic types." Veszelszki (2017) misconceives the semiotic nature of emoji when she explains that emoji lists explain depictions "on the basis of resemblance" (132). Such lists would be rather superfluous if resemblance really was that important: characters in the list would otherwise be self-explanatory. Moreover, the paraphrases given in most emoji lists contradict Veszelszki's point that emoji do not have any specifiable meaning without context. The crucial point regarding the semantics of emoji is not their resemblance to something else but the fact that there is a type for each instance of emoji use, organized in a system alongside numerous other types. Emoji occurring in messages are tokens, repeatable in various contexts; the types differ from each other, and the differences between them constitute their respective meanings. This type-token-relationship is a categorial difference between emoji and images such as photographs. Memes, for example, are copied and modified to convey complex references to popular culture (cf. Osterroth 2015), but the meaning of memes does not arise from differences between the types of a finite meme repertoire organized in a meme sign system or list embedded in a messenger software. Emoji, however, are ready-made elements utilizable for infinite iteration and creative recombination (cf. Christian 2017: 221). It is because of this quality that Danesi (2017: 53), talking of a "thesaurus effect", says that "emoji are selected from a standardized set available, like alphabet characters, on many keyboards or apps today. [...] So, the semantic nuances are already implicit in the prefabricated signs themselves." In this respect, emoji, even though their design is slightly more sophisticated than that of ASCII emoticons, can clearly be separated from photographs, video files or graphics.

3.2 A theory of symbols

The original form of the emoticon (as introduced by the computer scientist Scott Fahlman) is obviously motivated by the well-known smiley face, which had already been in use as a graphic design for about 20 years. A graphic, a sketch or a painting differs, according to Goodman (1976: 227 and 229), from an articulated artefact in its relative syntactic density; when looking at an image, "every difference in every pictorial respect makes a difference ... Any thickening or thinning of the line, its color, its contrast with the background, its size, even the qualities of the paper – none of these is ruled out, none can be ignored."

The transfer from graphic design to an element that is either a combination of keyboard characters or simply selectable from a menu bar constitutes the emoji as an element of a symbol scheme. The combination <:-) > consists of disjointed and finitely differentiated elements. Thus, its formal characteristics partly become contingent, or, as a matter of fact, become a question of available fonts. For the emoticon's use, it is crucial whether the bracket is opening or closing. It is secondary, however, to which degree that bracket is bent or how thick the line is. In this sense, the emoticon is – in contrast to the smiley face graphic – no longer a picture (cf. Goodman 1976: 230–231). Emoji, then, are not even a matter of font but rather of the system software or platform (cf. Miller et al. 2016).

Depictions are commonly characterized as resembling the depicted. Emoji, too, are commonly thought to convey meaning through their graphic resemblance to a physical object (Miller et al. 2016; cf also Veszelszki 2017: 132). For the actual use of pictorial signs, however, resemblance alone is not crucial: "knowing what the image resembles does not suffice for knowing how and what it represents" (Goodman & Elgin 1988: 113; see also Keller 1995: 124).

The shape of those emoji motivated by facial expressions or various objects such as groceries or animals enables them to be treated and understood as iconic signs. This does not, however, automatically allow for any further conclusions concerning their subsequent usage and communicative functions. A simple parallel can be found in the pictograms denoting public toilets: recognizing the resemblance with male and female bodies is not sufficient in order to know what might be expected behind the doors and for knowing the relevant norms of conduct.

By asserting that the resemblance of an emoji sign with a facial expression is not sufficient to explain its function in usage, the resemblance as such is not repudiated (cf. Dresner & Herring 2012: 66). The resemblance simply becomes less and less important, the more frequently an emoji is used, and the more it is used in different contexts. Resemblance cannot guarantee for the appropriate interpretation: "[i]ts apprehension does not assure, nor its absence preclude, understanding what a picture represents" (Goodman & Elgin 1988: 115). Rudi Keller also does not consider resemblance the most important characteristic of icons but the ability to trigger the intended association: "It [the icon] has to be able to create for the addressee the association intended by the 'speaker'" (Keller 1995: 125; translation mine). For a sign to count as an iconic sign, the interpreter of this sign must not be dependent on any special knowledge or rules.

A painting such as Leonardo da Vinci's "Mona Lisa", in Goodman's terminology, is syntactically and semantically dense throughout (cf. Goodman 1976: 136 and 153). Mona Lisa's smile is said to be mysterious, and the painting can be interpreted and re-interpreted over and over. Although it is a fairly typical example of Renaissance portrait painting in many aspects, it is still a unique piece of art. Emoji, in contrast, lack uniqueness of any kind and cannot be interpreted in the same way as da Vinci's painting. Emoji need to be interpreted as conventional signs (i.e., symbols) – just like lexemes, which may be vague or polysemous but are still characters of a notational symbol scheme (cf. Goodman 1976: 143–148; Giovannelli 2017) or, in other words, elements of a thesaurus.

Danesi's "thesaurus effect" mentioned above is the result of a process described by Rudi Keller as "symbolization" (German: *Symbolifizierung*; Keller 1995: 126). According to Keller, the categorical differences between indexical, iconic and symbolic signs do not result from their essential nature but from their usage (cf. Keller 1995: 113). As Keller (Keller 1995: 125) notes, an iconic sign must encourage and enable its recipient to achieve an interpretation associatively: "By using an icon, the sign emitting party expects of the addressee to draw a sensible conclusion from the graphic, phonetic or gestural expression of a sign by means of association. He [sic] must work out a plausible meaning associatively." (translation mine)

Generally, depictions of facial expressions hardly allow for an immediate interpretation based only on association. When "reading" emoji, however, one can rely on one's experience with previous encounters. Admittedly part of a huge, continuously supplemented pool of characters, the repertoire of important, frequently used emoji is rather straightforward. Indeed, this repertoire accounts for the symbolization which already affected original emoticons, as Keller (1995: 126; translation mine) also notes: "Apparently, there are repertoires of iconic signs in common use. Such ready-made repertoire icons, however, are very unstable specimen. They are, given a certain frequency of use, virtually damned to become symbols. Association turned to habit is no longer association." Keller gives various examples for either icons or "symptoms" (i.e. indexical signs) which end up as symbols because of their conventionalized use in communication. Such processes of symbolization are well known from ancient forms of writing. Ehlich (2002) describes the development of cuneiform scripts as a process of abstraction. At first, iconic shapes were transformed into a set of wedge profiles. Ehlich (2002: 990–100) explains:

> A new kind of shapes comes into being. It provides its own semiotic appeal, which is the appeal for graphic systematization. The following development is a comprehensive process of this semiotic systematization. The primal figural features get lost beyond recognition [...]. The result is a tertiary semiotic system – it is tertiary because first, the shapes were separated from the objects, then, the shapes were transformed to linear figures, and, finally, the transformed linear figures are changed into a completely abstract configuration of cuneiforms. Thus, a system of distinct semiotic structure arises.

In order to function efficiently as writing characters, visual signs need not have any iconic qualities. A sophisticated design has nothing to do with good legibility. The detailed design of hieroglyphics, for example, is of a pure calligraphic value (cf. Assmann 2002: 35). For their practicability in a writing system, the calligraphic quality is not important. Since iconic qualities require a certain effort during the production of signs, one advantage of symbolization is, as Keller (1995: 169) notes, the accuracy of the depiction becomes less important. With reference to the simplified writing system developed from the hieroglyphics for everyday purposes, Assmann (2002: 35) likewise points out that graphic qualities are not necessary for the operating of a writing system as long as the system remains closed.

Emoticons, in contrast to emoji characters, could be assembled from single characters of the keyboard layout. On the one hand, they thus allowed for creativity and playfulness. One could think of funny and original variations of the basic forms, clearly suggesting an iconic interpretation – i.e., suggesting using those signs as icons. On the other hand, the relevant and frequent forms were conventionalized from the beginning, so that in unspecific contexts the possibility to use them as icons became irrelevant. This development is also indicated by the fact that in many cases the original form <:-) > is reduced to the more abstract <:) > (cf. Albert 2015: 15). Keller (1995: 157) clearly describes a similar idea when he says that the process of conventionalization of communicative means is usually a process of demotivation.

To sum up, it can be said that in the common contexts of usage, emoticons and emoji predominately operate as symbolic signs. Their original iconicity is obvious but not relevant for interpretation.[2] Signs must not, according to Keller (1995: 148), automatically be classified as icons when they exhibit some relation of resemblance, but can nonetheless operate as arbitrary signs in principle. The symbolic character of emoji entails their conventionality, their unlimited repeatability, and their property of being arranged in a symbol scheme. Whereas the original emoticons have become symbolic signs because of their usage, the emoji characters were implemented as symbols right from the start. Due to their graphic qualities, the possibility to use them like images still remains but does not affect their most frequent use as conventional symbolic signs.

3.3 Differences between emoji and words

Having elaborated on the similarities between emoji and words, some decisive differences should be acknowledged, albeit only briefly here. In this regard, there are at least four properties of words which distinguish them from emoji. By the same token, there is one characteristic which distinguishes emoji from common logograms such as <$> and <&>.

A word of an alphabetic system, first of all, consists of discriminable graphemes and has a morphological structure, which means that it can be broken down into smaller units. Although many elements of single emoji characters can be found in other emoji, there are no definable constituents which can be selected individually and combined to a novel symbol.

Words, moreover, can be assigned to different lexeme categories by morphological, syntactic (functional) and semantic criteria. There are homonymous forms, which potentially belong to two different categories – *plan*, for example,

---

[2] See Keller (1995: 169) on this point: the "previous iconicity [is] still comprehendible ... But it no longer contributes anything to the interpretation of the signs in their present form." (translation mine)

is either a verb or a noun. The syntactic context, however, usually allows for an unambiguous categorization. Most instances of emoji usage cannot be categorized in an analogous way. Even so, emoji are sometimes used in place of a lexeme or an entire phrase (cf. Dürscheid & Siever 2017: 272). In such cases, one can sometimes decide which kind of constituent of the utterance has been replaced by the emoji, but there remains a lot more uncertainty than in the case of words.

Furthermore, a word may change its form depending on its respective syntactic properties – at least in inflexional languages. There are different forms such as *plan*, *plans*, *planned*, or *planning* belonging to the same lexeme (i.e., to the same type). Words may also be combined with bound morphemes in word formation processes (e.g., *plan* > *pre-plan*). For emoji, in contrast, there are obviously some basic regularities according to their syntactic distribution but no morphological features comparable to inflexion or word formation. The only formal modifications of emoji feasible by the users themselves are iteration and change of size.

Finally, words are grouped together to form more complex constituents, namely phrases. Phrases have hierarchical structures resulting in syntagmatic relations between the individual words, potentially affecting their inflectional form. Such relations are traditionally described in terms of government or, alternatively, in terms of dependency, according to the respective theory of syntax. Messages consisting of one or more emoji are far from having a syntax in this strict sense of the term. When it comes to syntax, one should note that the comparison has focussed on differences between words and emoji. If one was to compare emoji messages with clauses or sentences, phenomena such as tense or negation would add to these differences.

These four properties clearly distinguish emoji from words. However, they share all these differences from words with commonly known logograms. To differentiate between emoji and logograms, another feature can be taken into account. Dürscheid & Siever (2017: 267) point out that logograms are a fixed combination of a form and a pronunciation. There is, for example, only one (standard) pronunciation of <$>, namely [ˈdɔlaʁ]. Since there are no conventional pronunciations for emoji, they can also not be regarded as logograms. If several pronunciations are possible, the referential function might also be unclear: Is a floral emoji really used to refer to a cherry blossom (U+1F338) or could it also be an almond blossom? Does U+1F940 denote 'flower', 'rose', or 'tulip' (cf. Dürscheid & Siever 2017: 272)? Except cases of emoji replacing a single word (for example, *I ♡ you*), it is difficult to read them aloud (cf. Figure. 3.2), which is, after all, rather unusual when it comes to signs used in written discourse.

> Jetzt stehen wir in LU am Hbf 😭 10:45

Figure 3.2: Delayed train. In some contexts, punctuation marks might actually be pronounced. For example, one might end an utterance by saying *period* to stress one's determination. In contrast, it is rather unlikely that someone would utter *The train has stopped at LU main station – loudly crying face* (Private source).

4 Conclusion: Not so different after all?

Despite a long-lasting process of conventionalization, emoji occur beyond the limits of written standard language and thus remain a dynamic phenomenon. Trying to compile an exhaustive list of all possible functions and meanings is therefore not sensible. Polyfunctional elements are the normal case for any language, and a linguistic expression usually serves more than just one function at the same time. Nevertheless, one can safely say that the representation of feelings or moods is not the predominant function of emoji – not even of those depicting faces. In addition to their functions regarding pragmatic aspects and discourse organization, emoji invariably "add what can be called 'visual tone' to a message" (Danesi 2017: 10). In most cases, emoji serve as conventional symbolic signs rather than as stylized images. Their iconic features point to their origin but, since they are arranged as disjunctive and differentiated elements of a symbolic scheme, these iconic features are not crucial. Consequently, they have become more like the words alongside which they are used, and less like images. Notwithstanding, emoji are not to be equated with words but remain a phenomenon *sui generis* somewhere between images and logograms.

References

Albert, Georg. 2013. *Innovative Schriftlichkeit in digitalen Texten. Syntaktische Variation und stilistische Differenzierung in Chat und Forum.* Berlin: Akademie-Verlag.
Albert, Georg. 2015. Semiotik und Syntax von Emoticons. *Zeitschrift für angewandte Linguistik* 62(1). 3–22.
Arens, Katja & Nadine Nösler. 2014. Jaaaa:) alles klar!! bis morgen hdl:-*. Der Ausdruck von Emotionen in SMS. In Frieda Berg & Yvonne Mende (eds.), *Verstehen und Verständigung in der Interaktion. Analysen von Online-Foren, SMS, Instant-Messaging, Video-Clips und Lehrer-Eltern-Gesprächen*, 46–60. Mannheim: Verlag für Gesprächsforschung.

Assmann, Jan. 2002. Sieben Funktionen der ägyptischen Hieroglyphenschrift. In Erika Greber, Konrad Ehlich & Jan-Dirk Müller (eds.), *Materialität und Medialität von Schrift*, 31–50. Bielefeld: Aisthesis.

Bieswanger, Markus. 2013. Micro-linguistic structural features of computer-mediated communication. In Susan C. Herring, Dieter Stein & Tuija Virtanen (eds.), *Pragmatics of Computer-Mediated Communication. Handbook of Pragmatics Vol. 9*, 463–485. Berlin & Boston: de Gruyter.

Busch, Florian. 2017. Informelle Interpunktion? Zeichensetzung im digitalen Schreiben von Jugendlichen. *Der Deutschunterricht H. 4*. 87–91.

Christian, Alexander. 2017. *Piktogramme. Tendenzen in der Gestaltung und im Einsatz grafischer Symbole*. Köln: Halem.

Damasio, Antonio. 2000. *The feeling of what happens. Body and emotion in the making of consciousness*. Orlando et al.: Harvest.

Danesi, Marcel. 2017. *The semiotics of emoji. The rise of visual language in the age of the internet*. London & New York: Bloomsbury.

Dresner, Eli & Susan C. Herring. 2012. Emoticons and illocutionary force. In: Dana Riesenfeld & Giovanni Scarafile (eds.), *Philosophical dialogue: Writings in honor of Marcelo Dascal*, 59–70. London: College Publication.

Dürscheid, Christa & Karina Frick. 2014. Keyboard-to-Screen-Kommunikation gestern und heute: SMS und WhatsApp im Vergleich. In Alexa Mathias, Jens Runkehl & Torsten Siever (eds.), *Sprachen? Vielfalt! Sprache und Kommunikation in der Gesellschaft und den Medien. Eine Online-Festschrift zum Jubiläum für Peter Schlobinski* (= Networx 64). 149–181.

Dürscheid, Christa & Christina M. Siever. 2017. Jenseits des Alphabets – Kommunikation mit Emojis. *Zeitschrift für Germanistische Linguistik* 45(2),256–285.

Ehlich, Konrad. 2002. Schrift, Schriftträger, Schriftform: Materialität und semiotische Struktur. In Erika Greber, Konrad Ehlich & Jan-Dirk Müller (eds.), *Materialität und Medialität von Schrift*, 91–111. Bielefeld: Aisthesis.

Fiehler, Reinhard. 1990. *Kommunikation und Emotion. Theoretische und empirische Untersuchungen zur Rolle von Emotionen in der verbalen Interaktion*. Berlin & New York: de Gruyter.

Gerhards, Jürgen. 1988. *Soziologie der Emotionen. Fragestellungen, Systematik und Perspektiven*. Weinheim & München: Juventa.

Giovannelli, Alessandro. 2017. Goodman's aesthetics. In Edward N. Zalta (ed.), *The Stanford encyclopedia of philosophy* Fall 2017 edn. Available: https://plato.stanford.edu/archives/fall2017/entries/goodman-aesthetics/ (21 February, 2019)

Goodman, Nelson. 1976. *Languages of art. An approach to a theory of symbols*. Indianapolis & Cambridge: Hackett.

Goodman, Nelson & Catherine Z. Elgin. 1988. *Reconceptions in philosophy and other arts and sciences*. Indianapolis & Cambridge: Hackett.

Graßl, Constanze. 2014. Merkmale von Mündlichkeit und Schriftlichkeit in Forenbeiträgen. In Frieda Berg & Yvonne Mende (eds.), *Verstehen und Verständigung in der Interaktion. Analysen von Online-Foren, SMS, Instant-Messaging, Video-Clips und Lehrer-Eltern-Gesprächen*, 5–19. Mannheim: Verlag für Gesprächsforschung.

Herring, Susan C. & Ashley Dainas. 2017. "Nice picture comment!" Graphicons in Facebook comment threads. In Institute of Electrical and Electronics Engineers (ed.), *Proceedings of the fiftieth Hawaii international conference on system sciences* (HICSS-50). Available: http://ella.slis.indiana.edu/~herring/hicss.graphicons.pdf. (21 February, 2019)

Höflich, Joachim R. 2003. *Mensch, Computer und Kommunikation. Theoretische Verortungen und empirische Befunde*. Frankfurt a.M. et al.: Lang.

Imo, Wolfgang. 2015. Vom ikonischen über einen indexikalischen zu einem symbolischen Ausdruck? Eine konstruktionsgrammatische Analyse des Emoticons:-). In Jörg Bücker, Susanne Günthner & Wolfgang Imo (eds.), *Konstruktionsgrammatik V: Konstruktionen im Spannungsfeld von sequenziellen Mustern, kommunikativen Gattungen und Textsorten*, 133–162. Tübingen: Stauffenburg.

Keller, Rudi. 1995. *Zeichentheorie*. Tübingen & Basel: Francke.

Miller, Hannah, Jacob Thebault-Spieker, Shuo Chang, Isaac Johnson, Loren Terveen & Brent Hecht. 2016. "blissfully happy" or "ready to fight": Varying interpretations of emoji. In Association for the Advancement of Artificial Intelligence (ed.), *Proceedings of the 10th international conference on web and social media, ICWSM 2016*, 259–268. Available: https://experts.umn.edu/en/publications/blissfully-happy-or-ready-to-fight-varying-interpretations-of-emo (21 February 2019)

Osterroth, Andreas. 2015. Das internet-Meme als Sprache-Bild-Text. In *Image* 22(7). 26–46.

Pappert, Steffen. 2017. Zu kommunikativen Funktionen von Emojis in der WhatsApp-Kommunikation. In Michael Beißwenger (ed.), *Empirische Erforschung internetbasierter Kommunikation*, 175–212. Berlin & New York: de Gruyter (= Empirische Linguistik / Empirical Linguistics 9).

Runkehl, Jens, Peter Schlobinski & Torsten Siever. 1998. *Sprache und Kommunikation im internet. Überblick und Analysen*. Opladen & Wiesbaden: Westdeutscher Verlag.

Siever, Christina M. 2015. *Multimodale Kommunikation im Social Web. Forschungsansätze und Analysen zu Text-Bild-Relationen*. Frankfurt a.M. et al.: Lang (= Sprache – Medien – Innovationen 8).

Thome, Matthias. 2001. *Semiotische Aspekte computergebundener Kommunikation*. Saarbrücken (= Networx 20).

Veszelszki, Ágnes. 2017. *Digilect. The Impact of Infocommunication Technology on Language*. Berlin & Boston: de Gruyter.

Rachel Panckhurst and Francesca Frontini
4 Evolving interactional practices of emoji in text messages

1 Introduction

Several years ago, a pluridisciplinary team of linguists and computer scientists collected more than 88,000 French authentic SMS in Montpellier (http://www.sud4science.org/), within the context of a vast international project (http://www.sms4science.org/), coordinated by the CENTAL (UCL, Belgium). After semi-automatic treatment using natural language processing (NLP) techniques, the anonymized text messages were made available to the research community and the general public as a corpus, entitled *88milSMS*, in 2014 (http://88milsms.huma-num.fr) and in 2016 for the TEI/XML version (https://hdl.handle.net/11403/comere/cmr-88milsms) (Panckhurst et al. 2014, 2016a, 2016b).

In this article, we examine the usage of *emoji* in the *88milSMS* corpus. After differentiating between *emoji* and *emoticons*, we situate the context, indicate general statistics and mention press interest. Next, we address linguistic issues: are emoji used more often in addition (either redundantly or necessarily, sometimes as "softeners" (*adoucisseurs*, Détrie & Verine 2015) or for lexical replacement, denoting a reference/referential function (*Referenzfunktion*, Dürscheid & Siever 2017)? Concerning emoji insertion positioning, which is the most popular and what does this mean? Other researchers refer to "the emoji code" (Danesi 2016; Evans 2017), and emoji classifications have been proposed, including references to syntactic, semantic (Barbieri, Ronzano & Saggion 2016), semiotic, phatic and emotive/sentiment (Novak et al. 2015) levels. Are these satisfactory or do we need to redefine levels, contexts and potential ambiguity? Part-of-speech tagging (POS) and NLP software are then used to annotate SMS containing emoji within *88milSMS* in order to investigate the immediate grammatical environment. This allows us to conduct contextual analysis relating to syntactic linguistic functions of emoji. Finally, results from two questionnaires are explored: 1. sociolinguistic factors (age, gender) of the SMS donors having used emoji in *88milSMS*; 2. Comparison of SMS emoji usage with other instant messaging applications and social networks via a user-orientated questionnaire (Rascol 2017[1]).

---

[1] The authors would like to thank Stéphanie Rascol who conducted manual classification of the emoji appearing in *88milSMS* in her 2nd year Master's thesis (Rascol 2017).

2 Background

We differentiate between *emoji* (*e* 絵, "picture"; *moji* 文字, "character") 😀❤️😅😘😳😎😊😋❤️ and *emoticon* ("emotion" and "icon"), the latter corresponding to mainly "punctuation mark" usage, often requiring a 90° turn to the left :-) :) :p ;) :d :(:/ or to the right <3 in order to be interpreted, although sometimes a rotation is unnecessary, as indicated by the Japanese-influenced kaomoji emoticon ^^.

The *sud4science* text-message collection took place in 2011, and it was perfect timing: Apple introduced emoji inclusion on international smartphones that year (well after their 2007 marketing move for emoji on Japanese mobiles).

In *88milSMS*, around 30,000 total *emoticon* tokens and 30 different types[2] were used. The "top-ten" (see Figure 4.1) represent 94% of overall emoticon usage in the corpus. The emoticon which evolved the most compared to the previous *SMS4science* corpus moved from 21st (in 2004) to 2nd position (in 2011); interestingly enough, it is the "^^" emoticon, which seems to indicate increasing Asian influence in the up-and-coming emoji impact.

Compared to this, just under 400 *emoji* were used in *88milSMS*, i.e. slightly more than 1% of the overall combined emoticons+emoji. This exceedingly low percentage of emoji in our corpus is of course directly related to the Apple inclusion on iphones the same year as our text-message collection: usage was merely emerging. So, which emoji constitute our "top ten"? Is the heart classified number 1 as the media often indicates,[3] along with a recent widespread empirical scientific study conducted by Lu et al. (2016)? Do French speakers really use "hearts and broken hearts four times more than speakers of other languages"?[4] How does the 2015 Oxford "word of the year" emoji, namely 😂 ("face with tears of joy") rate in *88milSMS*?[5]

Precisely 378 emoji tokens and 69 emoji types were used in *88milSMS*. The "top-ten" descending percentages are also indicated in Figure 4.1 and they represent 50% of the overall emoji usage.

If one considers a combination of hearts (n° 2 "beating heart", n° 10 "black heart"), and also a combination of a smiling face with hearts (n° 7 "smiling face

---

2 *Types* refer to number of distinct items (e.g. differing dictionary entries); *tokens* refer to total number of occurrences.
3 See http://www.sud4science.org/?q=fr/node/5 for media documents related to emoji. (23.07.2019)
4 https://www.theguardian.com/technology/2016/mar/13/emojis-discussion-at-sxsw-emotions (23.07.2019)
5 https://languages.oup.com/word-of-the-year/word-of-the-year-2015 (01.08.2019)

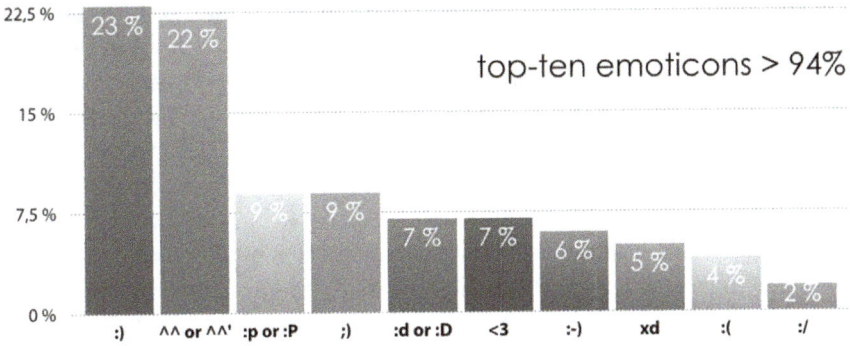

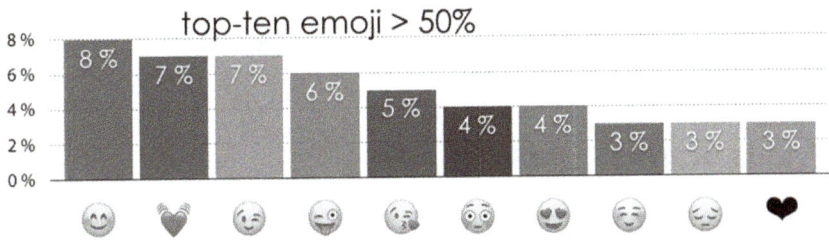

Figure 4.1: Top-ten" emoticon/emoji tokens: respectively 94% and 50% in *88milSMS*.

with heart eyes"), the heart(s) easily reap first place, but individually, the traditional 😊 "smiling face with smiling eyes" is number one. The 💗 ("growing heart") is in 13th position and the 💔 "broken heart", 💝 "heart with ribbon" and 💛 "yellow heart" are only inserted respectively thrice and twice in *88milSMS* (27th, 29th and 30th positions). Lu et al. (2016) used a "data set consist[ing] of over 400 million emoji-contained messages generated by more than three million users from 212 countries and regions", in which it transpired that the French are the most likely to use emoji in their messages per se (19.8%, Lu et al. 2016: 774) with heart-specific emoji being preferred. However, they do recognize that their study may include more younger persons' usage, since input from a Kika keyboard[6] was the sole focus of their study. So, sociolinguistic factors also need to be compared, in order to determine (at least) any age or

---

6 http://www.kika.tech/ (23.07.2019)

gender specific details. Also, the famous Oxford 2015 "word of the year": 😂 ("face with Tears of Joy") is only used once in our corpus, but we believe this particular emoji has evolved substantially over the past few years. Diachronic comparisons in future research are therefore essential (e.g. the Swiss *WhatsApp* project (http://www.whatsup-switzerland.ch/index.php/fr/) (Ueberwasser & Stark 2017) and the Belgian *Vos Pouces* (https://acougnon.wixsite.com/thumbs4science) (Cougnon et al. 2017) project).

Various media have shown broad interest in emoji evolution over the years, including the recent Sony Pictures film release ("The Emoji movie" 2017, http://www.theemoji-movie.com/). The *sud4science* team was interviewed by journalists for many written/online articles, radio broadcasts and television reports related to the SMS *sud4science* project, between 2011 and 2019 (http://www.sud4science.org/?q=fr/node/5). Interestingly enough, almost 50% of these title one of the following words (in French): "smiley", "emoticon", "emoji", and many mention the heart as being number one in France. This continuous media solicitation persuaded the researchers to conduct more in-depth scientific analysis.

3 Linguistic issues

This linguistic study focusses exclusively on emoji usage. Emoji generally indicate feelings which are expressed by emotions: sadness, anger, menacing acts, teasing, sentiments, tenderness, etc. Emoji sometimes, act as "softeners" (*adoucisseurs*, Détrie & Verine, 2015) or by allowing a playful way of re-introducing emotions into mediated digital discourse (henceforth MDD, "discours numérique médié", DNM, Panckhurst 2017), which may appear "dry", "harsh" or "dehumanised", without this sort of non-verbal, visual, inclusion. We posit that emoji usage provokes an enrichment of MDD, if combined simultaneously with textual data.

In preparing interviews accessible to journalists and the general public, an initial general "person/object" classification was adopted, in order to explain who and/or what the scriptor refers to when writing text-messages which include emoji:[7]

---

[7] Literal translation of examples from the *88milSMS* corpus: "Yuck 🤮"; "I'm not feeling well at all. My stomach feels upside down ... I don't know what to do 🤢"; "Great!! Thanks!! You're too kind!!!😇😈👿"; SMS n° 73717: "Haha I don't feel like working, so telling you off is fun 😏"; "With a cherry not tomato"; "She shut me out, the bitch. Thank goodness the front door wasn't locked. 😌" "Behind me, there's this dude who's trying to explain the crisis to a chick who asked him: "But "outraged by what?!" – Well, the "outraged" [referring to the best-seller Stéphane Hessel 2011 book, *Indignez-vous !, Time for outrage*] you know. – Right, but by

1. **Me**: Scriptor conveys own feelings to recipient:
   SMS n° 29370: Beurk 😨
   SMS n° 67195: Je me sens pas bien du tout. J'ai le ventre à l'envers complet... Je sais pas quoi faire 😰
2. **You/us**: Scriptor communicates with and refers to recipient and optionally includes her/himself:
   SMS n° 38419: Super !! Merci !! T'es trop gentille !!! 😠😠👿
   SMS n° 73717: Hihi j'ai pas envie de travailler, alors t'engueuler c'est fun 😏
3. **Object(s)/Other(s)**: Scriptor refers to third person(s)/object(s) and optionally includes her/himself and/or recipient:
   SMS n° 34761: Avec une cerise pas tomate 😊
   SMS n° 46499: Elle m à enfermé dehors la garce. Heureusement la porte d entrée était pas fermé à clef. 😁
   SMS n° 35548: Derrière moi, y a un ouaish qui essaie d'expliquer la crise à une piche qui lui a demandé : « Mais "indignés" par quoi ?! »
   - Bah les "Indignés" quoi.
   - Oui mais par quoi ??
   - Non mais "les Indignés"...
   Pfffffffff 😕
   SMS n° 60917: <pre_6> trouve que tu es très jolie mais comme tu ne sais que dire miaou, il faut qu'il réfléchisse 😏

In *88milSMS*, the category concerning the unequivocal link between scriptor and recipient is used most commonly. This implies that emoji are frequently used to maintain a connection or relationship between scriptors and recipients. Of course, conveying one's own feelings (1st category, "me": 28%) is also a way of bonding with the recipient, but text messages more often explicitly mention the second person in *88milSMS* (2nd category, "you/us": 57%). Including a third-party/object is also a way of creating a connivance with the recipient, but this is more infrequent (3rd category, "(s)he/it/them", 15%).

Emoticon and emoji functions can refer historically to Wilson (1993) and many authors have of course studied them (among others, for French, Cougnon 2015; Marccoccia & Gauducheau 2007; Pierozak 2007; for recent studies in multilingual Switzerland, Dürscheid & Siever 2017; Ueberwasser & Stark 2017). Marcoccia and

---

what?? – No, but the "outraged" ... Phew 😕"; "<6-letter-anonymized-first-name> finds you very pretty but since you only know how to purr, he wants to think about it 😏". Note that examples appear as written in corpus, i.e. including some variation on standardized forms.

Gauduchau (2007) (also summarized by Cougnon (2015: 53), analyse smileys/emoticons using a four-fold function classification system: 1. expressive, 2. humorous and ironic, 3. relational (closeness), 4. politeness. The first *expressive* instance indicates the scriptor's state of mind (sadness, mocking, anger, tenderness, etc., e.g. supra, SMS n° 67195: *Je me sens pas bien du tout. J'ai le ventre à l'envers complet… Je sais pas quoi faire* 😔). Humour and irony are classified in a second function, which refers to the *interpretative* nature of the message (e.g. supra, SMS n° 38419 : *Super !! Merci !! T'es trop gentille !!!* 😈😈😈). The third function is *relational* and indicates the bond between scriptor and recipient, in order to synchronize both parties' emotions (e.g. SMS n°60695:[8] … 😊 *Je t'aime aussi grand comme ça* 💗💜💛 !!!). Finally, a *politeness* function refers to the situation in which an emoji is added, and may work as a "softener", so that the recipient does not take the message literally (e.g., supra, SMS n° 73717: *Hihi j'ai pas envie de travailler, alors t'engueuler c'est fun* 😉).

Within the context of *88milSMS*, we observed three main situations – partly inspired initially by Marcoccia and Gauduchau 2007, Wilson 1993 – but which we redetermine as follows:[9]

1. *redundant addition*: an emoji is used as well as written text, but it is not required in order to understand the SMS (within the context of the exchange):
   [**Private SMS**]: Code dans la poche 🚗🚗!!!
2. *necessary addition*: an emoji is used as well as written text, and its inclusion is necessary in order to avoid misinterpretation:
   SMS n° 65641: Voleur de yaourts 😄
   SMS n° 66390: Pff toujours le même discours 😏😏😏
3. *lexical replacement*: an emoji is used instead of a word:
   [**Private SMS**]: OK. Courage et à demain. Nos ados sont des 😇.Non, plutôt des 😈😈
   [**Private SMS**]: Merci bcp Rachel gros 😘😘😘😘
   SMS n° 35642: Et si on prenait le 🚋 pour le Gaumont à 🕐 C'est que le 🎬 commence à 🕐 et je ne sais pas combien de temps il fait pour y arriver et puis je pense qu'il y aura du monde. Quel est ton avis sur ce point ?

---

[8] "… 😊 I love you also, as much as this 💗💜💛 !!!".
[9] The terminology ("redundant/necessary" addition, lexical replacement) is novel, but may need to be revised, as sociolinguists may deem it inappropriate. The term "disambiguation" could replace "necessary addition", from an interpretative viewpoint. Literal translation of examples: "(Road) code passed!!!"; "Yoghurt thief 😄" "OK. Courage and see you tomorrow. Our teenagers are 😇. No, rather 😈😈"; "Thanks alot Rachel big 😘😘😘😘"; "How about we take the 🚋 to the Gaumont at 🕐 The 🎬 starts at 🕐 and I don't know how long it takes to get there and I think there'll be lots of people. What's your viewpoint on this?".

We found that our double classification system, i.e., 1. emoji in SMS referring to person(s)/object(s); 2. addition/replacement was easier to implement for our manual analysis, because a clear distinction between *humour/irony* and *politeness* is not necessarily crystal clear in the context of our corpus. For instance, the following SMS could indeed be classified as a softener usage (Marcoccia and Gauducheau 2007):

SMS n° 71004: M'en parle pas 😳 😰! À vendredi alors :) bisous[10]

However, in the "Yogourt thief 😶" SMS n° 65641 (supra), it is difficult to differentiate between the politeness and the humour/irony classification. These two are therefore combined in our system and are classified in the "necessary addition" category.

Text messages containing superfluous emoji ("redundant addition", vis-à-vis the textual data) are the most common (66%). In this instance, emoji add a non-verbal, visual item to a text message, which in recent years is often interpreted as appearing more enticing than an SMS which is solely textual. The message can appear playful and more welcoming.

Emoji may refer to words, concepts, emotions... For instance, consider SMS n° 65148 below:[11]

SMS n° 65148: Et je préfère ta nouvelle coupe de cheveux... 💇

The 💇 emoji refers to a "redundant addition" and holds a paralinguistic rather than linguistic value, somewhat comparable to uttering the same sentence while mimicking hair-cutting with one's hand. Yet it is useful to distinguish such cases, in which the emoji has some sort of referential value, and can be seen as referring to a concept, if not a word ("haircut"), from those in which the emoji conveys an emotion, or clarifies the correct interpretation of a sentence ("necessary addition"). Following Danesi (2016: 167) in such cases emoji "add semantic nuances, [...] emphasize tone, [...] avoid potential misunderstandings, and [...] fulfil various phatic and emotive functions".

Some studies on emoji focus on quantitative usage and intercultural comparisons (Ljubešić and Fišer 2016, Lu et al. 2016). However, it is important to study emoji combined with the textual data appearing in the SMS,[12] since the

---

10 "Don't talk to me about it 😳 😰 See you on Friday then:) Kisses"
11 "And I prefer your new haircut... 💇"
12 In some rare instances, SMS are solely composed of emoji (4% of SMS in *88milSMS*, the most frequent being: 😍😂😭$_z$z^z).

context is vital in order to interpret them. Indeed, Ljubešić and Fišer (2016: 89) stress the importance of "understanding how emojis are included in natural language syntax". The second "necessary addition" category supra shows this (28%), supported by the study by Détrie and Verine (2015) on *insultes-mots doux* (insults which become tender words).

Lexical replacement is fairly rare in *88milSMS* (7%). The SMS which uses the most lexical replacements is repeated below:[13]

SMS n° 35642: Et si on prenait le 🚋 pour le Gaumont à 🕐 C'est que le 🎬 commence à 🕗 et je ne sais pas combien de temps il fait pour y arriver [...]

Nouns ("tram", "film") and numeral adjective + noun combinations ("7 heures", "8 heures") are replaced in this instance. NLP techniques will be applied to check preceding categories of these instances.

As emoji usage has evolved rapidly and radically in the past few years, it would be very interesting to compare it with more recent collections. In the authors' personal experience, as well as for other users,[14] lexical replacement has increased at the onset or the end of text messages, as openings or closures more often indicate today:[15]

[private SMS]: 👋 Je ne peux pas demain, la semaine prochaine ?... Et je suis partant pour mardi 8h15 (et lundi si besoin). Je vais te remplir la fiche. Bisous ! [private SMS]: Super! On finit de manger et on y va. 😘

Emoji positioning (opening, somewhere within SMS, closure) appears in Figure 4.2, below. Final closure positions of SMS and end of sentences are the most common places to insert emoji (87%), followed by a middle of SMS position (8%), and finally the onset (1%). The final 4% concern SMS containing solely emoji and no textual data (see note 12).

Part-of-speech tagging (POS) and NLP software are used (§4) to annotate SMS containing emoji in order to investigate the grammatical environment. This allows more in-depth analysis of linguistic functions and to check sociolinguistic factors.

---

[13] This may well have changed drastically since 2011, since emoji prediction is often proposed whilst writing messages with smartphones.

[14] In §5 of this paper we report on questionnaire data that provides evidence of increased usage of lexical replacement.

[15] "👋 [emoji replacing "Hi/hey", etc.] I can't tomorrow, next week? ... And I'm available for Tuesday 8.15 (and Monday if necessary). I'm going to fill out the form for you. Kisses!", "Great! We're finishing our meal then we'll leave. 😘" [emoji kiss instead of text].

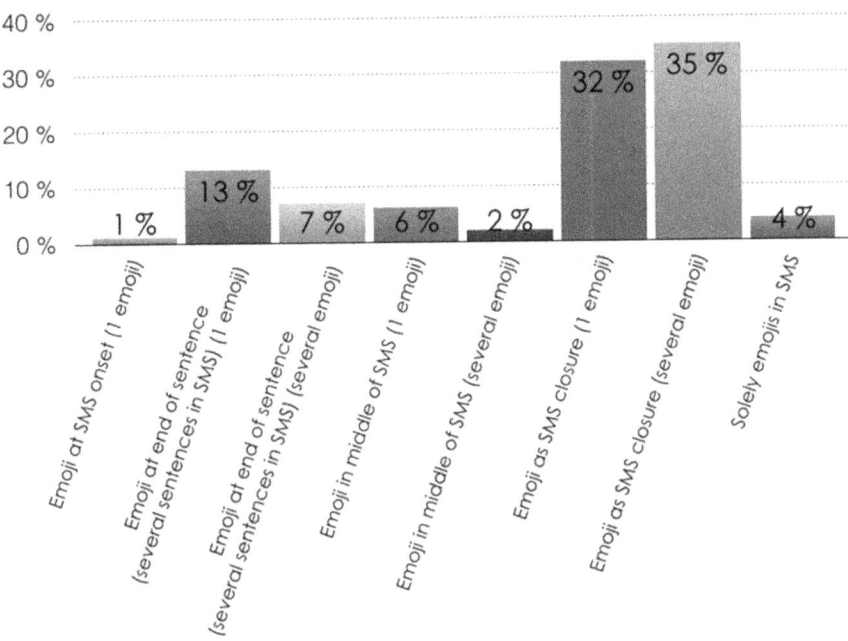

Figure 4.2: Emoji positions in SMS.

4 Context analysis

The availability of an SMS corpus[16] containing emoji, albeit of a limited size, allows us to tackle some basic methodological questions concerning the systematic study of emoji in context, from a corpus linguistics point of view.

To facilitate the context analysis, we automatically annotated all the SMS containing emoji with an automatic Part of Speech (PoS) Tagger trained for French (Treetagger[17]). The result is a text where words are recognised (tokenisation), lemmatised and annotated with their grammatical category.[18] Clearly the resulting annotation is not perfect (as we shall see below), but the outcome is sufficiently

---

[16] The following analyses may also apply to other types of corpora, including WhatsApp/ Messenger data.
[17] See www.cis.uni-muenchen.de/~schmid/tools/TreeTagger/ for complete documentation. (23.07.2019)
[18] See http://www.cis.uni-muenchen.de/~schmid/tools/TreeTagger/data/french-tagset.html for the French tagset. (23.07.2019)

precise to allow systematic inspection of the syntactic context surrounding emoji by means of targeted regular expressions.

The following analysis constitutes, to the best of our knowledge, the first attempt at studying emoji in their syntactic context. What syntactic function do emoji fulfil, if any? What are the correct tags to apply to emoji in different contexts?

We begin with an analysis of the tags automatically assigned by TreeTagger to the emoji appearing in our corpus[19] (see Figure 4.3 below).

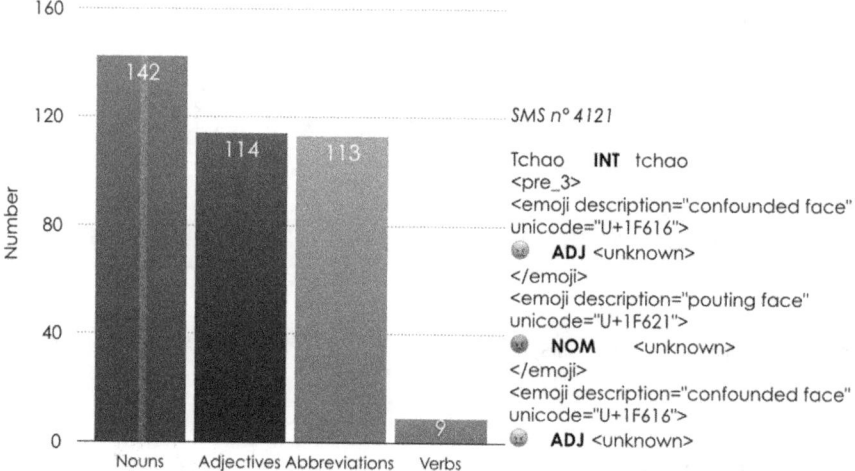

Figure 4.3: Tags automatically assigned to emoji by TreeTagger, with an example.

However, since TreeTagger was not initially designed to tag emoji they are often not correctly recognized as such. For instance, emoji are never assigned a punctuation tag. The automatically assigned tag is often inconsistent with the actual function of the emoji in the text but is somewhat influenced by the context, as TreeTagger is a statistical algorithm that decides on the category of a token based on the preceding tag assignments. Sequences of emoji may show particularly awkward tagging, since the choice of the first emoji tag may

---

[19] The standard output of TreeTagger is a tab separated file with three columns. Parameters used allowed skipping XML tags in the annotation process. Given this format, a regular expression such as for instance "<emoji.*\n.*\tNOM" will return all tokens that were marked up as <emoji> with a "NOM" tag assigned to them.

determine that of the following one(s); see for instance SMS n° 4121 (Figure 4.3), where noun and adjective tags alternate.

4.1 Left and right contexts

As we have seen (Figure 4.2), most emoji are inserted at the closure of a text message or at the end of a sentence within the SMS; sequences of several emoji are also common. Let us therefore first observe the textual context preceding the emoji.

As shown in Figure 4.4, of the 246[20] emoji that are preceded by text or typographical markers (thus excluding those at the beginning of an SMS (11 occurrences) and those that follow another emoji (121 occurrences)) we find that the preceding tag is often a punctuation mark, either a mid-sentence one (,:;), or a sentence-ending one (!? …) As for the other tags, they are distributed among principal parts of speech: a majority of nouns, followed by verbs, then adjectives, etc. Adverbs are not infrequent and are often represented by negation, ("pas", "plus"); the fact that emoji immediately follow a negation seems to confirm their use as softeners, as in the following example.

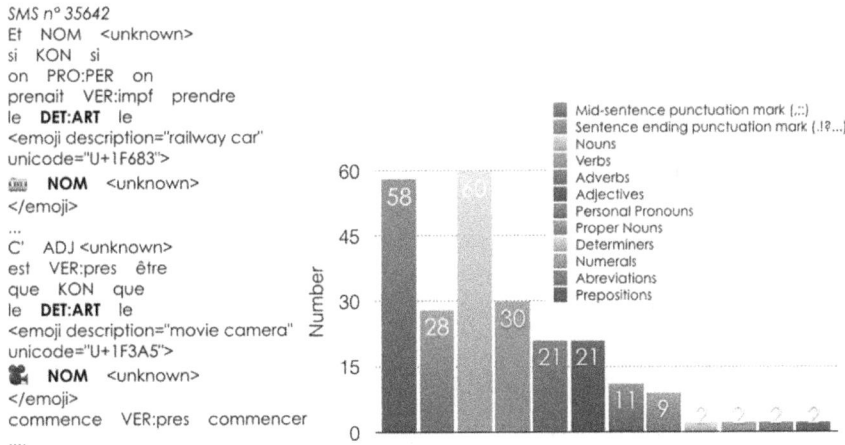

Figure 4.4: Tags assigned to tokens immediately preceding an emoji, with an example.

---

20 We use a regular expression ".*\t.*\t.*\n<emoji" that captures any token preceding the emoji, which gives 244 results. We then add two cases in which the preceding token is an anonymized name, replaced by an xml tag.

SMS n° 46528[21]
Je PRO:PER je
bosse VER:pres bosser
pas ADV pas
non ADV non
plus ADV plus
<emoji description="winking face" unicode="U+1F609">
😉 ADJ <unknown>
</emoji>

On the whole, manual inspection shows that the preceding context almost always coincides with a clause or phrase boundary, and no syntactic dependency links exist between the preceding context and the emoji. In some cases, explicit sentence marking is present:

SMS n° 1520[22]
Bon ADJ bon
dimanche NOM dimanche
à PRP <unknown>
vous PRO:PER vous
aussi ADV aussi
, PUN ,
plein ADJ plein
de PRP de
bisous NOM bisou
. SENT .
<emoji description="face throwing a kiss" unicode="U+1F618">
😘 ABR <unknown>
</emoji>

While in other cases the emoji is the sole closure marker:

SMS n° 1720[23]
Gros ADJ gros
bisous NOM bisou

---

[21] "I'm not working either 😉"
[22] "Have a nice Sunday, lots of kisses. 😘"
[23] "Big kisses auntie and have a nice evening you too 😘"

Tatie NAM <unknown>
et KON et
bonne ADJ bon
soirée NOM <unknown>
à PRP <unknown>
toi PRO:PER toi
aussi ADV aussi
<emoji description="face throwing a kiss" unicode="U+1F618">
😘 ADJ <unknown>
</emoji>

In some cases, the emoji is preceded by a proper noun, which may be anonymized in our corpus for privacy reasons (and replaced by an xml tag). In only 2 cases the preceding tag is a determiner, which clearly suggests the emoji is part of a noun phrase, thus pointing to a lexical replacement (SMS n° 35642, Figure 4.4). In such cases the emoji is well recognised by the tagger as being a noun by the contextual clue, despite the fact that emoji were almost certainly absent from the training set and thus unknown as possible tokens to the language model. This leads us to believe that the text immediately preceding the emoji may be used in future language models for improved emoji tagging.

On the contrary, the situation is much more uncertain when we examine the text following emoji; if we exclude those emoji that are at the end of an SMS and those that are followed by another emoji, we are left with 122[24] contexts. Figure 4.5 shows the category assigned to tokens immediately following the emoji. However, in this case the reliability of such figures is seriously diminished by tagging errors. In fact, the tagger assigns a tag to a token based on the combined probability of preceding tags and tokens; for instance in SMS n° 25783 below the preceding emoji is categorised as an unrecognised noun ("unknown" lemma).

In reality, in SMS n° 25783 (Figure 4.5) the emoji does not stand for a noun, and it functions among other things as an end of sentence punctuation mark, which the tagger fails to recognise. Thus, the second person subject pronoun "Tu" is mis-tagged as a proper noun as it is written with a capital letter following the emoji. This risk of incorrect tagging is frequent in our corpus, considering that 48 times out of 76 the word following an emoji is capitalised.

---

[24] </emoji>\n[^<]

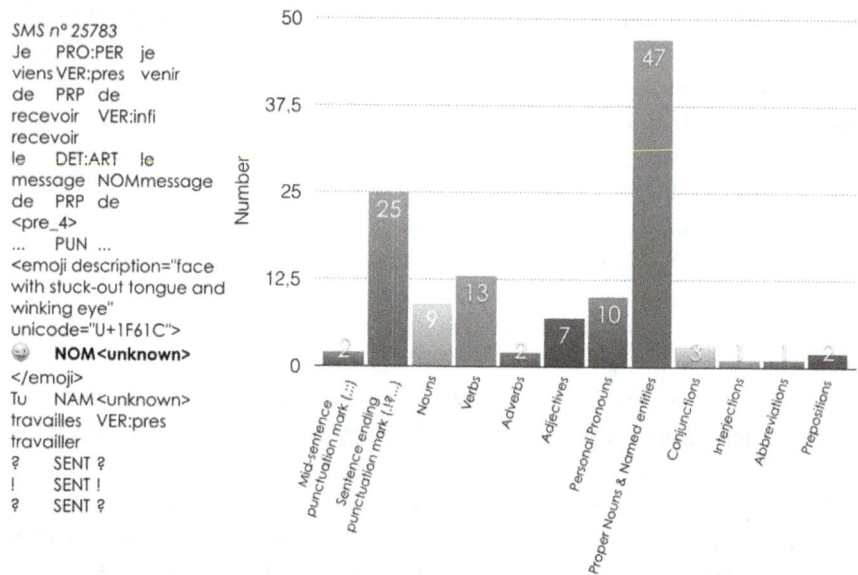

Figure 4.5: Tags assigned to tokens immediately following an emoji, with an example.

This seems to imply that in such cases the emoji also has some sort of end of sentence function for the scriptor, and this is not recognised by TreeTagger, since as specified above, emojis are never assigned a punctuation tag. In only 25 cases in our corpus emoji are followed by an explicit end of sentence marker.[25]

Mis-tagging often seems to affect interjections (see SMS n° 91447 below, last line), which are not correctly recognised. In such cases the error can either be caused by the preceding emoji or the language model itself, since it may not be properly trained for this type of register.[26]

SMS n° 91447
Tu   PRO:PER   tu
vas   VER:pres aller
le   PRO:PER   le
prendre VER:infi prendre
<emoji description="flushed face" unicode="U+1F633">

---

[25] </emoji>\n[^<]

[26] "You're going to take it 😳 Oh dear" In this instance, even without the emoji, "Oh dear" is not recognized, due to agglutination and absent diacritical signs.

😳 ADJ <unknown>
</emoji>
oulala NOM <unknown>

On the whole, just as we have seen for the preceding context, manual inspection shows that the sentence or phrase following an emoji is grammatically self-standing and the emoji does not transfer a syntactic function over to it. The exceptions are again the lexical replacements, as we have seen above. In SMS n° 35642, the prepositional phrase "pour le Gaumont" (for the Gaumont) is syntactically dependent on the noun phrase constituted by "le 🚋" (the tram).

Again, SMS n° 91447 above seems to indicate that at least in some cases emoji replace end-of-sentence punctuation, since, as we have seen they often occupy the last position in sentences and SMS.

4.2 Emoji and punctuation

Interaction between emoji and punctuation is explored here. In previous observations, we have already started to hypothesize that emoji may fulfil the role of clause or sentence-end marker. A clearer picture comes from searching all contexts in which an emoji is surrounded by words (thus excluding those placed as SMS openings or closures, or in emoji chains and crucially those preceded or followed by punctuation). The corresponding regular expression query[27] returns 37 results.

We note various cases. The emoji may represent a short pause, such as a comma:

SMS n° 7396[28]
Si NAM <unknown>
t' PRO:PER te
insistes VER:pres insister
<emoji description="face with stuck-out tongue and winking eye" unicode="U+1F61C">
😜 ADJ <unknown>
</emoji>
alors ADV alors

---

27 "\w+\t.*\t.*\n<emoji.*\n(.*\t.*\t.*\n)+</emoji>\n\w+"
28 "If you insist, then I'll come !!"

je   PRO:PER   je
viens VER:pres   venir
!   SENT !!   SENT !

Or it clearly stands for sentence ending, given the following capitalised subject personal pronoun.

SMS n° 24988[29]
Moi   NAM   <unknown>
c'   PRO:DEM   ce
était   VER:impf <unknown>
la   DET:ART   le
première NUM   <unknown>
fois   NOM   foi|fois
<emoji description="face with stuck-out tongue and winking eye" unicode="U+1F61C">
😜   ADJ   <unknown>
</emoji>
Je   PRO:PER   je
saurai   VER:futu savoir
mieux   ADV   mieux
faire   VER:infi faire
si   KON   si
j'   PRO:PER   je
y   PRO:PER   y
retourne VER:subp retourner
...   PUN   ...

To have a clearer picture of the interaction between emoji and punctuation we can also look at the opposite situation, namely cases in which the emoji is clearly not functioning as an end of sentence marker itself since it is either preceded or followed by an explicit end of sentence punctuation mark (SENT tags).

Twenty-five emoji are followed by an end of sentence token in our corpus, while twenty-eight emoji are preceded by an end of sentence token; in most of these cases the token is either an exclamation or a question mark. A possible hypothesis is that the emoji acts here as a softener or necessary addition to

---

29 "For me it was the first time 😜 I'll do better if I go back..."

clarify the interpretation of a question or an exclamation which may be misunderstood without it:

SMS n° 66390

Pff   NOM   \<unknown\>
toujours   ADV   toujours
le   DET:ART   le
même ADJ   même
discours   NOM   discours
\<emoji description="unamused face" unicode="U+1F612"\>
😒   ADJ   \<unknown\>
\</emoji\>
\<emoji description="smirking face" unicode="U+1F60F"\>
😏   ADJ   \<unknown\>
\</emoji\>
\<emoji description="face with stuck-out tongue and winking eye" unicode="U+1F61C"\>
😜   NOM   \<unknown\>
\</emoji\>
!   SENT   !
!   SENT   !
!   SENT   !

But manual inspection seems to show that the majority of these emoji are often redundant additions, like comments, with a paralinguistic value, replacing a gesture, or a facial expression.

SMS n° 61384[30]

Merde   NOM   merde
,   PUN   ,
tu PRO:PER   tu
m' PRO:PER   me
intrigues   VER:pres   intriguer
là ADV   \<unknown\>
\<emoji description="flushed face" unicode="U+1F633"\>
😳   ADJ   \<unknown\>
\</emoji\>

---

[30] "Shit, you're intriguing me there ?!"

? SENT ?
! SENT !

Only in some rare cases, the writer ending a sentence with an emoji feels the need to add a full stop, as would be expected in more formal written registers; in the majority of cases however end-of-sentence emoji have started to override full stops. This may mean that in the SMS register, the emoji may also function as a generic end of sentence marker, when no specific one ("!", "?") is required. It should be noticed that some authors (Dresner and Herring 2010) have already hypothesized a parallel between utterance-final punctuation marks and emoticon usage; this usage might have extended to emoji as well.

5 Questionnaires

Clearly this very limited analysis will have to be put to the test of a larger corpus. A comparison between corpora of different languages and, crucially, collected at different times, will help to see if some trends may be recognised in the emerging of new uses.

Another important aspect is of course the sociolinguistic one, since some social groups may be more innovative in their use of emoji. The 378 emoji extracted from the *88milSMS* corpus[31] may be linked up to a questionnaire, filled out by 95% of SMS donors. The questionnaire results provide useful sociolinguistic variables of emoji users such as gender (male: 44%; female: 56%) and age (average age, 27; drops to age 24 for top-five), however they may be considered biased, since the informants are all early adopters of this new technology and mostly young.

Another interesting factor to analyse would be the correlation between lexical replacement and age/gender; however, the number of lexical replacements in our emoji corpus does not allow us to draw any convincing conclusions. We identified lexical replacements manually, differentiating between openings (Private SMS: "👋 Je regarde après manger et je t'envoie un courriel 📧. Bises !" "👋 I'll look after eating and I'll send you an email 📧. Kisses" The 👋 emoji acts as an opening, such as "Hi"), closures (Private SMS: "Merci bcp Rachel gros 😘😘😘" "Thanks a lot Rachel lots of 😘😘😘" The 😘 emoji lexically replaces the noun "bisous/kisses") and mid-SMS (for instance an emoji replacing a noun, preceded by an article, such as "le 🚋" in SMS n° 35642).

---

[31] http://88milsms.huma-num.fr/references/emoji-88milsms.pdf (23.07.2019)

Indeed, the only two mid-SMS lexical replacements in the corpus are used by a 24-year old male in the same SMS, one of which corresponds to SMS n° 35642. Curiously enough, informant 422, a rather prolific one in our corpus, does not seem to make other such attempts. The other types of lexical replacements, while also quite rare (only 6 informants), seem more evenly distributed within the informants.

Has lexical replacement increased over time since the *88milSMS* corpus was collected? An online questionnaire conducted among French users of social media[32] within the framework of a Master's thesis (Rascol 2017) confirms that emoji use is now widespread in computer-mediated communication. Three-quarters of the informants declare using emoji always or most of the time, both in text messages and social media. However lexical replacement has not taken over other more paralinguistic functions. When asked the reason for using emoji, most informants answer that they use them to disambiguate potentially ambiguous/offensive messages and to stress the message (understanding: 81%; reinforcement: 71%; aesthetics: 52%; copying contacts' usage: 19%; shortened messages: 9%; trends/facts: 5%). At the same time 14% of informants declare using lexical replacement (although it is not clear how frequently), which seems to hint at an increase with respect to the *88milSMS* corpus.

These results resonate with everyday observations, which seem to show an increase in referential usages of emoji. This may also be linked to the fact that more "referential" emoji have been added over the past recent years, namely emoji representing things or actions rather than simply facial expressions or gestures.

6 Conclusion: Future directions

The results presented here are obviously very limited in size and they also represent a very early stage of adoption for a communicative device that has become extremely widespread over recent years. In future research, it will be essential to diachronically compare our results with more recent data, emanating from the Swiss *WhatsApp* project (http://www.whatsup-switzerland.ch/index.php/fr/) (Ueberwasser & Stark 2017) and Belgian *Vos Pouces* (https://acougnon.wixsite.com/thumbs4science) (Cougnon et al. 2017) project. Intercultural variation, crossplatform differences in graphical rendering (Miller et al., 2016) and "emoji

---

[32] 317 answers to the questionnaire were collected online; informants are mostly women, the average age is 37 and over 70% of them have been using emoji for 3 or more years.

semiotics" (Danesi 2016) will also be explored. This will enable one to visualize evolving mediated digital discourse several years down the track.

Moreover, diastratic and diamesic distribution of emoji usage will have to be taken into account. In particular, we need a thorough investigation in the differences of usage among generations, but also in the emerging differentiation among contexts of use, which now extends to varying mediums. It will be particularly interesting to compare emoji use in dialogic vs non (or less) dialogic contexts (e.g. instant messaging vs Social Media posts), synchronous vs asynchronous conversations (WhatsApp, email, Facebook posts), private vs public use (the latter now also including advertisements and other types of corporate communication).

Finally, these new types of corpora will help to tackle the practical implications for natural language processing and corpus linguistics of the widespread usage of emoji in various types of written texts. In this paper, we tried to address the question of how emoji are to be treated from the point of view of manual and automatic tagging. From what we have seen so far in our limited analysis, the correct tagging of emoji is crucial for the overall performance of the tagger. At the same time, emoji seem to fall into different grammatical categories, some of which are normally absent in written language and may require ad hoc tags. As we have seen in the "Background" paragraph of this paper mainstream press often refers to emoji as being a new type of words, or sometimes a new "language" form. But if we take into account our threefold classification (redundant addition, necessary addition, lexical replacement), only in the last case emoji seem to have the function of a canonical content word. In the other cases, they may be seen as fulfilling the same role as function words, interjections, punctuation or even replacing nonverbal communication such as gestures, prosody or facial expressions.

A promising perspective has recently been offered by Dürscheid and Siever (2017), who take up the classification of writing symbols by Gallman 1985. According to the authors emoji fall into the category of "Sonderzeichen", special characters, such as mathematical symbols (+%). From the grammatical point of view however such symbols may act as either ideograms, boundary signals ("Grenzsignale"), sentence signals ("Satzsignale"), or have an indexical function ("Indexikalische Funktion") helping the interpretation of the text. It remains to be seen whether even this sort of classification (which does not make assumptions as to communicative function of the emoji, contrary to the other ones cited in this paper), is sufficiently evident from a distributional point of view to be used for training a statistical PoS tagger.

What is clear from the examples seen in this paper, is that a correct classification of emoji with respect to the above four categories (Dürscheid & Siever

2017) seems to be necessary to accurately perform sentence splitting, PoS tagging, parsing texts containing emoji. In particular it is important to recognise the role of end-of-sentence emoji, in order to correctly recognise and parse sentences. Only in the case of proper lexical replacement, however, emoji may be treated as words, participating in the syntactic and semantic construction of a clause. In such cases they would be subject to most types of linguistic annotation (possibly to the exclusion of the morphology), such as constituency parsing, dependency parsing, semantic role labelling...

For instance, in SMS n° 35642 we can see a syntactic relation between "prendre" and 🚋, where 🚋 represents the object of the verb "prendre"; from the semantic point of view, using a FrameNet-like[33] representation, the semantic class of object 🚋 maps onto the "take + VEHICLE" frame, and thus selecting a given sense of the polysemous verb "prendre".

Such ideographic emoji can also be seen as having some sort of lexical semantic meaning, which may be analysed in terms of context semantics, just as occurs with alphabetic words. Some attempts in this sense have already been undertaken in projects such as in the EmojiNet project[34] and in Barbieri, Ronzano and Saggion (2016).

Thus, building new and better corpora of texts containing emoji becomes a necessity not only from the theoretical but also from the practical point of view, in order to train and test NLP algorithms that are capable of automatically processing such types of written communication.

This will imply collecting new and more balanced corpora, in terms of sociolinguistic, geographic and temporal variation, channel (public and private social media, emails, instant messaging), register (more or less informal). And also, the re-definition of our inventory of linguistic criteria, in order to be able to assign correct categories to emoji.

References

Barbieri, Francesco, Francesco Ronzano & Horacio Saggion. 2016. What does this emoji mean? A vector space skip-gram model for Twitter emojis. In Nicoletta Calzolari, Khalid Choukri, Thierry Declerck, Sara Goggi, Marko Grobelnik, Bente Maegaard, Joseph Mariani, Hélène Mazo, Asunción Moreno, Jan Odijk and Stelios Piperidis (eds.), *Proceedings of the Tenth International Conference on Language Resources and Evaluation (LREC 2016)*, pp. 3967–3972. Paris, France: European Language Resources Association (ELRA).

---

[33] https://framenet.icsi.berkeley.edu (23.07.2019)
[34] http://emojinet.knoesis.org/emosim508.php (23.07.2019)

Cougnon, Louise-Amélie. 2015. *Langage et sms: Une étude internationale des pratiques actuelles*. Presses universitaires de Louvain.

Cougnon, Louise-Amelie, Lenais Maskens, Sophie Roekhaut & Cedrick Fairon. 2017. Social media, spontaneous writing and dictation. Spelling variation. *Journal of French Language Studies* 27(3), 309–327.

Danesi, Marcel. 2016. *The semiotics of emoji: The rise of visual language in the age of the internet*. London/New York: Bloomsbury Publishing.

Détrie, Catherine & Bertrand Verine. 2015. Quand l'insulte se fait mot doux : la violence verbale dans les SMS. In Ulla Tuomarla, Juhani Härmä, Liisa Tiittula, Anni Sairio. Maria Paloheimo & Johanna Isosävi (eds.), *Miscommunication and verbal violence / Du malentendu à la violence verbale / Misskommunikation und verbale Gewalt* (Mémoires de La Société Néophilologique de Helsinki), vol. XCIII, 59–71. Société néophilologique.

Dresner, Eli & Susan C. Herring. 2010. Functions of the nonverbal in CMC: Emoticons and illocutionary force. *Communication Theory* 20(3), 249–268.

Dürscheid, Christa & Christina Margrit Siever. 2017. Jenseits des Alphabets – Kommunikation mit Emojis. *Zeitschrift für germanistische Linguistik* 45(2), 256–285.

Evans, Vyvyan. 2017. *The Emoji Code. How Smiley Faces, Love Hearts and Thumbs Up are changing the Way We Communicate*. London: Michael O'Mara Books.

Gallmann, Peter. 1985. *Graphische Elemente der geschriebenen Sprache. Grundlagen für eine Reform der Orthographie*. Reprint 2016. Berlin, Boston: De Gruyter.

Ljubešić, Nikola & Darja Fišer. 2016. A global analysis of emoji usage. *Proceedings of the 10th Web as Corpus Workshop*, 82–89. Berlin: Association for Computational Linguistics.

Lu, Xuan, Wei Ai, Xuanzhe Liu, Qian Li, Ning Wang, Gang Huang & Qiaozhu Mei. 2016. Learning from the ubiquitous language: An empirical analysis of emoji usage of smartphone users. *Proceedings of the 2016 ACM International Joint Conference on Pervasive and Ubiquitous Computing* (UbiComp '16), 770–780. New York, NY, USA: ACM.

Marcoccia, Michel & Nadia Gauducheau. 2007. L'analyse du rôle des smileys en production et en réception: un retour sur la question de l'oralité des écrits numériques. In Isabelle Piérozak (ed.), Glottopol (Regards Sur l'internet, Dans Ses Dimensions Langagières. Penser Les Continuités et Discontinuités. En Hommage à Jacques Anis) 10, 38–55.

Miller, Hannah, Jacob Thebault-Spieker, Shuo Chang, Isaac Johnson, Loren Terveen & Brent Hecht. 2016. "blissfully happy" or "ready to fight": Varying interpretations of emoji. *Proceedings of the 10th International Conference on Web and Social Media, ICWSM 2016*, 259–268. AAAI press.

Novak, Petra Kralj, Jasmina Smailović, Borut Sluban & Igor Mozetič. 2015. Sentiment of Emojis. *PLOS ONE* 10 (12).e0144296.

Panckhurst, Rachel, Mathieu Roche, Cédric Lopez, Bertrand Verine, Catherine Détrie & Claudine Moïse. 2016a. De la collecte à l'analyse d'un corpus de SMS authentiques : une démarche pluridisciplinaire. *Histoire Epistémologie Langage: Constitution de Corpus Linguistiques et Pérennisation Des Données*. 38(2),63–82.

Panckhurst, Rachel, Catherine Détrie, Cédric Lopez, Claudine Moïse, Mathieu Roche & Bertrand Verine. 2016b. 88milSMS. A corpus of authentic text messages in French. In Thierry Chanier (ed.), *Banque de corpus CoMeRe*. Ortolang : Nancy.

Panckhurst, Rachel, Catherine Détrie, Cédric Lopez, Claudine Moïse, Mathieu Roche & Bertrand Verine. 2014. *88milSMS. A corpus of authentic text messages in French*.

Panckhurst, Rachel. 2017. *Entre linguistique et informatique. Des outils de traitement automatique du langage naturel écrit (TALNE) à l'analyse du discours numérique médié (DNM)*. French habilitation diploma, Comue Université Paris-Est.
Piérozak, Isabelle (ed.). 2007. *Regards sur l'internet, dans ses dimensions langagières. Penser les continuités et discontinuités. En hommage à Jacques Anis*. Vol. Revue Glottopol-N°10 juillet 2007.
Rascol, Stephanie. 2017. L'évolution de l'utilisation des emojis de la sphere privée à la sphere publique. Université Paul-Valéry Montpellier 3.
Ueberwasser, Simone & Elisabeth Stark. 2017. What's up, Switzerland? A corpus-based research project in a multilingual country. *Linguistik Online* 84(5).
Wilson, Andrew. 1993. A pragmatic device in electronic communication. *Journal of Pragmatics* 19(4), 389–392.

Part 2: **The social life of images**

Sirpa Leppänen
5 Revisualization of classed motherhood in social media

1 Introduction

As a particular type of the strategy of recontextualization (Bauman & Briggs 1990: 73; Blommaert 2005: 47; Leppänen & Kytölä 2016), revisualization refers to the ways specific socially, culturally, and historically situated, unique aspects of visual discourse are taken up and reinserted in a new context and, as part of this process, the images are modified in some way. Revisualization can involve particular styles of visual representation, design and communication, but also ways of selecting and zooming on particular contents. Further, it can be accompanied and complemented in different ways by textual recontextualization. In this chapter, I argue that in current social media practices, revisualization is an increasingly common practice – it has a significant role in for example interest-driven, humorous and activist social media practices (van Zoonen 2005; Leppänen & Häkkinen 2013). More specifically, I will discuss revisualization in action with the help of two examples from Finland-based social media: blogs dealing with the shifting and contested social category of motherhood. Firstly, to contextualize my analysis, I will briefly discuss historical and current discourses of motherhood in Finland, as well as one their vehicles, so called homing blogs – a popular, largely visual blog genre in Finland produced by young women who have retreated from the labour market to the private sphere of the home (Jäntti et al 2018). Finally, I will show how the discourse of homing blogs has been revisualized (and recontextualized) in social media – in the guise of parodic motherhood blogs.

The investigation of motherhood blogging is worthy of analysis because – as I will show in both cases discussed here – the imagery and styles of visual representation used construct a particular version of motherhood. In so-called homing blogs, the version (or vision) produced is of a contemporary, idealized middle-class motherhood. In parodic mother blogs, meanwhile, we see visualizations of lower class motherhood. I will demonstrate how these revisualizations of motherhood are deeply ambiguous. On the one hand, they appear as a form of transgressive political critique which uses parody to ridicule traditional discourses and (visual) ideologies of gender, class and motherhood. On the other hand, these blogs can also be interpreted as attacking, from a moralistic educated middle-class perspective, the lifestyles and tastes of lower-class women. From this perspective, bloggers present a grotesque version of the idealized middle-class motherhood, representations that in recent theoretical and empirical work on gender and class have been found typical of working class and underclass femininity in media discourses, public debates and politics (Skeggs 1997; Tyler 2008; Tyler and Bennett 2010; Hatherley 2018). Ultimately, therefore, I argue that otherwise parodic representations of motherhood end up disparaging non-conformist motherhood, thus signalling affinity with classist media spectacles of lower class motherhood that also Finnish audiences "have loved to hate" (Tyler 2008).

2 Revisualization as an aspect of recontextualization

As I say above, I am approaching revisualization as an extension of the concept of recontextualization originally suggested by Bauman & Briggs (1990) and Silverstein & Urban (1996). Emerging at the intersection of performance studies, anthropology and discourse studies, entextualization involves two related processes of discourse generation: decontextualization – taking discourse material out of its context – and recontextualization – integrating and transforming this material so that it fits in a new context. According to Bauman & Briggs (1990: 75–6), there are six dimensions that are relevant in de-/recontextualization; these are: (i) *framing* (i.e. the metacommunicative management of the recontextualized text); (ii) *form* (i.e. formal transformation from one context to another); (iii) *function* (i.e. transformation of the function of discourse); (iv) *indexical grounding* (i.e. shifts of for example deictic markers of person, spatial location and time); (v) *translation* (i.e. both interlingual and intersemiotic translation); and (vi) the *emergent structure of a new context* (i.e. the way in which discourse is shaped by and shaping context by the process of recontextualization). In contrast to the notion of intertextuality that has traditionally been understood as relationships among texts – how texts refer to, draw upon, and/or are shaped by earlier texts – entextualization highlights the processual aspects of intertextuality (Trester 2012: 243), the way in which, in Blommaert's (2005: 47) words, intertextuality turns into "an empirical research programme".

In entextualization processes, communicative actors are active agents for whom entextualization is a means of discursive navigation and "an act of control" through which they can claim a degree of social and discursive power (Bauman and Briggs 1990: 76). This power shows in their access to the activity of entextualization, in the legitimacy of their claims to reuse existing discourse material, in their competence in such reuse, and in the differential values attached to various types of discourse. Entextualization provides a tool for investigating "empirically what means are available in a given social setting, to whom they may be available, under what circumstances, for making discourse into text" (Bauman & Briggs 1990, 74; see also Leppänen et al. 2014). For many scholars of computer-mediated discourse, entextualization has indeed proved a fruitful concept for the discussion of the trajectories, uptake and transformation of semiotic content, forms and styles that are now pervasive in digital discourse, communication and interactions (see e.g. Leppänen 2012; Rymes 2012; Androutsopoulos 2013; Leppänen et al. 2014).

The aspect of entextualization that is particularly useful for my current purposes is that it makes possible a conceptualization of, and focus on, the analysis of the uptake and transformation of not only verbal or textual stuff, but also other types of semiotic material. In the case under investigation here, the material that is interesting is visuality – the content of images, their aesthetic, design and photographic dimensions, and their interplay with verbal text. In particular, I am interested in the ways in which the uptake and modification of visual material and styles generate new meanings with respect to a cultural phenomenon – motherhood – being recontextualized. In these ways, my chapter highlights how entextualization in digital practices also involves the crossing and integration of semiotic boundaries as one aspect of the contemporary "realities of the semiotic landscape" (Kress & van Leeuwen 1996: 34). In other words, I am concerned with the ways digital practices are inherently social multimodal practices with which people make sense of and construct their social and cultural realities, identities and relationships online and around social media (Thurlow 2013; Leppänen et al. 2017).

3 Femininity, motherhood and social class

Femininity and motherhood as classed have long historical roots (Poovey 1984; Skeggs 2001). For example, in Britain, according to Poovey (1984), the notion of ideal femininity emerged in the 18th century. As an image it indexed the habitus of the upper classes, a category of pure, white heterosexuality. Later this image of femininity translated into an ideal for middle-class women that was then disseminated and enforced through conduct books and magazines. As argued by Hatherley (2018: 358), this image of femininity has proved to be very resilient and powerful. Even in the 21st century, working-class, black and/or non-heterosexual women who do not have the financial resources to successfully perform femininity in these idealized or hegemonic ways are still excluded from its realm, demonized and "cast down into the realms of the grotesque" (see also Skeggs 1997;

Gillies 2006; Tyler 2008). In a similar vein, feminist research has shown how motherhood has also been characterized by diverse positions and meanings, and how few mothers can or will submit to "the (white, middle-class, heterosexual) norms of good mothering" (Kawash 2011: 979). Regardless, social class continues to matter in various ways, both in creating or constraining the mothers' material and social opportunities and in shaping the values, goals, and identities that mothers bring to raising their children (Lareau 2003).

Similar processes characterize the history of classed femininity and motherhood in Finland. The discourses of modern motherhood have distinguished "good" motherhood from "bad" according to the mother's social class and wealth (Satka 1996; Nätkin 1997; Helén 1997; Berg 2008). In the 19th and early 20th century, motherhood in Finland became a right that working class women had to struggle for, whereas for upper class women this right was a given. Servants and country women, left-wing, "red" working class mothers and civil war widows were considered particularly immoral and unsuitable as mothers (Nätkin 1997: 42; Satka 1996: 88–91). "Bad" motherhood was seen as ignorance, lack of education or indifference – all characteristics associated with working class and poor mothers. Poverty itself, the material circumstances in home and the poor hygiene in rural and working-class homes were also taken to symbolize insufficient motherhood. At the same time, mothers' employment outside the home was also stigmatized (Sulkunen 1987, 1989) as a form of deviance or even as a crime against women's "true" vocation, motherhood, and the active moral education of children that it was taken to entail. However, alongside with the modernization of the society in the 1960s and 1970s, ideal motherhood began to be challenged. Attitudes and norms concerning different types of motherhood – single mothers, widows, divorced, common law and married mothers – became more liberal, means of birth control increased, abortion became legalized and sexual culture freer. In addition, an increasing number of mothers began working outside the home (Nätkin 1997). Thus, the ideologies and norms of "good" motherhood became less compelling, and it was increasingly regarded not as a set of mutually exclusive choices, but as individual value choices (Nätkin 1997: 250; Berg 2009). Currently, motherhood in Finland can in principle take many different forms. Most significantly, stay-at-home motherhood is just one of the possible positionings available to women; by the same token, working outside the home and having a career is, in principle, not stigmatized. In fact, as a Nordic welfare state, Finland has actively supported women's participation in the labour market for decades (Brunila & Ylöstalo 2015).

The freedom for individual mothers to make their own choice is, however, not a categorical given in spite of these developments. Nowadays, social, political, economic and discursive forces can still corral mothers into particular life trajectories, and, in practice, powerfully delimit their actual options. As discussed in detail by Jäntti and her colleagues (2018), in line with developments in other Western welfare societies (e.g. Porter 2012), it is justified to argue that Finland has witnessed a "feminized recession" (Adkins 2012: 629). For example, there have been cuts in social services, such as communal day care, accompanied by the loss of jobs for women in the public sector, making them more vulnerable. These economic and social changes have also been accompanied by a conglomerate of neoliberal, conservative and post-feminist ideologies in gender discourses that re-articulate the importance of the woman's place in the private sphere of the home and nuclear family (Hayden 2002, Blunt and Dowling 2006). One outcome of these developments has, in fact, been that some individual, modern, educated women have retreated back to home, and that these moves have been rationalized and justified as a "natural" and legitimate choice that women themselves make, rather than the outcome of a range of structural, economic and ideological factors (Jäntti et al. 2018: 890).

These developments are interesting from the point of view of social class: it seems that the women who have been retreating to the home are primarily middle-class women ("modern, educated women"), who "can negotiate and share their "return" to the private sphere of the home with their peers" via, for example, blogging about it (Jäntti et al. 2018: 890). Blogging, for them, thus offers a collective means for synthesizing and blurring the public and the private (Thurlow (2013: 244), for justifying and authenticating their "choice"(Jäntti et al. 2018). The classed nature of these mediatized re-enactments of domesticity can, however, also imply that there are other women – women who may not be (seen as) equally "modern and educated" – who do not have a similar motivation or set of resources to make their situations publicly as visible and sharable via social media.

4 Setting the standard: Homing blogs as a visualization of middle-class motherhood

Homing blogs are a popular women's genre. As single authored diary-like updates of the personal lives of bloggers (Blood 2002; Myers 2010; Rettberg 2013), they constitute a particular sphere of semi-public digital agency (Jäntti et al. 2018:890). They are "semi-public" in that they represent an extension of the bloggers' homes and, by publicly displaying details of their authors' private lives (Noppari & Hautakangas 2012). In this sense, they could be seen as a continuation of the tradition of life-writing, but, unlike traditional diaries, they have a strong emphasis on visual photographic representation of the self, domestic spaces and activities. In the same way as other social media aimed at parents (such as the Mumsnet discussed in Mackenzie 2019), homing blogs also provide mothers with opportunities for negotiating their position in relation to discourses of motherhood, and serve as a means for seeking identification, connectedness, groupness and communality with other mothers (see Leppänen et al. 2017; Zappavigna 2011).

Most significantly, in light of my focus here, homing blogs are indexical of particular social, cultural and gendered identities, distinctly depicting middle-class motherhood. In so doing, bloggers speak of social class as taste, as sets of preferences of style, manners, patterns of consumption, and cultural values. This Bourdieusean view of social class (Bourdieu 1984; Bourdieu & Wacquant 1992; Skeggs 1997, 2015; Gronov 1997; Purhonen et al. 2014) points to people's ability to judge what is beautiful, good and proper as a socially distinctive practice. Thus, different social classes come to have different cultural tastes and to consume culture differently; they also decide what is not liked or from which preferences one should disidentify (see e.g. Purhonen et al. 2014).

Against this backdrop, homing blogs can be seen as a discursive arena for doing classed, sometimes elitist notions of motherhood, where the legitimation of privilege/inequality is discursively organized and sustained (Thurlow & Jaworski 2017: 246). In particular, they seem to draw on and mobilize images of well-organized domestic life and clean, well-ordered homes. While in the early 20th century such imagery was promoted for the education of mothers on the importance of health and hygiene (Saarikangas 2002; Nätkin 1997), in the 21st century they have more to do with the ideologies of "good" motherhood, still displayed prolifically in public media discourses of different kinds. For example, Berg (2009: 172) has argued that currently a typical image of motherhood in the media is the super-mother – a mother who is competent, energetic and diligent. In homing blogs, the modern ideals of middle-class motherhood and the investment mothers make are very visible.

What we often see in homing blogs[1] are carefully crafted visualizations of private dreams that are broadcast to a blogger audience. Often, the emphasis on the private as the core substance shows in the blogger's point of view, for example: the blogs include a first-person singular position, manifest in both the photographic perceptual focus (i.e. showing viewers what the author sees), and in the narration (i.e. telling viewers what the author thinks). In this way, audiences are given an account of experiences in, and reflections on, the everyday life of the women bloggers – a verbalized and visualized insight into their view of the world. Figure 5.1 offers an illustration of this kind of private experience being publicly

---

[1] I'm very grateful to all the bloggers who each gave me a permission to use their posts as my data examples in this article.

5 Revisualization of classed motherhood in social media — 113

Figure 5.1: http://mminulta.blogspot.com, accessed 12 February, 2019.

disseminated – here we see a carefully colour coordinated picture of the blogger's feet on a rug.

Most bloggers do not include their own pictures in their profile. When they do so, we find photographs like 5.1, or pictures that have been shot or edited so that they cannot be identified. An example of this can be seen in 5.2 below. This kind of images emphasize the bloggers' role as an observer whose main task is to

Figure 5.2: http://saapasjalansalonki.blogspot.com, accessed 1 February, 2019.

record and represent details of their lifeworld, but in a way that backgrounds themselves. In this sense, they differ a great deal from for example fashion bloggers who regularly pose for their own cameras (Duffy & Hund 2015).

While the bloggers avoid including pictures of themselves, they emphatically focus on giving their audiences aestheticized visions of the spaces, details, objects and the material reality of their homes. In these ways, they display publicly intimate moments of their family lives. For example, blog posts often include pictures of children as in Figure 5.3. At other times, they often suggest a retreat to a simpler, downshifted and ecologically aware life. For example, there are pictures of mundane activities, such as making handicrafts, baking, knitting, tending plants, preparing meals, or enjoying a cup of tea in settings indicating austerity and modesty. At the same time, everything in the pictures conveys a particular

Figure 5.3: https://aitiydenaika.blogspot.com, accessed 3 February, 2019.

sense of style – the objects and furnishings may be old and recycled, but they are (presented as) beautiful in their contours, colours and materiality; this is what we see in Figures 5.4, 5.5 and 5.6:

Figure 5.4: http://mminulta.blogspot.com, accessed 12 February, 2019.

It seems that, in these kinds of homing blogs, beauty, harmony and balance are central values. This shows in the poetic and aesthetic depictions of the bloggers' everyday lives inside or in proximity of their homes. The pictures are carefully edited so that they are dominated by soft muted colours shading into black, often, however, with flecks of sunlight as an important element in them. There are posts depicting picturesque details of the bloggers' homes, close-ups of unfinished handicrafts and household chores, children playing, houseplants, and pets. Bloggers or other adults seldom feature in pictures. Likewise, there are few images taken in urban settings, or involving technological gadgets, cars or computers. It is as if the pictures depict life decades ago. The overall impression of the entries thus is that of nostalgia and melancholy. The visual depiction of these young women's domestic lives seems, in fact, to be in stark contrast with the everyday epiphanies and moments of happiness that the

Figure 5.5: http://mminulta.blogspot.com, accessed 12 February, 2019.

Figure 5.6: http://irmastiina.blogspot.com, accessed 28 February, 2019.

bloggers' textual entries suggest they enjoy (Jäntti et al. 2018). In these respects, they resemble a great deal rhetorical strategies that Mapes (2018: 217) has shown to be typical of elite authenticity in food discourse, another discourse central in the construction and mediatization of classed identity: simplicity, lowbrow appreciation, pioneer spirit, locality and sustainability.

5 Visual parody: The revisualization of homing blogs

While homing blogs arguably display aestheticized images of industrious, but melancholic and romanticized or nostalgic middle-class motherhood, they nowadays also have their counter-genre. In Finland, such a counter-blog is *Shitty Mother's Diary* ("Paskaäidin päiväkirja").[2] This particular diary was launched in 2007 by an anonymous group of bloggers. A key goal in their blogs and other social media posts is that they use parody to challenge the ideological assumptions concerning the nuclear family, notions of "good" mothering, and the aesthetics of home conveyed in, for example, homing blogs.[3]

In *Shitty Mother's Diary*, we find a mother figure who is familiar from comic and critical representations in the media: the "relaxed" mother.[4] According to Berg (2009: 129), relaxed motherhood is the opposite of the mother who sacrifices everything for her child and family. As examples of relaxed motherhood, Berg refers to celebrity mothers who have, among other things, described stay-at-home motherhood as a "brain-dead activity" and "confessed" to being a "bad mother" who makes sure they have time for themselves and their needs. However, in *Shitty Mother's Diary* this vision of the relaxed mother is also presented as an explicitly classed being, as a critical travesty of the middle-class motherhood one example of which is visible in the homing blogs discussed above.

This parodic criticality of *Shitty Mother's Diary* no doubt has a political undertone. It can, in fact, be seen as an example of new forms of activism that in the context of ludic and memic participatory cultures increasingly rely on playful transgressions as their key strategies (van Zoonen 2005; Leppänen & Häkkinen 2012; Häkkinen & Leppänen 2014). Along the lines suggested by Janks (2003: 2), their transgressiveness derives from how they both go beyond the bounds of norms and, in doing so, highlight the very same norms in a deeply "reflective act of denial and affirmation." As will be shown in more detail below, *Shitty Mother's Diary* tackles the figure of the middle-class mother, bringing this this figure in an elevated position down to "the comic plane of parody and travesty" (Bakhtin 1981: 54).

---

2 http://paskamutsi.vuodatus.net, accessed 12 January, 2019
3 Social media parodies of motherhood are not an exclusively Finnish phenomenon; for example, there is a similar blog in Sweden, *Dåliga mammans blogg*, ("The bad mother's blog", https://inaskrev.blogspot.com/) and in the UK: *The Diary of a Pompey Chavette* (https://shadesofpompeychav.wordpress.com).
4 Similar depictions of bad mothers can be found on other media as well – in Finnish TV comedy, for example.

The transgressive stance taken in *Shitty Mother's Diary* is very clear in this early entry from the year 2007. What we see in this entry is a picture of a young child who is placed in a dog carrier.

The picture in Figures 5.7 is accompanied by a verbal entry which, in its own way, also flouts our expectations of what a blog entry typically contains:

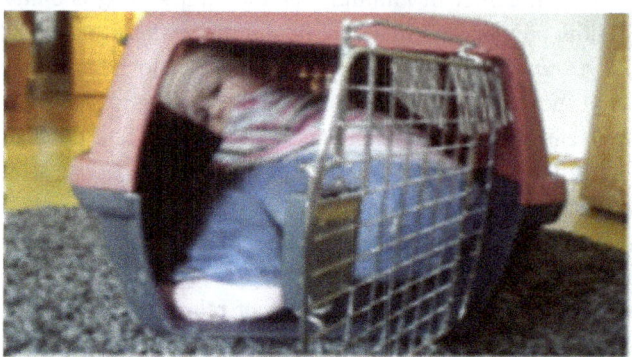

Figure 5.7: http://paskamutsi.vuodatus.net, accessed 12 January, 2019.

Extract 5.1 – Translation of verbal framing of Figure 5.7[5]

"I'm the summer cat of the shitties Nicittä now and I was given the task of choosing my favourite out of reder mail, so here goes!

Esmeralda Ariel's piece first caught my eye SUCH A LOVELY princess-like name *tasting it* Esmeralda Ariel <3 I wonder if it is a birth name or an artist name? [...] Some ybercool fridge magnetism [...],

One mother also sends us an idyllic picture with a useful tip to those who are traveling with kids."

In Figure 5.7, the picture suggests that children can be treated in the same way as dogs. In addition, the picture does not present the child in an aesthetically pleasing way. Rather, it is made to look like a low-quality snapshot that has not been self-consciously or deliberately designed at all – which may, in fact, be a strategy exploited more generally in social media in broadcasting material supposedly documenting "authentic" everyday life (Berliner 2014: 298). All the other visual aspects of this entry also highlight ways in which this blog deviates from the typical conventions of homing blogs. These include the ample use of emoticons, the choice of the Comic Sans Serif as the font (a font originally designed

---

5 All the translations from the original Finnish texts to English are by SL. Due to space limitations, the original Finnish texts were excluded from this chapter.

for cartoons), and the seemingly random use of typeface colours. The overall impression of the page is that it is cluttered, unorganized and messy. The contents of the text entry also amplify the impression of a lack of design and control: the entry gives us a fairly incoherent string of comments and reactions to alleged reader mail, all of which remain quite opaque to the reader.

The same transgressive theme is apparent in other entries. Figures 5.8 and 5.9, for example, are pictures taken inside a car wash, describing how, during the children's school break, the mother has come up with the idea of taking the children along for entertainment.

Figure 5.8: http://paskamutsi.vuodatus.net, accessed 12 January, 2019.

Extract 5.2 – Translation of the verbal framing of Figures 5.8 and 5.9

"I've almost done my bird with the school break. And it is not as if it isn't nice to spend several days in a row with the kids the only thing that bothered me was the constant cooking, normally they eat at school during the day. It is a constant problem to figure out activities for the energetic offspring and secondly everything costs in this world so it is not an easy concept this. But as a hint to others, too that you don't always have to pay to have fun as long as you are an inventive person. =)"

As in Figure 5.7, the entry here includes seemingly happenstance pictures illustrating what the textual entry describes: that taking the children to car wash can be meaningful "quality time" with mother. These examples also exemplify another typical feature of the verbal content of posts: they are written in vernacular or "slangy", speech-like Finnish, with frequent misspellings, missing

Figure 5.9: http://paskamutsi.vuodatus.net, accessed 12 January, 2019.

punctuation and unorthodox syntax. In addition, every compound word is written as two separate words. In this way, and akin to the "non-aesthetic" pictures and visual design, the verbal content thus becomes an evocative index of the allegedly non-normative mother identity. The desired overall impression seems to be that either the blogger's competence in blogging, photographing and writing is not very strong, or, that she is not too concerned with following the usual or expected rules.

In the same way as in homing blogs, the "shitty mother" herself is seldom in the pictures. Instead, there are entries that give or ask for tips relating to home decoration, handicrafts, cooking, or activities with children. Typically, the pictures depict the end results of the mother's activities, showing the products as somehow warped, shoddy or shocking. For example, there are pictures about rotten food, or burnt or otherwise sad looking baked goods. With irony, however, the verbal comments frame the content of the images as if they were impeccable and attractive. Figure 5.10 illustrates this kind of a blog entry, picturing a smoothie that the "shitty mother" had prepared as a Mother's Day surprise:

Extract 5.3 – Translation of the verbal framing of Figure 5.10

"**Mother's day surprise !**
Hello and an energetic Mother's Day to everyone <3 :) :)
    In the morning I got a lovely surprise when I found in the fridge a green smoothie that I had buzzed together a few weeks ago. :)
    It was in a good shape and breathed easily in a Rooster jar by Arabia [a Finnish design brand]. It is absolutely the top this way of super foods and fresh nutrition. :) :) :) I recommend it to all of those who have doubts! :)
    <3 <3 <3 <3 <3"

Figure 5.10: http://paskamutsi.vuodatus.net, accessed 12 January, 2019.

The stance taken in the pictures and verbal entries is constative or positively emotional – they depict or evaluate the details in the "shitty mother's" life. Seemingly innocently, the posts thereby engage in the display of, and commentary on, mothering in the best traditions of normative middle-class motherhood, suggesting that the mother simply has tried to do the right, correct and proper thing. At the same time, bloggers nevertheless display none of the careful, aestheticizing design and flair with visual presentation and photography characteristic of for example homing blogs. Figures 5.11 and 5.12 offer other examples of this type of "shitty mother" entries. In these cases, we see a mother's home-decorating project:

Extract 5.4 Translation of verbal framing of Figures 5.11 and 5.12

"DIY RURAL ROMANTIC CUPBOARD. Our reader Hot Romance -85 sent us a tip on home decorating: Now that it is almost Christmas, you often want to refurbish your home but the price is often too high. I just thought to do it myself and saved a lot of money' ... You can find inspiring pictures in web flea markets and magazines for interior decoration :) A big thank you to Hot Romance and wishes for a wonderful time preparing for Christmas to all of our other readers, too."

The example in Figures 5.11–2 and Extract 5.4 builds on a contrast between middle-class aesthetics and its subversion. Figure 5.11 includes a picture of a beautiful country romantic cupboard, of the kind that is often featured in magazines of interior decoration. At the same time, as Figure 5.12 shows, the blog entry also includes a picture of a cupboard that seems to be redecorated

Figure 5.11: http://paskamutsi.vuodatus.net, accessed 12 January, 2019.

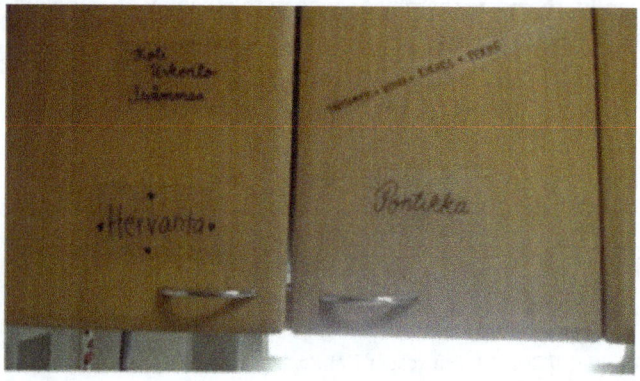

Figure 5.12: http://paskamutsi.vuodatus.net, accessed 12 January, 2019.

according to the model provided by the country romantic cupboard. However, the social and cultural indices of this particular cupboard are all "wrong": instead of the French calligraphic inscription on a stylish cupboard suggesting an upper class, elitist taste, it has Finnish words written in shaky block letters by a felt tip pen on a standard issue, shabby kitchen cupboard. Further, instead of the inscribed reference to a romantic shop in Paris selling hosiery and shoes ("Bonnetterie & Chaussures"), the re-fashioned cupboard refers to a working-class suburb of Hervanta in the city of Tampere, Finland. In addition, it shows inscriptions whose connotations are far from the prestigious ones of the model cupboard: they include a reference to Finnish homemade moonshine ("pontikka"); a nationalist right-wing slogan ("Koti, Uskonto ja Isänmaa", 'Home, Religion and Fatherland') and an iconic extract from Finnish rock lyrics ("Työttömyys, viina, kirves ja perhe", 'Unemployment, spirit alcohol, axe, family'). As in the case of the other examples discussed above, the verbal framing of the images 5.11 and 5.12 stands in an ironic contrast with the pictures, seemingly earnestly complimenting a reader for her frugal home decorating tip that can help others to renovate and beautify their homes. In sum, like the other entries, this example explicitly highlights and transgresses the norms of motherhood; while imitating these normative discourses and practices, it also constitutes a parodic version of these.

Finally, Figure 5.13 illustrates yet another key activity of good home making. The design for the picture seems deliberate: we are given a gloomy view of dead flowers, with an empty beer can as an additional adornment in the composition. The verbal framing, in turn, includes a deadpan plea for help in gardening. Once more, the entry transgressively highlights one of the norms of good motherhood – the skill of tending flowers – simultaneously flagging its absurdity with respect to the alleged life style choices of the "shitty mother".

Figure 5.13: http://paskamutsi.vuodatus.net, accessed 12 January, 2019.

Extract 5.5 – Translation of verbal framing of Figure 5.13

"Help with plucking flowers.
  Garden life is at its peak now and I have a problem. When I bought this flower the sales person said that I had to pluck the dead flowers off, otherwise it won't make new flowers. So which ones of these I should have plucked off? Initial situation: (relatively dry already)."

Part of the transgressive business of *Shitty Mother's Diary* is that the entries appear to be commented on by followers. In their own ways, the comments develop the themes and contents of the entries, amplifying and directing the reader's attention to the transgressiveness of the actions of the alleged mother. Comments of this kind are illustrated by Extract 5.5:

> Extract 5.6: – Translation of comments on Figure 5.14/Extract 5.5
>
> "Well that's not true. I almost had a Freudian. I thought that you had started drinking coke. :)))))))))). Well now I can say this when I learnt the truth."
> "Aulikki come ooooooon!!!!!"
> "Oh yes if anyone has any time to do something to the grass, the neighbour is getting noisy so that friends please move this way, alias the garden needs more than plucking"
> "I know, I know! From those flowers in the hanging pot in the lower picture you need to bluck all flowers one by one, so you learn if loved or not. (...) These are the lessons by ancient folks. (is that a compound word BTW?) (...) i've become so careful with this compounding and hyphens, better to ask if you're not quite sure cos there's always so good advice here for everything. ♥ ♥"

Extract 5.6 shows how none of the (alleged) commentators, except the last one, actually responds to the blogger's call for help with her flowers. Instead, they attend to the beer can as the most salient detail in the picture, voicing relief over the realization that the can is after all not Coke but beer. The image of the mother as the one who is air-headed, and more interested in beer than flowers, cooking or even children gets its confirmation and legitimation by the assumed collective of other like-minded "shitty mothers" connecting with each other through the channel of *Shitty Mother's Diary*.

To summarize, *Shitty Mother's Diary*, in principle, depicts, discusses and comments on similar topics as the homing blogs. However, in all other respects its relationship with homing blogs is a parodic one: it constantly relies on transgressive revisualizations and recontextualizations of the themes and styles for representing motherhood in homing blogs. This shows in every aspect of its design: the pictures which are deliberately "non-aesthetic", snapshot-like, with little colour coordination, filtering or editing, as well as the layout which is usually cluttered, unorganized and peppered with excessive emoticons. In terms of its language and verbal features, a similar impression of a lack of control and refinement is produced through spelling mistakes, the use of vernacular Finnish or slang, and the lack of conventional punctuation. This is a vision/version of mother that is altogether less refined than the mother emerging in the homing blogs: she is (presented as) less educated, frivolous, untidy, boozy, and even immoral.

6 Conclusion: Ambiguity of the revisualized mother

In this chapter I have had three main aims. Firstly, building on the notion of recontextualization, I have argued that, in informal and interest-driven digital media, revisualization is an increasingly pervasive phenomenon. Secondly, I have demonstrated revisualization in action with the help of two examples of Finland-based mother blogs: first, homing blogs and then *Shitty Mother's Diary* posts. I have showed how, in the latter, the imagery and visual styles typical of homing blogs are taken up and transformed. Thirdly, I have argued how in *Shitty Mother's Diary* revisualization, along with its associated textual recontextualizations, served the purpose of subverting the norms and discourses of middle-class motherhood and the ways in which these continue to be recirculated, evaluated and legitimated in different public and media discourses. In doing so, the bloggers behind the *Shitty Mother's Diary* both display their familiarity with, and meaningfully deviate from the "appropriate" genre conventions, content preferences and modes of representation of homing blogs. More specifically, they do this on at least three levels:

a) To create parody, they imitate, exaggerate and/or invert visual, linguistic, stylistic and content choices typical of homing blogs (see also Halonen & Leppänen 2017).
b) To drive home their transgressive messages, they often create an ironic contrast between the visual and textual content of the blog entries.
c) By transgressively re-articulating the norms and ideals of middle-class motherhood, they both highlight the pervasiveness of these discourses and critically tackle them.

This final point deserves to be discussed in more detail. On the one hand, *Shitty Mother's Diary* could indeed be seen as a form of political critique that uses parody to ridicule normative discourses and (visual) representations of gender, class and motherhood. At the same time, it could be seen as an attempt to giving voice to the lower-class mother, and to being unashamed of how she deviates from the ideals of motherhood. Following Hatherley (2018:358), the contents and styles of representation in *Shitty Mother's Diary* could be seen as voicing "an alternative femininity, via an "Anti-Pygmalion" aesthetic" that deliberately transforms and resists the hegemonic middle-class preferences. In this sense, *Shitty Mother's Diary* could even be argued as an act of the lower-class mother writing back and re-seizing the weapon of taste that Bourdieu & Wacquant (1992: 114) have argued to have been in possession of the elite in the struggle for social status and power.

On the other hand, *Shitty Mother's Diary* could also be interpreted as attacking, from an educated middle-class perspective, the lifestyles and tastes of lower-class women. This interpretation has a lot to do with authenticity. In homing blogs, we see accounts, stories, and representations that are created and disseminated by real women in the context of their lifeworlds. The messages they give us may be aesthetized, filtered and edited, but in their blog entries what we witness are *their* words, thoughts, predicaments, perceptions and visions. In *Shitty Mother's Diary*, in contrast, we are given the perspective of the imagined or at least anonymized "shitty mother" who is most likely a fictional creature. If this is indeed the case, it could be asked, what or who are actually being disparaged. It is possible, for instance, to conclude that "the shitty mother" emerging in the blog entries is a grotesque continuation of the bad – working class and poor – motherhood that used to be highlighted in modern Finnish discourses, in other words, a mother branded by ignorance, lack of education and indifference.

On a more general level, it should be noted that the ambiguity highlighted by *Shitty Mother's Diary* is actually a recurrent feature of parodic recontextualization on social media. It seems that, while the ambiguity of parody can function as a useful strategy to attract different audiences, it also raises the question of what is the context according to which audiences should/could orient to and make sense of it. In social media, it is often the case that what gets disseminated, sometimes in viral ways, is the spectacular meme, but not its societal, cultural, and political code. However, as Beverley Skeggs (2004: 29) argues, ambivalence itself can be valuable and essential for many forms of social reproduction in late-modern societies (see also Kolehmainen 2017). In this way, ambivalence, too, can serve as a means for destabilizing existing power relations.

References

Adkins, Lisa. 2012. Out of work or out of time? Rethinking labor after the financial crisis. *South Atlantic Quarterly* 111(4), 621–641.
Androutsopoulos, Jannis. 2013. Localizing the global on the participatory web. In Nicholas Coupland (ed.), *The Handbook of Language and Globalization*, 300–324. Blackwell Publishing: Malden, MA, Oxford, Chichester.
Bakhtin, Mikhail M. 1981. From the Prehistory of Novelistic Discourse. In Michael Holquist (ed.), *The Dialogic Imagination*. Trans. C. Emerson & M. Holquist. Austin: U of Texas Press.
Bauman, Richard & Charles L. Briggs. 1990. Poetics and performance as critical perspectives on language and social life. *Annual Review of Anthropology* 19, 59–88.

Berg, Kristiina. 2008. *Äitiys kulttuurisina odotuksina* ["Motherhood as cultural expectations"]. Helsinki: Väestöntutkimuslaitoksen julkaisusarja D 48.
Berg, Kristiina. 2009. Kulttuuriset odotukset äitiyden rakentajina ["The construction of motherhood by cultural expectations"]. *Janus* 17(2), 170–5.
Berliner, Lauren S. 2014. Shooting for Profit: The Monetary Logic of the YouTube Home Movie. In Laure Rascaroli, Gwenda Young & Barry Monahan (eds.), *Amateur Filmmaking: The Home Movie, the Archive, the Web*, 289–300. London: Bloomsbury Academic.
Blommaert, Jan. 2005. *Discourse: A critical introduction*. Cambridge: Cambridge University Press.
Blood, Rebecca. 2002. Introduction. In John Rodzvilla (ed.), *We've got Blog: How Weblogs are Changing our Culture*, ix–xiii. Cambridge: Perseus Publishing.
Blunt, Alison & Robyn Dowling. 2006. *Home: Key Ideas in Geography*. London: Routledge.
Bourdieu, Pierre. 1984. *Distinction: A social critique of the judgment of taste*. London: Routledge & Kegan Paul.
Bourdieu, Pierre. 1994/1998. *Practical Reasons: On the Theory of Action*. Cambridge: Polity Press.
Bourdieu, Pierre & Loïc Waquant. 1992. *An Invitation to Reflexive Sociology*. Chicago, IL: University of Chicago Press.
Brummette, John, Marcia DiStaso, Michail Vafeiadis & Marcus Messner. 2018. Read all about it: The politicization of "Fake news" on Twitter. *Journalism & Mass Communication Quarterly* 95(2), 497–517.
Brunila, Kristiina & Hanna Ylöstalo. 2015. Challenging gender inequalities in education and in working life – a mission possible? *Journal of Education and Work* 28(5), 443–460.
Duffy, Brooke E. & Emily Hund. 2015. "Having it all" on social media: Entrepreneurial femininity and self-branding among fashion bloggers. *Social Media + Society* 1(2), 1–11.
Gillies, Val. 2006. *Marginalised Mothers: Exploring Working-Class Experiences of Parenting*. Abingdon: Routledge.
Gronow, Jukka. 1997. *Sociology of Taste*. London: Routledge.
Halonen, Mia & Sirpa Leppänen. 2017. "Pissis stories": The self and the other as gendered, sexualized and class-based performance on social media. In Sirpa Leppänen, Elina Westinen & Samu Kytölä (eds.), *Social media discourse, (dis)identifications and diversities*, 39–61. New York: Routledge.
Hatherley, Frances. 2018. A working-class anti-Pygmalion aesthetics of the female grotesque in the photographs of Richard Billingham. *European Journal of Women's Studies* 25(3), 355–370.
Hayden, Dolores. 2002 [1984]. *Redesigning the American Dream: The Future of Housing, Work and Family Life*. New York: W.W. Norton.
Helén, Ilpo. 1997. *Äidin elämän politiikka. Naissukupuolisuus, valta ja itsesuhde Suomessa 1880-luvulta 1960-luvulle* ["Mother's life politics: women, power and the view of the self in Finland from the 1880s to the 1960s"]. Tampere: Tammer-Paino Oy.
Häkkinen, Ari & Sirpa Leppänen. 2014. YouTube meme warriors. Mashup videos as satire and interventional political critique. *eVarieng* 15.
Jenks, Chris. 2003. *Transgression*. New York: Routledge
Jäntti, Saara, Tuija Saresma, Sirpa Leppänen, Suvi Järvinen & Piia Varis. 2018. Homing blogs as ambivalent spaces for feminine agency. *Feminist Media Studies* 18(5), 888–904.
Kawash, Samira. 2011. New directions in motherhood studies. *Signs: Journal of Women in Culture and Society* 36(4), 969–1003.

Kolehmainen, Marjo. 2017. The material politics of stereotyping white trash: Flexible classmaking. *The Sociological Review* 65(2), 251–266.
Kress, Gunther & Theo van Leeuwen. 1996. *Reading Images: The Grammar of Visual Design*. Abingdon: Routledge.
Lareau, Annette. 2003. *Unequal Childhoods: Race, Class, and Family Life*. Berkeley: University of California Press.
Lehto, Mari & Suvi-Sadetta Kaarakainen. 2016. Epäonnistunut sodanjulistus ja pullantuoksuiset äidit. Hyvä äitiys Äitien Sota -tv-sarjassa ["A failed call for war and mothers smelling of cake: Good motherhood in the TV series Mothers' War"]. *Kasvatus & Aika* 10(1), 87–99.
Leppänen, Sirpa. 2012. Linguistic and discursive heteroglossia on the translocal internet: the case of web writing. In Mark Sebba, Shahrzad Mahootian & Carla Jonsson (eds.), *Language Mixing and Code-switching in Writing: Approaches to Mixed- language Written Discourse*, 233–254. London: Routledge.
Leppänen, Sirpa & Ari Häkkinen. 2012. Buffalaxed superdiversity: Representations of the other on YouTube. In Jan Blommaert, Ben Rampton, Karel Arnaut & Massimiliano Spotti (eds.), *Diversities. A special issue on sociolinguistics and superdiversity*, 14(2), 17–33.
Leppänen, Sirpa, Henna Jousmäki, Samu Kytölä, Saija Peuronen & Elina Westinen. 2014. Entextualization and resemiotization as resources for identification in social media. In Philip Seargeant & Caroline Tagg (eds.), *The language of social media: communication and community on the internet*, 112–138. Basingstoke: Palgrave.
Leppänen, Sirpa & Samu Kytölä. 2016. Investigating multilingualism and multi- semioticity as communicative resources in social media. In Marilyn Martin-Jones & Deirdre Martin (eds.), *Researching Multilingualism: Critical and Ethnographic Approaches*, 155–171. London: Routledge.
Leppänen, Sirpa, Samu Kytölä, Elina Westinen & Saija Peuronen. 2017. Introduction: Social media discourse, (dis)identifications and diversities. In Sirpa Leppänen, Elina Westinen & Samu Kytölä (eds.), *Social media discourse, (dis)identifications and diversities*, 1–36. New York: Routledge.
Mackenzie, Jai 2019. *Language, gender and parenthood online: Negotiating motherhood in Mumsnet talk*. Abingdon & New York: Routledge.
Mapes, Gwynne. 2018. (De)constructing distinction: Class inequality and elite authenticity in mediatized food discourse. *Journal of Sociolinguistics* 22(3), 265–287.
Myers, Greg. 2010. *The Discourse of Blogs and Wikis*. London: Continuum.
Noppari, Elina & Mikko Hautakangas. 2012. *Kovaa Työtä Olla Minä: Muotibloggaajat Mediamarkkinoilla* ["Hard work to be me: Fashion bloggers in the media market"]. Tampere: Tampere University Press.
Nätkin, Ritva. 1997. *Kamppailu suomalaisesta äitiydestä. Maternalismi, väestöpolitiikka ja naisten kertomukset*. ["The struggle over Finnish motherhood: Maternalism, population politics and women's stories"]. Helsinki: Gaudeamus.
Poovey, Mary. 1984. *The proper lady and the woman writer: Ideology as style in the works of Mary Wollstonecraft, Mary Shelley, and Jane Austen*. Chicago: University of Chicago Press.
Porter, Ann. 2012. Neo-conservatism, neo-liberalism and Canadian social policy: Challenges for feminism. *Canadian Woman Studies* 29(3), 19–31.
Purhonen, Semi, Jukka Gronow, Riie Heikkilä, Nina Kahma, Keijo Rahkonen & Arho Toikka. 2014. *Suomalainen maku. Kulttuuripääoma, kulutus ja elämäntyylien sosiaalinen*

eriytyminen. ["The Finnish taste. Cultural capital, consumption and the social diversification of lifestyles"]. Helsinki: Gaudeamus.

Rymes, Betsy. 2012. Recontextualizing YouTube: From macro-micro to mass-mediated communicative repertoires. *Anthropology & Education Quarterly* 43(2), 214–222.

Saarikangas, Kirsi. 2002. *Asunnon muodonmuutoksia. Puhtauden estetiikka ja sukupuoli modernissa arkkitehtuurissa.* ["Transformations of the home. The aesthetics of purity and gender in modern architecture"]. Helsinki: SKS.

Satka, Mirja. 1996. *Making Social Citizenship: Conceptual practices from the Finnish Poor Law to Professional Social Work.* Jyväskylä: SoPhi.

Silverstein, Michael & Greg Urban (eds.). 1996. *Natural Histories of Discourse.* Chicago: The University of Chicago Press.

Skeggs Beverley. 1997. *Formations of Class and Gender: Becoming Respectable.* London: Sage.

Skeggs, Beverley. 2001. The toilet paper: Femininity, class and mis-recogntion. *Women's Studies International Forum*, Vol. 24(3/4), 295–307.

Skeggs, Beverley. 2004. *Class, Self, Culture.* London: Routledge.

Skeggs, Beverley. 2009. The moral economy of person production: the class relations of self-performance on "reality" television. *The Sociological Review* 57(4), 626–644.

Skeggs, Beverley. 2015. Introduction: Stratification or exploitation, domination, dispossession and devaluation? *The Sociological Review* 63, 205–222.

Sulkunen, Irma. 1987. Naisten järjestäytyminen ja kaksijakoinen kansalaisuus ["Women's organization and dualistic citizenship"]. In Risto Alapuro (ed.), *Kansa liikkeessä*, 157–172. Helsinki: Kirjayhtymä.

Sulkunen, Irma. 1989. *Naisen kutsumus. Miina Sillanpää ja sukupuolten maailmojen Erkaantuminen.* ["Woman's vocation, Miina Sillanpää and the differentiation of gendered worlds"]. Helsinki: Hanki ja Jää.

Thurlow, Crispin. 2013. Fakebook: Synthetic media, pseudo-sociality and the rhetorics of Web 2.0. In Deborah Tannen & Anne M. Trester (eds.), *Discourse 2.0: Language and New Media*, 225–248. Washington, DC: Georgetown University Press.

Thurlow, Crispin & Adam Jaworski. 2017. Introducing elite discourse: The rhetorics of status, privilege, and power. *Social Semiotics* 27(3), 243–254.

Trester, Anne M. 2012. Framing entextualization in improv: Intertextuality as an interactional resource. *Language in Society* 41(2), 237–258.

Tyler, Imogen. 2008. Chav mum chav scum: Class disgust in contemporary Britain. *Feminist Media Studies* 8(1), 17–34.

Tyler, Imogen. 2013. *Revolting Subjects: Social Abjection and Resistance in Neoliberal Britain.* London: Zed Books.

Tyler, Imogen & Bruce Bennett. 2010. Celebrity chav: Fame, femininity and social class. *European Journal of Cultural Studies* 13(3), 375–393.

Walker Rettberg, Jill. 2013. *Blogging.* Cambridge: Polity Press.

Zappavigna, Michele. 2011. Ambient affiliation: A linguistic perspective on Twitter. *New Media & Society* 13(5), 788–806.

Zoonen, Liesbet van. 2005. *Entertaining the Citizen: When Politics and Popular Culture Converge.* New York: Rowman & Littlefield.

Axel Schmidt and Konstanze Marx
6 Making Let's plays watchable: An interactional approach to gaming visualizations

1 Introduction: The watchability of Let's Plays

Entering the keyword 'Let's Play' on YouTube results in over 170 million hits. This is a genre that has become very popular in a very short period of time. Here, gamers document their gaming in films, so called Let's Plays, and tens of thousands of other people watch via YouTube. What is interesting about this relatively new phenomenon is that video games are not only played, but the playing is presented to a (potential) mass audience where viewers do not play the game but watch others do. Normally, the interactivity of a video game is one of its most outstanding, appealing features. In Let's Play, however, this interactivity can only be experienced vicariously by the audience. For this reason, Let's Players must support their audience's vicarious experience by strategically commenting verbally on their play moves and by deploying specific visual presentation techniques. In this chapter, we are interested in how the core activity of playing a computer game is transformed into a "platform format" (Goffman 1983) by verbal, embodied and visual means. In short, we ask what practices players use to make Let's Play watchable?

A prevalent practice used by players on Let's Play is to continuously comment verbally on their game moves. If game activities are accountable in their own right (see section 3), one can ask, why they have to be explained or commented on verbally in addition to the visible action on screen. Our thesis is as follows. On the one hand, continuous commenting fulfills the main objective of Let's Plays which is to present active gameplay. Comments should therefore generate an added value, not simply making gameplay visually accessible. This itself indicates how the presentation of the game alone is not sufficient. Often – as we will show – a player's own game actions are explicated verbally which makes the game play more transparent as an action and thus more attractive for viewers. In other words, how players make Let's Plays watchable for viewers. It is our contention that the watchability of video gaming depends to a large extent on the degree of viewers' insights into the players's motivations for action and the player's experience of the game.[1] To this end, we examine a case-study example of a Let's Play with respect to its player's linguistic and embodied practices and the ways in which there (self-experienced) interactivity of video games is made accessible to others. It is in this way that media formats (i.e. video games) not primarily designed for watching, are transformed into watchable presentations.

In the sections which follow we give a brief overview of Let's Plays and their typical characteristics (section 2) followed by an outline of our data and method (section 3). Then, in section 4, we examine some of the key strategies of players with reference to selected extracts from our Let's Play case-study. In short, it becomes clear that the central practice in Let's Plays – that is, formulating one's own acts – is closely related to the specific kind of multimodal nature and form of visual presentation of Let's Plays.

2 What are Let's Plays?

Let's Plays are defined simply as "playing videogames for the internet" (Hale 2013: 3). However, as we say, the game is not only played but also commented on verbally by players who usually appear in a facecam. In addition, both the playing process and any verbal comments are recorded and uploaded to video hosting websites like YouTube. The following stills show a Let's Play embedded in YouTube (Figure 6.1a) and in full screen mode (Figure 6.1b):

Let's Plays first appeared in 2006 and nowadays have very high "click rates". The German player *Gronkh* for instance has about 4.5 million subscribers, while the world's most popular player, *PewDiePie*, has over 60 million subscribers.

Previous studies of video-gaming show that players and their spectators used to talk with each other, commenting on game play while playing the game (cf. Baldauf-Quilliatre & Colon de Carvajal 2019; Piirainen-Marsh 2012; Tekin and Reeves 2017). Furthermore, phases "in the game" and "out of the game" are ordinarily distinguishable and lead to different concepts of time ("game time" vs. "interaction time") and, in turn, different forms of involvement (cf. Mondada 2013). By contrast, Let's Plays adopt a different participation framework. Instead of a shared physical setting where every co-present person

---

[1] In contrast to other well-known games like chess, many video games are self-generated and therefore particularly opaque to observers.

6 Making Let's plays watchable — 133

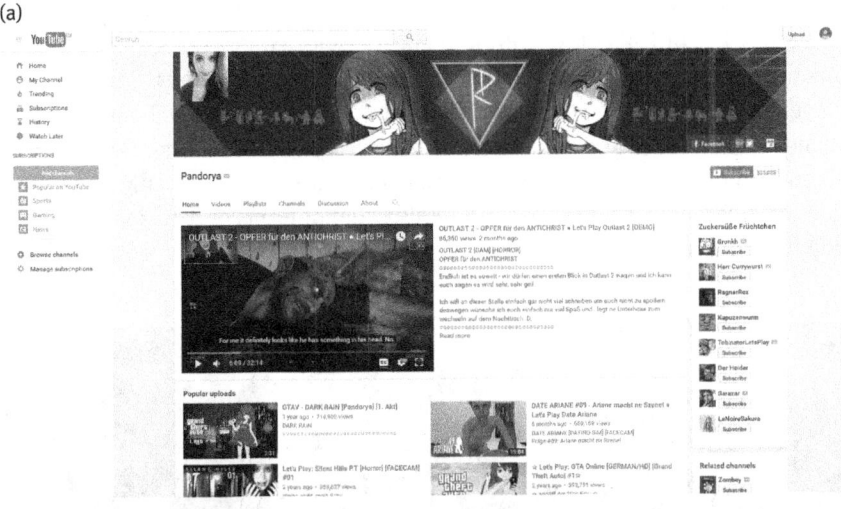

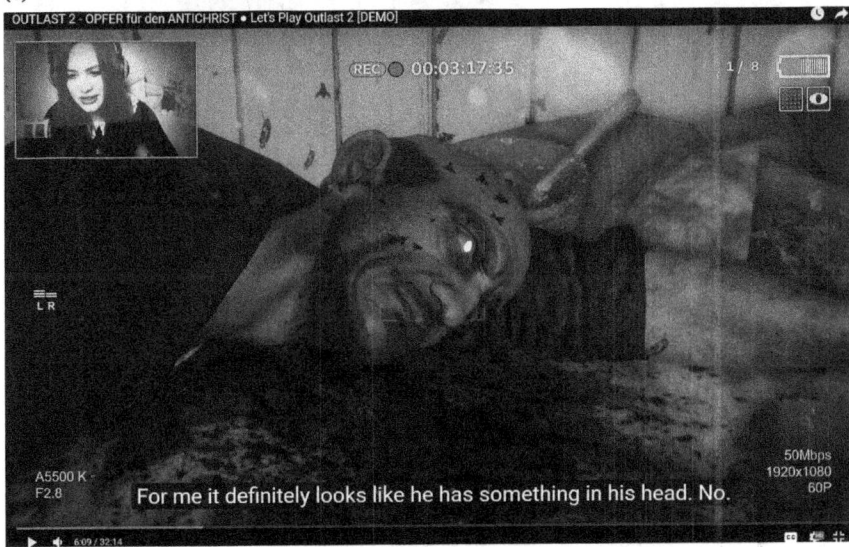

Figure 6.1: (a) Pan embedded in YouTube. (b) Pan in full-screen mode.

is able to participate, Let's Plays entail a unidirectional form of communication that excludes the viewer from direct feedback.[2]

---

2 We refer here to recorded Let's Plays uploaded to video portals like YouTube. Such Let's Plays have the status of films (they are "fixed products") and, as uploads, they are

Before we go into detail, we give an impressionistic overview of the main characteristics of Let's Plays with reference to selected moments in a Let's Play uploaded on YouTube on the 15th of June 2016 by a famous German Let's Player called *Pandorya* (nickname: *Pan*). In this case, Pan is playing a demo version of the survival horror game *Outlast 2*.[3] At the beginning, *Pan* refers to an audience by uttering "*a warm welcome to Outlast 2*" accompanied by a look into the facecam (see Figure 6.2), all reminiscent of forms of para-social interaction (cf. Horton & Wohl 1956, Ayaß 1993).

Figure 6.2: Pan's audience address.

Also right at the beginning, Pan emphasizes her individual experience and general attitude by categorizing herself (ironically) as a "*miserable fan-girl*". During the whole Let's Play she shows many affective reactions conveyed visually by means of the integrated facecam (e.g. scared, as in Figure 6.3).

---

permanently available to a dispersed, potentially mass audience. Due to the affordances of the medium, feedback from viewers can only be given in written form afterwards (cf. Dynel 2014, Frobenius 2014). Such commentary activities are not included in this article. We also do not consider the opportunity used by many players to distribute their Let's Plays live (e.g. on *Twitch*), where viewers can chat with them during the game (cf. Recktenwald 2017).

3 The actual Let's Play discussed here can be found (21.07.2019) at: https://www.youtube.com/watch?v=P9StHBpbnlA&t=186s.

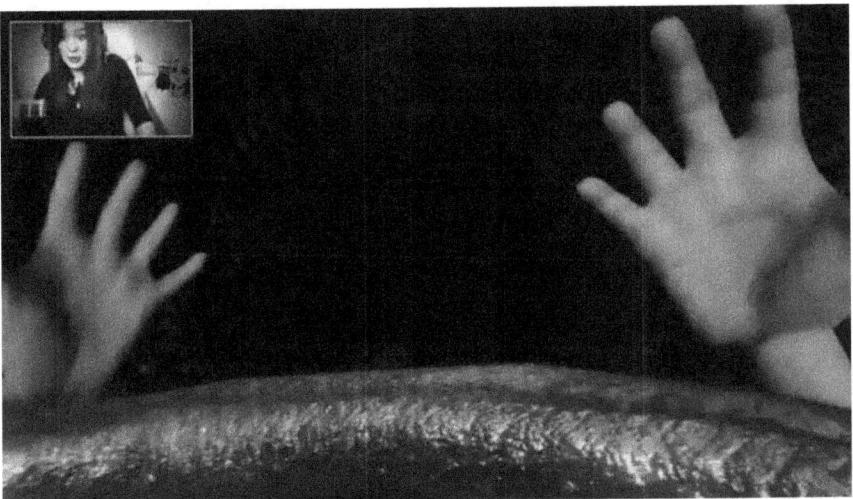

Figure 6.3: Frightening.

Overall, her verbal moderation of the game play uses a spontaneous language and takes place partly as an ad hoc reaction to events emerging in the game; there is obviously no post-editing. Finally, and interestingly, Pan problematizes the moderation itself: about 13 minutes after the start of the game, she says, "*hey, how do you present it now?*"[4] Evidently, the need to make one's own playing attractive to others is also a concern for players themselves (and not only for analysts like us). A key reason for this is that Let's Plays are recorded and thus fixed products. As such, targeted viewers can no longer play the game, but only watch how others play it. The game itself unavoidably loses its interactivity therefore. For players, thus, the challenge is to make watching the game attractive – in other words, to make it watchable.

3 Data and method

In order to demonstrate core strategies and practices of making Let's Plays watchable we draw on the same case already introduced. This is an example of a so-called *blind play* (i.e. the game has not been played before by this player)

---

[4] In the German original Pan uses the expression *moderieren* which explicitly signals broadcasting contexts.

by the popular German player Pan who presents a current computer game from the *adventure-action*-genre. The combination of *blind play* and the *adventure/action* genre promises situations that are potentially unpredictable, surprising and in the need of explanation since players are typically confronted with obscure settings. Selecting a popular Let's Play player offers us a chance to pin-point more typical, well-established practices in this community of Let's Player.

Our contribution follows an interactional perspective, or more precisely a multimodal extended EMCA approach, which asks *how* participants create social reality. EMCA stands for Ethnomethodology and Conversation Analysis (cf. Heritage 1984a). By multimodal expansion, we mean attention is paid not only to talk, but also to embodied actions, including the use of objects, of media technology and of space (cf. Deppermnann 2013, Mondada 2008, Streeck/Goodwin/LeBaron 2011). Specifically, our analytic focus is on the strategies or practices by which players design their Let's Plays to be attractive, engaging and therefore watchable. EMCA research on mediated interaction in general (cf. Arminen, Licoppe, & Spagnolli 2016, Schmidt & Marx 2017) and video games in particular (cf. Reeves, Greiffenhagen, and Laurier 2016 for an overview) has emphasized that the mediation of a given interaction is not determined by technical circumstances alone. Rather, mediation is taken to be an interactional achievement. Within media settings, and following Arminen, Licoppe & Spagnolli (2016), participants' use of technology also reflects their notion of a reasonable *accountable* handling of the technology. In short, the way practical problems are solved in mediated settings is related to the manner in which interaction is shaped by the specific affordances of the technology. For example, video players in co-present multiplayer settings only turn their bodies halfway around in order to react to other players in their backs thereby at the same time being able to turn back quickly to their own running video game. Through the half turn of the body, what Schegloff (1998) coined "body torque", players simultaneously display their temporary double involvement, which makes their action accountable for others and at the same time reflects the specifics of the media setting.

According to Reeves, Greiffenhagen, and Laurier (2016) there are thus *two levels of accountability* in video game settings: First "real world actions" like the above mentioned body orientations within the game setting, but also steering the game and possible verbal conduct (concerning the game play or anything else). Secondly and additionally in comparison to face-to-face-settings, there are (inter-)actions in the virtual world conducted by player-driven avatars. The latter is illustrated by Reeves, Greiffenhagen, and Laurier (2016) using the case of a cooperative multiplayer game in which one of the avatars kneels down. This visible action is read by the (competent) co-players as a display that the player's avatar is about to set a trap. They, in turn, display their understanding by embodied actions of their avatars (in this case they form a semicircle behind and around the trapper). In this way, the game itself produces socially organized and comprehensible interactions based on the control actions of the players.

In order to reconstruct how participants produce Let's Plays, we use multimodally extended GAT2-transcripts that show the use of different modal resources in their temporal interplay.[5] In the transcripts (see extract 6.1 and Figure 6.4) speech and pauses appear bold and provide the temporal framework for aligning physical activities, game events (after the abbreviation GE), game sounds (after the abbreviation GS) and status displays (after the abbreviation SD). The alignment is done with special characters (%, *, +, etc.), one symbol indicates the beginning (%), a double symbol (%%) the end and the double-headed arrow (—≫) a continuation beyond the transcript of an activity/event.

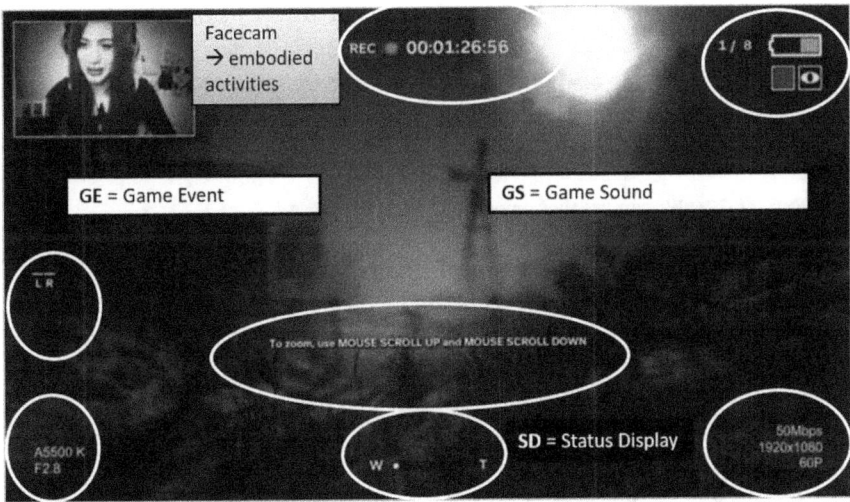

Figure 6.4: Relevant events for transcription.

---

[5] See Selting et al. (2011) for GAT 2-conventions; Mondada (2014) for conventions of multimodal transcription; and Recktenwald (2017) for the transcription of LP- and Twitch-formats. A selection of the GAT 2-conventions we use is provided below.

Extract 6.1: A transcript example

```
1    PAN      und äh wir können die *%+KAmer~a%% be~~nutzen?
              and äh we can use the camera
                                       %nods
     GE                                *camera use--->>
     SD                                +camera symbol--->>
     GS                                ~bleeping
```

4 Making Let's Plays watchable

In this section, we present three key practices, two talk-based and a visual one, used by players in the overall attempt of making Let's Play engaging and, therefore, watchable for viewers; we do so with reference to the same case-study example of Pan playing the demo version of the survival horror game *Outlast 2*.

4.1 Commenting on self-generated actions in Let's Plays

We start with a simple example to show how moderation works in principle. In the following extract, *Pan* uses the integrated camera function at the very beginning of her game play:

Extract 6.2: "We can use the camera"

```
1    PAN       und äh wir können die *KAmera benutzen?#
               and uh we can use the camera
     GE/DS                            *camera use/camera symbol--->>
2    PAN       wir KENN_das ja in outlast–
               we already know that from outlast
3    PAN       wir *können wieder** RANzoomen,
               we can zoom in again
     GE                *zoom in/zoom out
4    PAN       und ich kann *natürlich auch die NIGHTvision anmachen?
               and of course I can also put on the night vision
     GE                                *night vision -->>
```

For now, we focus on just the visual impressions in order to highlight the particular use of verbal comments. First of all, potentially relevant objects of perception are attended to; for example, a landscape, a fence, a wind pump and a house in the distance as well as conditions of perception, here especially the relative darkness, are noticeable. In addition, the image frame moves, it gets bigger and smaller, changes color etc. (see Figure 6.5a-c).

(a)

Figure 6.5a: Objects, conditions of perception.

(b)

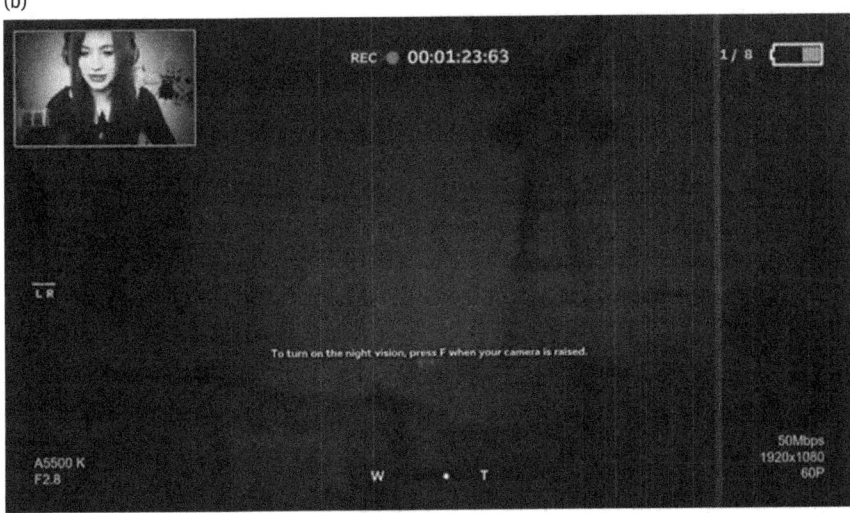

Figure 6.5b: Zoom.

(c)

Figure 6.5c: Night Vision.

Depending on the player's background knowledge, game features can be recognized (for instance point-of-view-perspective, in-game-camera etc.). Altogether, however, specific action context is not easily inferred, except perhaps that someone might be looking for something. Even then, viewers would not easily discern what the exact focus or purpose is. Accordingly, what viewers get to see remains inaccessible and therefore less attractive.

This changes completely when we look at the same extract in conjunction with its verbal comments. Viewers learn *what* Pan is doing (that she uses the camera and its features); more than this, however, they also learn what her *purpose* it is: she uses the camera to *demonstrate* her functions and is not looking for anything as one might have otherwise imagined. This framing of the sequence as a demonstration is not obvious from the images alone – regardless of how much expert knowledge one might have about the game or about video games in general. In addition, the "demonstration frame" (cf. Goffman 1986, 66) shifts attention away from the visual content to the way it is technically captured and conveyed by using and demonstrating functions of the game-integrated camera. As such, the focus is not on the events in front of the camera, but about the camera action itself which is made (also by means of accompanying words) accountable in a specific way.[6] The sequence is thereby segmented into three units concerning technical control over the game: camera, zoom, and night vision.

Furthermore, as the above case illustrates, another moderator effect is that the player identifies certain visual events as *self-generated results of their own actions*. Figure 6.6 demonstrates this relation. Since the deployment of the simulated camera is done during Pan's utterance *"and, uh, we can use the camera"* the visually conveyed game event becomes understandable as *her* action.[7]

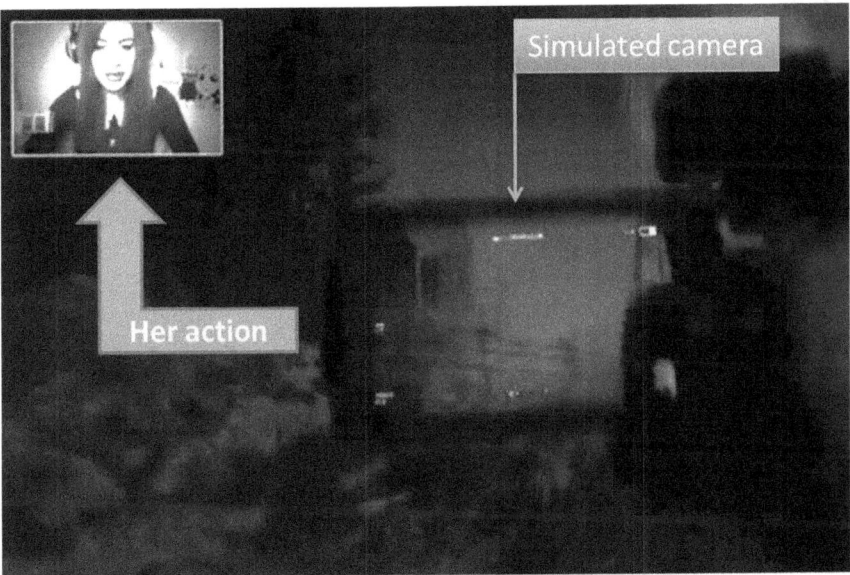

    und äh wir können die Kamera# benutzen
    and, uh, we can use the camera

Figure 6.6: Self-generated events.

This raises two fundamental questions. First, which activity forms the basis for Let's Plays? Second, how is this activity presented visually?

First of all, the core activity in Let's Plays (i.e. computer gaming) is a form of human-machine communication usually described as a *cybernetic control loop*, as illustrated in the following Figure (6.7).

---

6 See also Laurier & Reeves (2014) who discuss the accountability of the camera use in different video games.
7 The hash (#) in our transcripts defines the exact location where a still image was drawn.

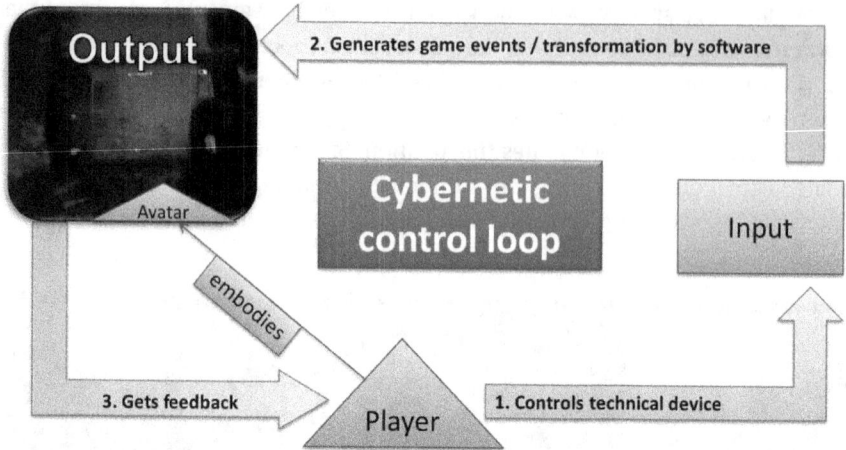

Figure 6.7: The cybernetic control loop of gaming.

As Figure 6.7 shows, playing a computer game entails generating game events by controlling a technical device which transforms software-based inputs into on-screen outputs whereby the latter serves as a feedback for the player. Since inputs are controlled and adjusted on the basis of outputs, gaming follows the model of a cybernetic control loop. Together with the audio-visual point-of-view-aesthetic, the technical ability to effect or cause events is fundamental for embodying one's avatar in a virtual world.

4.2 Visualization of self-generated actions in Let's Plays

The *visual presentation* of activities in Let's Plays rearranges the physical-spatial configuration of the real game situation which is usually body-/face-to-screen and hands-on-controller. First of all, the activity of controlling the game is not represented, so hands–on-controller does not usually appear in Let's Plays. Instead, via facecams, players' bodies are reduced to the face which appears smaller at the edge of the screen; by contrast, game play fills the entire screen and is thus marked as the main focus. As a result, player and gameplay appear simultaneously in a split-screen-optics spatially next to each other. Mondada (2009) has described the use of split-screen as a re-arrangement of interactional space. In our case, the use of the facecam together with the split screen makes players appear more like recipients than controllers of the game. Nevertheless, the control loop clearly remains crucial since the person who appears in the facecam generates, perceives and reacts to what is happening in the game (see Figure 6.8).

Figure 6.8: Visual representation of self-generated events.

It is precisely this self-generation of the gameplay that makes video games appear/feel attractive, interactive and immersive (cf. Calleja 2011). However, because this core aspect is missing when the gameplay is presented in Let's Plays, an additional orientation is needed for giving viewers an insight into the cycle of self-control. One solution to this problem is very frequent verbal references by players to their own actions. That means, players are not only playing but also simultaneously *formulating* their game actions, as in the example above where Pan, while using the camera, also formulates her actions verbally. Following Schegloff's (1972) "formulating place" and Goodwin & Goodwin's (1996) "formulating planes", we call this strategy "formulating gameplay". A particular problematic action in terms of comprehensibility for viewers is *seeing* or *visual perception*. Although seeing is an indispensable activity of playing a video game, seeing is difficult to convey for viewers on the basis of the images alone. Visual impressions alone never reveal whether seeing is a relevant activity at any moment – as opposed to some other activity like walking, fighting, opening a door, etc.. If it is relevant, nor is it clear what the focus is, how it is to be interpreted and how it leads to or is connected to subsequent actions.[8] Players therefore face the fundamental challenge of making their perception perceptible to viewers. This brings us to the third (and last) of our three practices for making Let's Plays watchable.

---

[8] Goodwin (1994, 1995, 1996, 2000), in particular, has attended to "seeing as an activity".

4.3 Formulating perception in Let's Plays

In a further example we take a closer look at the ways processes of visual perception are formulated. In the following extract Pan explores the entrance area of a wooden house:

Extract 6.3: "Delicious"

1	PAN	*was ham wir HIER–
		what do we have here
	GE	*hardly perceptible game object
2	PAN	=Ä&ähä:;
	GE/DSSD	&camera use/camera symbol
3		%(0.6)%%(0.53)*(1.00)&
	pan	%looks down to the right
	GE	*camera focus on game object
	GE/SD	night vision/symbols
4	PAN	°h LECker,
		°h yummi
5	PAN	&%ich HAbe es ver*MISST;
		I have really missed it
	GE/SD	&end of camera use/camera symbol disappears--->>
	pan	%looks to facecam
	GE	*focus on door
6	PAN	ich LIE+be ++outlast.
		I love outlast
		+looks to facecam

Here, we are most interested in three aspects of this short extract: *visual impressions*, the role of *deixis*, and the verbally expressed *perspective* of Pan's visual perception.

Referring only to visual impressions, the viewer has two clues for reconstructing Pan's perception. First, the facecam conveys the direction of her *gaze*. For example, in Figure 6.9 she is seen looking straight down (6.9a), diagonally downwards (6.9b,) and straight into the facecam (6.9c).

It is not possible to know exactly what Pan is looking at; only her looking into the facecam is easily understood as an audience address.[9] Secondly, Pan's point-of-view-perspective conveys what she is visually focusing on in the game.

---

9 To discover the real objects and intentions of Pan's gaze we would need access to the physical setting. From interviews, however, we know that a gaze straight downwards is directed at events on screen whereas a gaze diagonally downwards is directed to status displays. In Figure 6.9a, therefore, the gaze straight downwards is understandable as game gaze (cf. Aarseth 2004, Atkins 2006) and thus as the default mode for someone involved in the game.

6 Making Let's plays watchable — 145

Figure 6.9a: Gaze direction diagonally downwards.

Figure 6.9b: Gaze direction straight downwards.

Figure 6.9c: Gaze direction in facecam.

Hence, the player sees what the avatar sees and viewers see what the player-avatar-hybrid sees (in this case, a kind of bucket).[10] This is enhanced by the viewfinder of the camera indicating what is currently focused by a grey square inserted in the display (see Figure 6.10).

---

[10] See also Baldauf-Quilliatre & Colon de Carvajal (2015).

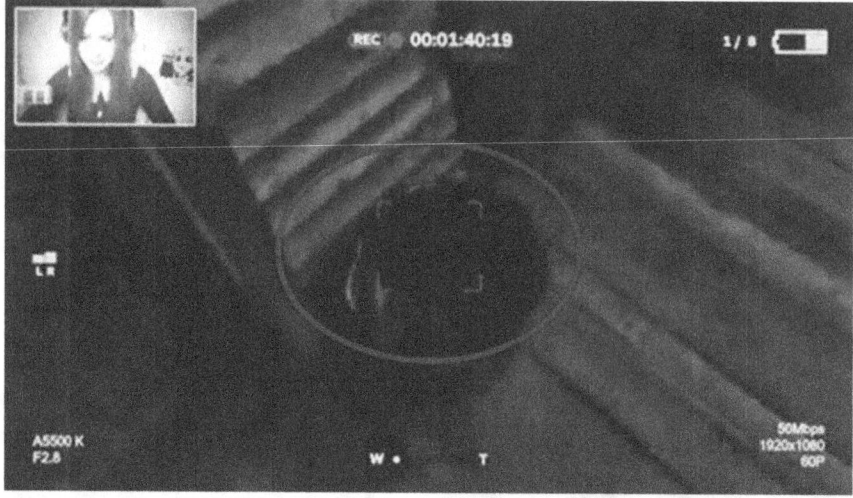

Figure 6.10: We see what is seen.

The images thereby simulate the "perception of perception" – in other words, giving a sense of what another person is noticing or looking at.

As we say, images alone are apparently never sufficient. To further mark seeing *as* seeing players rely on the verbal resource of *deixis*. In the example above, Pan makes her perception a relevant action in line 1 by uttering "*what do we have here*". These exploratory announcements are very frequent in Let's Plays and they indicate that visual perception is currently relevant. In particular, this is achieved by the local deictic "*here*" which serves as a cue for specifying the context produced by *here* (cf. Hausendorf 2003). In face-to-face interaction this is usually done by means of pointing gestures (cf. Goodwin 2007); however, these are clearly not available in this mediated instance. Instead, and as we have argued above, viewers rely on the point-of-view-perspective for discerning the player's vision. Thus, the point-of-view-vision acts as a pointing instrument which indicates what Goodwin (1994) calls a "domain of scrutiny".

Exploratory announcements like "*what do I/we have here*" are usually fulfilled subsequently by formulating visual impressions. Those verbalizations again specify the perspective of perception. What is striking about the current case is that even though an announcement of exploration makes the identification of a scrutinized object pertinent, there is no such investigation. That is, no referent is verbally specified such as "a bucket with guts". This leads to a sort of mystery which itself creates tension and contributes to making Let's Plays engaging and watchable. Instead, what Pan reveals verbally is reduced to assessments. First, in line 2, we have a response cry (Goffman, 1981) – *ähhhh* – for conveying disgust and which reflects her immediate experience. This is followed in line 4 by a positive evaluation term (*delicious*), accompanied by a smile evoking the sensual qualities of the object in question. *Delicious* is also presented in direct contrast to disgust. Although the choice of words and prosody suggest irony, subsequent events show how Pan is concerned also with the aesthetics of the game. In this regard, note how she no longer refers to the concrete object of scrutiny ("the bucket") with the pronoun *it* in "*I missed it*" (line 5), but refers rather generically to a type concept – namely the look or design of the game *Outlast*. The visual impression she stresses thereby becomes a trademark for the game itself. This is clearly shown in the euphoric evaluation of the game in line 6 of the extract ("*I love Outlast*"). Only through the accompanying words do viewers have access to Pan's personal perspective on the events unfolding visually, which are indicated as a typical feature of a game-specific aesthetic.

5 Summary

We started with the claim that Let's Plays transform an interactive video game into a fixed, broadcast-like product. This process can be understood as "de-interactivisation" (cf. Ackermann 2016). The playing of the game itself, however, remains interactive. As we have argued, the basic activity structure of Let's Plays is a "cybernetic control loop" which cannot be readily made accessible by drawing only on visual presentations. Thus, the main problem for players consists of how to make this "black box" accessible for viewers. Based on two typical cases we have shown how the players in Let's Plays deal with this problem. A pervasive practice throughout Let's Plays is to formulate one's own actions.[11] Thereby players make the gameplay comprehensible and at the same time watchable. This applies in particular – as we have shown – to formulations of visual perception, which make the self-organizing control loop of playing a video game transparent by creating a connection between prospective relevancies (like the above mentioned exploratory announcements) and retrospective evaluations of actions (like response cries or explicit verbalizations such as

---

[11] There are other settings in which participants formulate their actions; for example, when think-aloud-methods are used in writing research (cf. Marx & Schmidt 2019 for a discussion of this aspect).

delicious). This relation cannot be conveyed solely through the visuals. Only the verbal comments are able to transform a stream of visual events into comprehensible actions. Let's Plays are thus an interesting case of re-mediated visualizations (cf. Bolter and Grusin 2000), which needs additional verbalization to be attractive for viewers. In addition, our example analysis has shown how a fully multimodal practice (i.e. Let's Plays) is visualized in specific ways and, thereby, how communicative processes are embedded. This way, visualization not only fulfils representational purposes (i.e. showing something), but is also used to simulate core processes of multimodal interaction such as using the in-game camera to indicate the direction of a player's gaze.

GAT 2 Transcription conventions (selection)

°h / h°	in- / outbreaths
(.)	micro pause
and_uh	cliticizations within units
uh, uhm	hesitation markers
=	fast, immediate continuation with a new turn or segment (latching)
:	lengthening
SYLlable	focus accent

Final pitch movements of intonation phrases

?	rising to high
,	rising to mid
–	level
;	falling to mid
.	falling to low

References

Aarseth, Espen. 2004. Genre trouble: narrativism and the art of simulation. In Noah Wardrip-Fruin & Pat Harrigan (ed.), *First person. New media as story, performance, and game*, 45–57. Cambridge: MIT Press.

Ackermann, Judith (ed.). 2016. *Phänomen Let's Play-Video: Entstehung, Ästhetik, Aneignung und Faszination aufgezeichneten Computerhandelns. Neue Perspektiven der Medienästhetik*. Wiesbaden: Springer VS.

Arminen, Ilkka, Christian Licoppe & Anna Spagnolli. 2016. Respecifying mediated interaction. *Research on Language and Social Interaction* 49 (4), 290–309.
Atkins, Barry. 2006. What are we really looking at? The future-orientation of video game play. *Games Cult* 1 (2), 127–140.
Ayaß, Ruth. 1993. Auf der Suche nach dem verlorenen Zuschauer. In Werner Holly & Ulrich Püschel (eds.), *Medienrezeption als Aneignung*, 27–41. Opladen: Westdeutscher Verlag.
Baldauf-Quilliatre, Heike & Isabel Colón de Carvajal. 2015. Is the avatar considered as a participant by the players? A conversational analysis of multi-player videogames interactions. *PsychNology Journal* 13 (2–3), 127–147.
Baldauf-Quilliatre, Heike & Isabel Colón de Carvajal. 2019. Interaktionen bei Videospiel-Sessions: Interagieren in einem hybriden Raum. In Konstanze Marx & Axel Schmidt (eds.), *Interaktion und Medien*, 219–254. Heidelberg: Winter.
Bolter, Jay David & Richard Grusin. 2000. *Remediation: understanding new media*. Cambridge: MIT Press.
Calleja, Gordon. 2011. *In-game: from immersion to incorporation*. Cambridge: MIT Press.
Deppermann, Arnulf. 2013. Multimodal interaction from a conversation analytic perspective. *Journal of Pragmatics* 46, 1–7.
Dynel, Marta. 2014. Participation framework underlying YouTube interaction. *Journal of Pragmatics* 73, 37–52.
Frobenius, Maximiliane. 2014. Audience design in monologues: How vloggers involve their viewers. *Journal of Pragmatics* 72, 59–72.
Goffman, Ervin. 1981. Response cries. In Ervin Goffman (ed.), *Forms of talk*, 78–122. Philadelphia: University of Pennsylvania Press.
Goffman, Erving. 1983. The interaction order. *American Sociolocical Review* 48 (1), 1–17.
Goffman, Erving. 1986. *Frame analysis*. Boston: Northeastern Univ. Pr.
Goodwin, Charles. 1994. Professional vision. *American Anthropologist* 96 (3), 606–633.
Goodwin, Charles. 1995. Seeing in depth. *Social Studies of Science* 25, 237–274.
Goodwin, Charles. 1996. Transparent vision. In Elinor Ochs, Emanuel Schegloff & Sandra A. Thompson (eds.), *Interaction and grammar*, 370–404. Cambridge: Cambridge University Press.
Goodwin, Charles. 2000. Practices of seeing visual analysis: An ethnomethodological approach. In Theo van Leeuwen & Carey Jewitt (eds.), *Handbook of visual analysis*, 157–182. London: Sage.
Goodwin, Charles. 2007. Enviromentally coupled gestures. In: Susan D. Duncan, Justine Cassell & Elena T. Levy (eds.), *Gesture and the dynamic dimension of language: essays in honor of David McNeill*, 195–212. Amsterdam: John Benjamins.
Goodwin, Charles & Marjorie Harness Goodwin. 1996. Seeing as situated activity: Formulating planes. In Yrjo Engeström & David Middleton (ed.), *Cognition and communication at work*, 61–95. Cambridge: Cambridge University Press.
Hale, Thomas. 2013. From jackasses to superstars: A case for the study of 'Let's Play'. Available online at: https://www.academia.edu/5260639/From_Jackasses_to_ Superstars_A_Case_for_the_Study_of_Let_s_Play_September_2013_ (21 February, 2019).
Hausendorf, Heiko. 2003. Deixis and speech situation revisited: the mechanism of perceived perception. In Friedrich Lenz (ed.), *Deictic conceptualisation of space, time and person*, 249–269. Amsterdam, Philadelphia: John Benjamins.
Heritage, John. 1984. *Garfinkel and ethnomethodology*. Cambridge: Polity Press.

Horton, Donald & Richard R. Wohl. 1956. Mass Communication and para-social interaction: Observations on intimacy at a distance. *Psychiatry* 19, 215–229.

Laurier, Eric & Stuart Reeves. 2014. Cameras in video games: Comparing play in Counter-Strike and Doctor Who Adventures. In Mathias Broth, Eric Laurier & Lorenza Mondada (ed.), *Studies of video practices: Video at work*, 181–207. Hoboken: Taylor and Francis.

Marx, Konstanze & Axel Schmidt. 2019. Let's Play (together) oder schau mal, wie ich spiele – (Interaktive) Praktiken der Attraktionssteigerung auf YouTube. In Konstanze Marx & Axel Schmidt (eds.), *Interaktion und Medien*, 319–352 Heidelberg: Winter.

Mondada, Lorenza. 2008. Using video for a sequential and multimodal analysis of social interaction: Videotaping institutional telephone calls [88 paragraphs]. In *Forum Qualitative Sozialforschung / Forum: Qualitative Social Research* 9 (3), Art. 39.

Mondada, Lorenza. 2009. Video recording practices and the reflexive constitution of the interactional order: Some systematic uses of the split-screen technique. *Human Studies* 32 (1), 67–99.

Mondada, Lorenza. 2012. Coordinating action and talk-in-interaction in and out of video games. In Ruth Ayaß & Cornelia Gerhardt (eds.), *The appropriation of media in everyday life*. pp. 231–270. Philadelphia: John Benjamins.

Mondada, Lorenza. 2013. Coordinating mobile action in real time: The timely organization of directives in video games. In Pentti Haddington, Lorenza Mondada & Maurice Nevile (eds.), *Interaction and mobility: language and the body in motion*, 300–341. Berlin; New York: de Gruyter.

Mondada, Lorenza. 2014. Conventions for multimodal transcription. Available: https://franzoesistik.philhist.unibas.ch/fileadmin/user_upload/franzoesistik/mondada_multimodal_conventions.pdf (26 March, 2018)

Piirainen-Marsh, Arja. 2012. Organizing participation in video gaming activities. In Ruth Ayaß & Cornelia Gerhardt (eds.), *The appropriation of media in everyday life*, 197–230. Philadelphia: John Benjamins.

Recktenwald, Daniel. 2017. Toward a transcription and analysis of live streaming on Twitch. *Journal of Pragmatics* 115, 68–81.

Reeves, Stuart, Christian Greiffenhagen & Eric Laurier. 2016. Video gaming as practical accomplishment: Ethnomethodology, conversation analysis, and play. *Topics in Cognitive Science* 9 (2), 308–342.

Schegloff, Emanuel A. 1972. Notes on a conversational practice: Formulating place. In David Sudnow (ed.), *Studies in social interaction*, 95–119. New York: Free Press.

Schmidt, Axel & Konstanze Marx. 2017. Interaktion und Medien. *Sprachreport* 33, 4, 22–33.

Selting, Margret, Peter Auer, Dagmar Barth-Weingarten, Jörg Bergmann, Pia Bergmann, Karin Birkner, Elizabeth Couper-Kuhlen, Arnulf Deppermann, Peter Gilles, Susanne Günthner, Martin Hartung, Friederike Kern, Christine Mertzlufft, Christian Meyer, Miriam Morek, Frank Oberzaucher, Jörg Peters, Uta Quasthoff, Wilfried Schütte, Anja Stukenbrock & Susanne Uhmann. 2011. A system for transcribing talk-in-interaction: GAT 2. [trans. by Elizabeth Couper-Kuhlen & Dagmar Barth-Weingarten.] *Gesprächsforschung – Online-Zeitschrift zur verbalen Interaktion (*www.gespraechsforschung-ozs.de*)* 12, 1–51.

Streeck, Jürgen, Charles Goodwin & Curtis D. LeBaron. (eds.). 2011. *Embodied interaction. Language and body in the material world*. New York [u.a.]: Cambridge University Press.

Tekin, Burak S. & Stuart Reeves. 2017. Ways of spectating: unravelling spectator participation in Kinect play. In *Proceedings of the 2017 CHI Conference on Human Factors in Computing Systems*, 1558–1570.

Dorottya Cserző
7 Intimacy at a distance: Multimodal meaning making in video chat tours

1 Introduction

Dorottya: Have you ever given a virtual tour to somebody?

Dina: Yeah when I moved into my new house, my whole family. I was running around with my iPad and showing "this is the bathroom, this is my room, this is the hall, this is the kitchen". You know because they might never come down here and visit. So, to be able to show them virtually...They feel happier because they're like "oh we know where she's living and we can put a picture in our minds now". You feel a lot more comfortable rather than it's just like "she lives in a house".

Dina is a university student I interviewed about her video chat habits as part of larger research project on domestic video chat use. When I asked whether she had ever given a virtual tour during a video chat, there was no need to explain what I meant by this phrase. At this point in the interview, I already knew that she had started using video chat to keep in touch with her family after she had moved to a different city to attend university. Dina's account indicates that under these circumstances, giving a video chat tour of her new home was expected. This account was by no means exceptional: video chat tours were mentioned in almost half of the interviews (14 out of 29), usually in the context of moving to a new place or while travelling.

The research project combined inductive qualitative interview analysis (Mason 2002; Gibbs 2007) with a multimodal micro-analysis (Norris 2016; Norris 2004) of video recorded video chat interactions under the framework of nexus analysis (Norris & Jones 2005; Scollon 2001). Video chat was designed to be, and still essentially seen as, a phone call plus video (Neustaedter et al. 2015; Harrison 2013). Since practices of talking on the phone have been studied extensively (for example Drew & Chilton 2000; Weilenmann 2003; Rettie 2009; Hutchby & Barnett 2005; Schegloff 2004), the main focus of the video chat project was the use of visual resources during video chats. As demonstrated by Dina's quote, making use of the visual resources by giving a virtual tour can have great emotional value within a domestic video chat. Although virtual tours are common practice in video chats (Kirk et al. 2010; Buhler et al. 2013; Zouinar & Velkovska

https://doi.org/10.1515/9781501510113-008

2017; Licoppe & Morel 2014; Licoppe & Morel 2012), only two of the videos collected for the project contained virtual tours. The first one, which took place in a video chat conducted in fulfilment of university coursework requirements, was analysed in a chapter of a previous edited volume (Cserző 2016). In this chapter, I review some of the key features of video chat tours and present an analysis of the second tour, which occurred in a video chat between Kate and her brother, Charlie.

2 Features of video chat tours

During video chat tours the show-er moves the camera around so that the viewer can observe her physical space. Thus, video chat tours make relevant the interactional roles of *show-er* and *viewer*. Similarly to *caller/called* or *guide/guided*, the roles of show-er and viewer are associated with specific rights and obligations (Licoppe & Morel 2014; Licoppe & Morel 2012; De Stefani & Mondada 2014). The show-er claims the right to take an extended multimodal turn in a similar manner to the way story tellers claim the right to produce a narrative, and she is required to produce a video sequence that is intelligible, relevant, coherent, and interesting (Licoppe & Morel 2012; Licoppe & Morel 2014; Zouinar & Velkovska 2017). The viewer is required to pay attention and produce appropriate reactions (primarily verbally as the show-er may not always be able to see non-verbal reactions during a video chat tour). As the show-er adjusts the tour based on the responses of the viewer, the tour is jointly produced moment by moment (Licoppe & Morel 2012; Licoppe & Morel 2014). However, unlike the static roles of *caller/called* or *guide/guided*, *show-er* and *viewer* are transient roles which can change multiple times during a video chat comparable to *speaker/listener* or *narrator/audience*.

Virtual tours are common in personal video chats (Kirk et al. 2010; Buhler et al. 2013; Zouinar & Velkovska 2017; Licoppe & Morel 2014; Licoppe & Morel 2012), which is notable because they do not align with the intended use of the medium: the video chat systems in use today are designed to support conversation, focusing the camera on the individual user rather than capturing a wider shot of the environment (Neustaedter et al. 2015). This means that showing large areas is tricky, and virtual tours can be seen as a negotiated reading of the affordances of video chat (Shaw 2017). I suggest that video chat users have good reasons for engaging in virtual tours because these tours can fulfil important interactional and relational goals.

One function of video chat tours is that they are a good way of demonstrating joint attention, which is problematic in video chat. Attention is at the heart of human communication (Jones 2005, p.152; Norris 2004: 4), but due to the affordances of video chat monitoring, showing attention is more difficult than in face to face encounters, and the joint attentional frame is more fragile (Licoppe 2017b; de Fornel & Libbrecht 1996; Rosenbaun et al. 2016). Mondada (2014b) noted that during guided visits a common focus of attention is maintained throughout, and as video chat tours are similar to guided visits, this can be extended to video chat tours as well. Both guided visits and video chat tours rely on one participant showing the other participant various features of the environment and entails extended evaluation of the shown features. Thus both types of interaction involve discussions of a series of stance objects, which has also been linked to expressing joint attention (Du Bois 2007: 159).

The other important function of guided tours is creating intimacy. Zouinar and Velkovska argue that video chat tours contribute to a sense of closeness between the interactants because

> the type of relationship between participants is highly consequential on what is shown, especially concerning person's body and local environment, and how is it shown. Moreover, shared history and mutual knowledge that characterize close social relationships are important resources participants rely upon to make sense of what they see on the screen (2017: 402).

Thus, video chat allows users to exercise or negotiate their 'right to see' (Kirk et al. 2010; Longhurst 2013; Harper et al. 2017) and explore or define the boundaries of their relationships. When mundane objects or areas are shown, the act of showing can be more meaningful than what is being shown.

Lastly, video chat tours are relevant because video chat creates a unique spatial configuration. In face to face interaction the environment is shared and can always be relied on as a source of small talk (Coupland & Ylanne 2006). In distance communication technologies there are two (or more) separate environments, and depending on the affordances of the technology they impact the interaction in different ways. In calls between landlines, the locations are given. Sometimes there can be noises heard from the surroundings which can lead to a discussion about the environment (Drew & Chilton 2000). In calls to mobile phones, location is a central concern as it impacts on availability (Weilenmann 2003). During a video chat, the 'where' is revealed visually by default. Therefore, the question is not 'where are you?' but 'how is it where you are?' and the novelty of video chat compared to the phone is that the answer can be *shown* rather than *described*.

3 Charlie's video chat tour

The video chat tour analysed in this chapter was part of a video chat between Kate and her brother Charlie. The recording was created with the freely downloadable screen capturing software Debut Video Capture, which recorded the entire screen of Kate's laptop together with the sound, creating a video file of the video chat interaction. In this set-up the camera acts both as a medium of communication for the participants and a recording device for the researcher. The names have been changed, and the participants have consented to the use of screenshots and transcripts in publications.

At the time of the recording, Kate was living in the UK while Charlie was spending a year in Thailand. During this period, they regularly used video chat to keep in touch with each other. The tour starts 8 minutes into the video chat and the conversation preceding the tour reveals that Charlie has only recently arrived in Thailand and is currently in temporary accommodation. Charlie also tells Kate that he has found a place to stay for the rest of his trip and is due to move in one week. In the course of their conversation, Charlie decides to send Kate a link to someone's facebook profile (this appears as turn 1 in the transcript). His first attempt fails, and as Kate is waiting for something else to show up in the chat box below the video feed she seems to notice the colour of the room for the first time (turn 13). It is this noticing that prompts Charlie to produce the video chat tour which is the focus of the following analysis.

The analysis is based on the methodology of conversation analysis (Hutchby & Wooffitt 1998), incorporating multimodal analysis (Norris 2004; Mondada 2016). First, the verbal and paralinguistic elements were transcribed through repeated viewing of the video using the Jeffersonian transcription system (Atkinson & Heritage 2006). Then, multimodal actions were added to the transcript by inserting verbal descriptions of the actions in double parentheses. Before the start of the tour, these refer to actions taken by clicking the mouse or typing. During the tour the descriptions convey the way Charlie moves the camera to produce the tour. The transcript also contains five images which are all screen shots from the video recording. The positioning of the images in the transcript indicates where they are in relation to the surrounding utterances, so Figure 7.1 is a screenshot taken just between turns 12 and 13, Figure 7.2 is between turns 16 and 17, and so on. These images were chosen because they represent key points in the tour. The first image shows what Kate saw on her screen before she pointed out the colour of the room. The following images show the objects that Charlie highlights by pointing the camera in different directions (he shows the room by rotating his laptop on the spot, without getting up from his bed). These images are clearly intentional, as Charlie holds the laptop steady long enough to produce a clear image of them. This contrasts with the video sequences between the images shown, where the quick movement of the camera produces blurry footage that is difficult to interpret. In the analysis, I will show that the images featured in the transcript are also highlighted as meaningful through Charlie's accompanying narrative. During the tour, Charlie explains to Kate not only what she should look at, but also the 'right way' to see the objects (Licoppe et al. 2017; Licoppe 2017a). Kate's video is shown in Figure 7.1 to provide more context, but it has been omitted from the later images as the analysis focuses on the tour.

4 Transcription conventions

[words]	simultaneous or overlapping speech and actions
?	questioning intonation
(.)	untimed short pause
(2.0)	pause timed in seconds
((cough))	paralinguistic features and multimodal actions
(example)	unintelligible speech
hi:	lengthened syllable

5 Tour of the red room

1. Charlie: here we go (.) I think you might be able to see it I dunno we'll see
2. (6.5)
3. Charlie: there you go ((sends link))
4. Kate: ((clicks on link))
5. (3.0)
6. Kate: uh clicky (.) it's thinking about it
7. (6.0)
8. ((browser opens))
9. Kate: whoa ((page loads, content not available)) no
10. Charlie: come up?
11. Kate: content is currently unavailable it says
12. Charlie: yeah no worries I can do it this way then ((hums a tune)) uh::

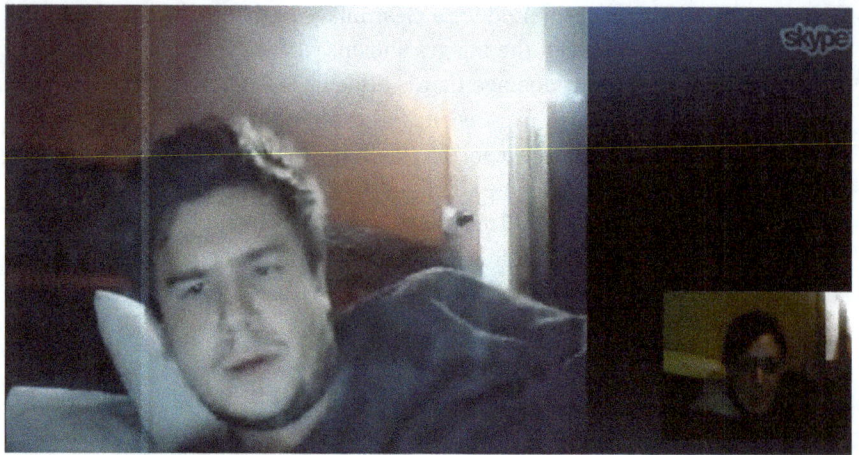

Figure 7.1: The starting point.

13. Kate: is your room red?
14. Charlie: yeah it's horrible it's like a sex dungeon
15. Kate: ((laughs))
16. Charlie: honestly it's so gross I have two mirrors look at this ((starts turning laptop to show room)) it's so weird look (.) I have a mirror (.) at bed length

Figure 7.2: The first mirror.

7 Intimacy at a distance: Multimodal meaning making in video chat tours —— 157

17. Kate: ey?
18. Charlie: and then there's another mirror (.) at bed length

Figure 7.3: The second mirror.

19. Kate: that is so weird
20. Charlie: there's my there's my telly

Figure 7.4: The television.

21. Charlie: and there's my bathroom [(it's untidy)] ((starts turning laptop back towards himself))

Figure 7.5: The bathroom door.

22. Kate: [that's real bizarre][why have you got two mirrors]
23. Charlie: [yeah it's ( )]ha? ((laptop is now back in the original position))
24. Kate: why have you got two mirrors that's so pervy
25. Charlie: I really don't know
26. Kate: oh [no]
27. Charlie: [right] how do I send um how do I send you a picture on Skype

The transcript shows that the tour is motivated by a *noticing* from Kate ('is your room red?'), which turns the room into a *stance object* (Du Bois 2007) to be jointly evaluated by the two of them throughout the tour. A noticing can be defined as an action that 'makes relevant some feature(s) of the setting, including prior talk, which may not have been previously taken as relevant' (Schegloff 2014: 219). Such actions have social significance because not every feature or prior turn is singled out for being noticed (Keisanen 2012: 201); for example the colour of Kate's room is not discussed.

The tour is introduced gradually in turns 13–16. It is made relevant by Kate's noticing in turn 13, but the immediate response is a verbal evaluation of the room (turn 14) which elicits laughter from Kate (turn 15) and is then expanded into a multimodal evaluation sequence beginning in turn 16. It is difficult to pinpoint the exact beginning of the tour, as Charlie only starts moving the camera after saying 'look at this'. He then produces blurry images which are difficult to interpret, providing the first clear shot (shown in Figure 7.2) after the second 'look' (still in turn 16). This shot is held steady while he provides a gloss ('I have a mirror at bed length') until Kate produces a reaction (turn 17).

The showing of the next object of interest (the second mirror, featured in Figure 7.3 follows the same structure with a still shot coinciding with the description of what is shown (in turn 18) and held until a response is produced (turn 19). At this point the tour could finish as the two objects projected in turn 4 have been shown and acknowledged. However, Charlie continues the tour showing some features that are quite mundane (an old-fashioned television shown in Figure 7.4 and a closed door shown in Figure 7.5) and at odds with the previous features and the evaluation. When he shows these features (turns 20 and 21) he still produces a clear shot of the objects he is naming, but he does not wait for a reaction from Kate between the two. After showing the bathroom door, he starts turning the laptop back towards himself, projecting the end of the tour. At the same time, Kate produces another evaluation of the mirrors (turn 22), ignoring the ordinary features of the room shown in the last two clear images. After a short repair sequence (turns 22–24), they finish discussing the room (turns 25–26) and Charlie introduces a new topic with a framing move (Sinclair & Coulthard 1992) in turn 27 ('right').

6 Evaluating the red room

Throughout the extract discussed above Kate and Charlie express alignment with each other by jointly evaluating the stance object (Du Bois 2007): Charlie's room. The evaluation of the room starts in turn 13 with Kate's noticing ('is your room red?') with a prosody indicating surprise. In a literal sense, this is merely a question about the colour of Charlie's room. However, there is an undeniable implication that a red room is surprising, potentially even sinister or in poor taste. Charlie's immediate response ('yeah it's horrible, it's like a sex dungeon') indicates that he takes Kate's noticing as a criticism. It is possible that this interpretation draws on British stereotypes about Bangkok as a destination for sex-tourism in addition to Kate's tone of voice. Furthermore, Charlie's comment also reveals that he has no problem with evaluating his room in such a negative way.

There is a stark contrast between Kate's implied judgment in turn 13 and Charlie's explicit evaluation in turn 14. In the analysis below, I will demonstrate that this contrast is characteristic of the exchange as a whole in addition to the opening phase quoted here. Kate points out an unusual feature without overtly committing to an evaluation, exploiting the potential ambiguity of noticings and stance taking (Jaffe 2009; Thurlow & Jaworski 2011; Goodwin & Goodwin 2012). Depending on Charlie's reaction, the colour of the room could be framed as amusing, puzzling, strange, or exotic. It transpires that her caution is unwarranted, as Charlie immediately launches into a series of harsh comments, evidenced by pointing the camera at the 'offending' objects in turn. It is also notable that although the tour reveals that Kate's initial assessment is inaccurate (only the wall behind the bed is red, the other walls are white as seen in Figures 7.2–7.5), this is not discussed at any point. This (together with the lack of reaction to the mundane features of the room) indicates that focus of this interaction is relational rather than factual as features that do not support the joint stance are not elaborated.

The negative evaluation of the room serves a positive relational goal by allowing Kate and Charlie to bond over their shared stance. Even though some of the comments are quite harsh and would be viewed as insults in other contexts, here they contribute to signalling and creating intimacy and solidarity as they are accompanied with laughter and are exchanged in a relaxed conversation (Culpeper 2011; Bernal 2008). Furthermore, it appears that transgressive sexual topic (which is even more of a taboo between siblings) is used as a means to construct intimacy, similarly to the rude stories analysed by Coupland and Jaworski (2003). All of this is possible because the participants exploit the ambiguity of the situation: although Charlie is accountable to some degree for the design of the room as he is occupying it, the accountability is limited because he is staying in the room for only a brief period and may have had little choice or control over the room. Therefore, any criticism that is made can be interpreted as disapproval of the unknown designer of the room rather than Charlie. This is observable in the specific lexical choices as shown in the analysis below.

In the analysis of Table 7.1 I show how the language used by both Charlie and Kate contributes to a favourable interpretation of the impolite expressions. To support the analysis, all turns that relate to the tour are separated into clauses. Although three of Kate's contributions (4, 11, and 23) are not clauses, they are included in this table for the sake of completeness. Each clause was assigned a value (neutral, contextual, or negative) and an expression of ownership (unexpressed, possessive determiner, or possessive process) as appropriate. The two final clauses (22 and 23) did not relate directly to the room and were thus excluded from this categorization along with clause 19 which is unfortunately unintelligible. The classification (first according to value then ownership) and interpretation is discussed below.

7 Intimacy at a distance: Multimodal meaning making in video chat tours — 161

Table 7.1: Value and ownership analysis.

	Speaker	clause	value	ownership
1	Kate	is your room red	neutral	possessive determiner
2	Charlie	it's horrible	negative	unexpressed
3	Charlie	it's like a sex dungeon	negative	unexpressed
4	Kate	((laugh))	contextual	
5	Charlie	honestly it's so gross	negative	unexpressed
6	Charlie	I have two mirrors	contextual	possessive process
7	Charlie	look at this	contextual	unexpressed
8	Charlie	it's so weird	negative	unexpressed
9	Charlie	look	contextual	
10	Charlie	I have a mirror at bed length	contextual	possessive process
11	Kate	ey	contextual	
12	Charlie	and then there's another mirror at bed length	contextual	unexpressed
13	Kate	that is so weird	negative	unexpressed
14	Charlie	there's my there's my telly	neutral	possessive determiner
15	Charlie	and there's my bathroom	neutral	possessive determiner
16	Charlie	(it's untidy)	negative	unexpressed
17	Kate	that's real bizarre	negative	unexpressed
18	Kate	why have you got two mirrors	contextual	possessive process
19	Charlie	yeah it's () ha?		
20	Kate	why have you got two mirrors	contextual	possessive process
21	Kate	that's so pervy	negative	unexpressed
22	Charlie	I really don't know		
23	Kate	oh no		

The clauses are assigned one of three values: neutral, contextual, or negative. The clauses labelled 'neutral' express no negative (or indeed positive) judgement, whether implicit or explicit. Clause 1 is classed as 'neutral' rather than 'contextual' because as argued above, the ambiguity of this opening turn is an important feature in this interaction. Although in light of the later interaction this clause can be heard as an implicit judgement, more favourable interpretations are also possible at the time it is uttered. Furthermore, as this is the first turn relating to the room, the context is yet to be established. The other neutral clauses relate to the ordinary features of the room (the TV and the bathroom).

In contrast, the clauses grouped into the 'contextual' category are not inherently negative but carry a negative evaluation within the context of the interaction. This is mostly achieved by referring to objects that have been explicitly linked to negative evaluations in the previous clauses (such as the mirrors). In addition, Kate's non-committal laughter and ejective (4 and 11) indicate alignment with Charlie without furthering the evaluation. This is the category with the most clauses, nine in total.

Finally, eight of the clauses were classed as 'negative' because they contain expressions that signal an explicitly negative evaluation. These clauses have a very similar grammatical structure ('[object] is [adjective]'), but they are not all equally harsh. The negative evaluations range from 'it's so weird' and 'it's untidy' to 'it's so gross' and 'that's so pervy'. In terms of the overall pattern, Kate does not commit to an explicitly negative evaluation until clause 13, and even then she chooses relatively mild words ('weird' in clause 13 and 'bizarre' in clause 17) until clause 21, where she finally evaluates the room as 'pervy'. Contrastingly, Charlie starts off by using harsh evaluative language, which is toned down over the course of the tour.

The distribution of evaluation and ownership expressions is systematic if not strategic, and it contributes to the positive interpretation of the impolite expressions. Firstly, most of the clauses are in the 'unexpressed' ownership category, which means that they refer to the room or a part of the room without expressing Charlie's ownership. Instead of using a possessive determiner (your/my room), they use deictic terms (it/this/that), which obscure the owner of the object. Similarly, in clause 12 Charlie uses the construction 'there's another mirror' instead of 'I have another mirror', which would mark him as the owner of the mirror explicitly. In fact, possessive determiners are only used in three clauses, all of which have been assigned the 'neutral' value category. The third ownership category contains four clauses (two of them identical) which are variations of 'Charlie has mirrors'. This category was labelled 'possessive process' following the classification of the systemic functional approach (Halliday & Matthiessen 2004). The clauses in the 'possessive process' and 'possessive determiner' all highlight Charlie's ownership of the room, although with different linguistic constructions. As with the value categorization, some clauses could not be placed in any of the categories.

Thus, a close analysis of the language used shows that the negative evaluation of the room is led by Charlie. Kate's opening noticing implies that there is something remarkable about the room, but she does not say anything explicitly negative until clause 13 ('that is so weird'), which is quite mild in comparison with the other evaluations. In contrast, Charlie starts with a negative evaluation ('it's horrible') and continues with negative or contextually negative evaluation until clause 14 ('there's my telly').

As noted above, the participants only use possessive determiners in neutral value statements. In addition, all the negative value statements leave the ownership unexpressed. The contextual statements are spread across the 'unexpressed', 'possessive process', and unclassified categories. The overall effect is that Charlie can distance himself from his room by using impersonal constructions, especially when discussing negative aspects of the room. This allows him to align himself with Kate as a viewer of the room, rather than its owner. They can both express their negative judgement of the room, as this is never attributed to Charlie personally on the linguistic level. In fact, Kate is encouraged to make a negative evaluation of the room by Charlie's numerous negative comments. These evaluations are balanced out by the ordinary elements of the room (the TV and the bathroom), which Charlie does claim ownership for.

7 The showing sequence

In video chat tours, the two main resources at the disposal of the show-er for the production of the tour are camera movement and speech. The two modes work together to create meaning, and neither is *fully* intelligible without the other for participants and analysts alike (Jewitt 2016; Norris 2016). In the analysis above, I have shown how these two modes work together to produce meaningful sequences. For example, when Charlie produces a clear shot of an object (as in Figure 7.2), he names the object of interest (e.g.: 'I have a mirror at bed length') at the same time. Thus, Charlie lets Kate know that the image of the mirror is intentionally produced, and she is expected to react in some way. This unit of showing and telling is exactly what Dina evokes in the re-enactment of her video chat tour ("this is the bathroom, this is my room, this is the hall, this is the kitchen"). Video chat tours, therefore, are comprised of a series of multimodal showings and evaluations.

Verbal glosses are crucial for domestic video chat tours because the video footage alone is often difficult to interpret. Firstly, video chat tours are live and unedited which means that they necessarily include some video sequences that are the by-product of moving the camera into place rather than something the show-er intends to focus on. Such 'by-product' sequences are especially common at the beginning of a video chat tour if the show-er needs to turn the device (and thus the camera) around (Licoppe & Morel 2014; Licoppe & Morel 2012). Although the camera is moved strategically and purposefully by the show-er, the viewer may 'misinterpret' some motions, especially when there is ambiguity in whether a given shot is the end in itself or just the means to arrive at another shot. In addition, the resolution of video chat cameras is relatively poor, which means that images can be pixelated even if there is sufficient light and the internet connection is fast. Figures 7.1–5 demonstrate the poor quality of the video analysed in this chapter: the screenshots are difficult to decipher, even though they were taken in the moments when the footage was the most clear.

8 Pointing in video chat tours

Pointing gestures are crucial in the organisation of physical guided tours (De Stefani & Mondada 2014; Mondada 2013) because they are resources for introducing new objects and establishing joint attention towards them. However, pointing a finger is of little use in video chat, because participants do not share the same space. Instead, they must use alternative ways of pointing to accomplish the same goal. Pointing to something at the distant location is best done verbally, while pointing to something in the immediate environment can be done through the use of the camera.

The analysed extract demonstrates how powerful verbal pointing can be. In the video, it is Kate's noticing that makes the tour relevant. Similarly, the video chat tour analysed in Cserző (2016) is also occasioned by a noticing ("Where are you? Is that your kitchen?"). In addition, noticings can also compel the distant participants to change what is shown during a video chat tour (Licoppe & Morel 2014). Similarly, in physical tours guided participants can initiate reorientations during the tour by producing noticings combined with pointing gestures (De Stefani & Mondada 2014).

Pointing with the camera can be done by moving the camera, as Charlie does in this video, or by bringing small objects to the camera (Licoppe 2017a). Whichever method is chosen, pointing with a camera is more powerful than a pointing gesture because short of looking away from the screen, the viewer cannot help but look at what the camera focuses on. In contrast, a successful pointing gesture requires active co-operation on the part of the viewer (Kendon 1990; Luff et al. 2003; Mondada 2014a).

Pointing in video chat tours functions in the same way as in amateur tourist videos in that it serves to locate the self in a particular moment and location and facilitates the sharing of an experience through the medium of video (Thurlow & Jaworski 2014). However, the criteria for determining what is worthy of being shown is completely different in these two genres. In tourist videos participants aim to capture spectacular public locations in footage that can be played on multiple occasions and for different audiences (Thurlow & Jaworski 2014). In contrast, virtual tours in video chat are ephemeral real-time exchanges which typically focus on private domestic spaces. Often there is nothing intrinsically interesting about the spaces and objects they show: the video is worthy of being shared simply because it represents the show-ers every day lived experience.

9 Conclusion

In video chat tours the physical space becomes a resource for video chat users to make claims about their own and each other's identity and their relationship to each other. This is true of video chats in general, but comes into focus during video chat tours, which highlight the constructed nature of space (Thurlow & Jaworski 2011; Lefebvre 1991). The video chat tour between Charlie and Kate reaffirms the intimacy of their familial relationship, in which video chat from a bed is unremarkable, and comments such as 'your room is pervy' are a light-hearted joke. The analysed extract illustrates the personal nature of video chat tours, which are often improvised for an audience of one.

The construction and assessment of space is done partly through conversation and partly by the show-er's manipulation of the frame to direct the attention of the viewer in a way that is not possible in face-to-face situations. Show-ers have a very powerful tool in their hands which allows them to literally share their point of view. However, the accompanying descriptions are also crucial for delineating meaningful and incidental shots. Furthermore, viewers are active co-producers, shaping the tour through noticings and evaluations. Pointing is a crucial resource for establishing joint attention towards the stance objects (Du Bois 2007), but in video chat tours pointing must be accomplished verbally or through the use of the camera rather than through gestures.

Thus, video chat tours are joint interactional achievements relying on multimodal meaning making practices. Although video chat tours in domestic settings share many features of amateur tourist videos, they operate on a different logic: the goal is not to capture something spectacular, but to share an everyday experience. By showcasing private spaces, producers of video chat tours also blur the boundaries between public and private, bringing a genre linked to spectacular public spaces into an ordinary environment. While tourist videos tend to feature places that are considered to have intrinsic value, video chat tours show spaces that become "showable" due to the people inhabiting them. As illustrated by the opening quote from Dina, sharing these private spaces can have great emotional value for loved ones living far away.

Video chat is an intimate medium in the sense that it is mostly used in close relationships: between partners, relatives, and friends (Miller & Sinanan 2014; Longhurst 2017; O'Hara et al. 2006; Rintel 2013; Kirk et al. 2010). The average number of people my participants contacted via video chat was much lower than those they contacted by text messaging, phone calls, email, instant messaging, or social media. Thus, it appears that turning on the camera is an act of intimacy in the context of domestic video chat. Participants certainly use their webcams in strategic ways during a video chat, but there is always a potential that the camera will also reveal something else in addition to what is intended. In close relationships, this is a welcome affordance because it creates an opportunity for discussing incidental details, topics that perhaps do not warrant telling but are nevertheless meaningful in the context of the particular relationship (Tannen 2006; Zouinar & Velkovska 2017; Sacks 1995). By noticing such details, video chat users can show each other that they care, maintaining intimacy at a distance.

Acknowledgements: I would like to express my thanks to the volume editors for their invaluable comments on the previous drafts of the chapter. This research would not have been possible without financial support from The Sidney Perry Foundation, The Gen Foundation, The Sir Richard Stapley Educational Trust, The Humanitarian Trust, and The Allan & Nesta Ferguson Charitable Trust and the time and trust of my participants. I am also grateful to Virpi Ylänne and Tereza Spilioti for their insightful and constructive feedback on my research. Any remaining shortcomings are my own.

References

Atkinson, Maxwell J. & John Heritage. 2006. Jefferson's transcript notation. In Adam Jaworski & Nikolas Coupland (eds.), *The discourse reader*, 158–165. New York: Routledge.

Bernal, María. 2008. Do insults always insult? Genuine impoliteness versus non-genuine impoliteness in colloquial Spanish. *Pragmatics* 18(4), 781–802.

Du Bois, John W. 2007. The stance triangle. In Robert Englebretson (ed.), *Stancetaking in discourse*, 139–182. Amsterdam and Philadelphia: John Benjamins Publishing Company.

Buhler, Tatiana, Carman Neustaedter & Serena Hillman. 2013. How and why teenagers use video chat. *Proceedings of the 2013 Conference on Computer Supported Cooperative Work*

SE – CSCW '13 February (10). Available: http://clab.iat.sfu.ca/pubs/ BuhlerTeenVideoChat.pdf (21 February, 2019)

Coupland, Justine & Adam Jaworski. 2003. Transgression and intimacy in recreational talk narratives. *Research on Language and Social Interaction* 36(1), 85–106.

Coupland, Nikolas & Virpi Ylänne. 2006. Relational frames in weather talk. In Adam Jaworski & Nikolas Coupland (eds.), *The discourse reader*, 349–361. London and New York: Routledge.

Cserző, Dorottya. 2016. Nexus analysis meets scales: An exploration of sites of engagement in videochat interviews. In Jaspar Naveel Singh, Argyro Kantara & Dorottya Cserző (eds.), *Downscaling culture: Revisiting intercultural communication*, 337–365. Newcastle-upon-Tyne: Cambridge Scholars.

Culpeper, Jonathan. 2011. *Impoliteness: Using language to cause offence*. Cambridge: Cambridge University Press.

Drew, Paul & Kathy Chilton. 2000. Calling just to keep in touch: regular and habitualised telephone calls as an environment for small talk. In Justine Coupland (ed.), *Small talk*, 137–162. Harlow: Longman.

Fornel, Michel de & Liz Libbrecht. 1996. The interactional frame of videophonic exchange. *Réseaux. The French journal of communication* 4(1), 47–72.

Gibbs, Graham. 2007. *Analysing qualitative data*. London: SAGE.

Goodwin, Marjorie H. & Charles Goodwin. 2012. Car talk: Integrating texts, bodies, and changing landscapes. *Semiotica* 2012(191), 257–286.

Halliday, Michael A. K. & Christian M. I. M. Matthiessen. 2004. *Halliday's introduction to functional grammar* 4th edn. London and New York: Routledge.

Harper, Richard, Sean Rintel, Rod Watson & Kenton O'Hara. 2017. The "interrogative gaze": Making video calling and messaging "accountable." *Pragmatics* 27(3), 319–350.

Harrison, Steve R. 2013. Parallel universes of teleconferencing. *The Electronic Journal of Communication*, 23.

Hutchby, Ian & Simone Barnett. 2005. Aspects of the sequential organization of mobile phone conversation. *Discourse Studies* 7(2), 147–171.

Hutchby, Ian & Robin Wooffitt. 1998. *Conversation analysis: Principles, practices and applications*. Malden, MA: Polity Press.

Jaffe, Alexandra. 2009. Introduction: The sociolinguistics of stance. In Alexandra Jaffe (ed.), *Stance: Sociolinguistic perspectives*, 3–28. Oxford: Oxford University Press.

Jewitt, Carey. 2016. Multimodal analysis. In Alexandra Georgakopoulou & Tereza Spilioti (eds.), *The Routledge handbook of language and digital communication*, 69–84. London and New York: Routledge.

Jones, Rodney H. 2005. Sites of engagement as sites of attention: time, space, and culture in electronic discourse. In Sigrid Norris & Rodney H. Jones (eds.), *Discourse in action: Introducing mediated discourse analysis*, 141–154. London and New York: Routledge.

Keisanen, Tiina. 2012. "Uh-oh, we were going there": Environmentally occasioned noticings of trouble in in-car interaction. *Semiotica* 2012(191), 197–222.

Kelly, Clare. 2015. "Let's do some jumping together": Intergenerational participation in the use of remote technology to co-construct social relations over distance. *Journal of Early Childhood Research* 13(1), 29–46.

Kendon, Adam. 1990. *Conducting interaction: patterns of behavior in focused encounters*. Cambridge: Cambridge University Press.

Kirk, David B., Abigail Sellen & Xiang Cao. 2010. Home video communication: mediating "closeness." *Proceedings of the 2010 ACM conference on Computer supported cooperative work – CSCW '10*, 135–145. Available: https://dl.acm.org/citation.cfm?id=1718945 (28.03.2019)

Lefebvre, Henri. 1991. *The production of space*. Malden, Oxford, and Victoria, Oxford, and Victoria: Blackwell Publishing.

Licoppe, Christian, Paul K. Luff, Christian Heath, Hideaki Kuzuoka, Naomi Yamashita & Sylvaine Tuncer. 2017. Showing objects: Holding and manipulating artefacts in video-mediated collaborative settings. *Proceedings of the 2017 CHI Conference on Human Factors in Computing Systems – CHI '17*, 5295–5306. Available: http://dl.acm.org/citation.cfm?doid=3025453.3025848 (21 February, 2019)

Licoppe, Christian. 2017a. Showing objects in Skype video-mediated conversations: From showing gestures to showing sequences. *Journal of Pragmatics* 110, 63–82. Available: http://dx.doi.org/10.1016/j.pragma.2017.01.007 (21 February, 2019)

Licoppe, Christian. 2017b. Skype appearances, multiple greetings and "coucou". The sequential organization of video-mediated conversation openings. *Pragmatics* 27(3), 351–386. Available: https://benjamins.com/online/prag/articles/prag.27.3.03lic (21 February, 2019)

Licoppe, Christian & Julien Morel. 2014. Mundane video directors in interaction: Showing one's environment in Skype and mobile video calls. In Mathias Broth, Eric Laurier & Lorenzo Mondada (eds.), *Studies of video practices: Video at work*, 135–160. New York and London: Routledge.

Licoppe, Christian & Julien Morel. 2012. Video-in-interaction: "Talking Heads" and the multimodal organization of mobile and Skype video calls. *Research on Language & Social Interaction* 45, 399–429.

Longhurst, Robyn. 2017. *Skype: bodies, screens, space*. London and New York: Routledge.

Longhurst, Robyn. 2013. Using skype to mother: Bodies, emotions, visuality, and screens. *Environment and Planning D: Society and Space* 31(4), 664–679.

Luff, Paul, Christian Heath, Hideaki Kuzuoka, Jon Hindmarsh, Keiichi Yamazaki & Shinya Oyama. 2003. Fractured ecologies: Creating environments for collaboration. *Human–Computer Interaction* 18(1–2), 51–84.

Mason, Jennifer. 2002. *Qualitative researching* 2nd edn. London: Sage Publications.

Miller, Daniel & Jolynna Sinanan. 2014. *Webcam*. Cambridge: Polity Press.

Mondada, Lorenza. 2016. Challenges of multimodality : Language and the body in social interaction. *Journal of Sociolinguistics*, 20(3), 336–366.

Mondada, Lorenza. 2013. Displaying, contesting and negotiating epistemic authority in social interaction: Descriptions and questions in guided visits. *Discourse Studies*, 15(5),597–626.

Mondada, Lorenza. 2014a. Pointing, talk, and the bodies: Reference and joint attention as embodied interactional achievements. In Mandana Seyfeddinipur & Marianne Gullberg (eds.), *From gesture in conversation to visible action as utterance*, 95–124. Amsterdam/Philadelphia: John Benjamins Publishing Company.

Mondada, Lorenza. 2014b. Shooting as a research activity: The embodied production of video data. In Mathias Broth, Eric Laurier & Lorenza Mondada (eds.), *Studies of video practices: Video at work*, 33–62. London and New York: Routledge.

Neustaedter, Carman, Carolyn Pang, Azadeh Forghani, Erick Oduor, Serena Hillman, Tejinder K. Judge, Michael Massimi & Saul Greenberg. 2015. Sharing domestic life through long-term video connections. *ACM Transactions on Computer-Human Interaction*, 22(1), 1–29.

Norris, Sigrid. 2004. *Analyzing multimodal interaction: A methodological framework*. New York and London: Routledge.

Norris, Sigrid. 2016. Concepts in multimodal discourse analysis with examples from video conferencing. *Yearbook of the Poznan Linguistic Meeting*, 2(1), 141–165.

Norris, Sigrid & Rodney H. Jones (eds.). 2005. *Discourse in action: Introducing mediated discourse analysis*. London and New York: Routledge.

O'Hara, Kenton, Alison Black & Matthew Lipson. 2006. Everyday practices with mobile video telephony. *Proceedings of the SIGCHI conference on Human Factors in computing systems*, 871–880. Available: http://portal.acm.org/citation.cfm?doid=1124772.1124900 (25 February, 2019)

Rettie, Ruth. 2009. Mobile phone communication: Extending goffman to mediated interaction. *Sociology* 43(3), 421–438.

Rintel, Sean. 2013. Video calling in long-distance relationships: The opportunistic use of audio / video distortions as a relational resource. *The Electronic Journal of Communication*, 23(1,2).

Rosenbaun, Laura, Sheizaf Rafaeli & Dennis Kurzon. 2016. Blurring the boundaries between domestic and digital spheres: Competing engagements in public Google hangouts. *Pragmatics*, 26(2), 291–314.

Sacks, Harvey. 1995. *Lectures on conversation*. Edited by Gail Jefferson. Oxford, UK & Cambridge, USA: Blackwell publishing.

Schegloff, Emanuel A. 2004. Answering the phone. In Gene H. Lerner (ed.), *Conversation analysis: Studies from the first generation*, 63–107. Amsterdam and Philadelphia: John Benjamins Publishing Company.

Schegloff, Emanuel A. 2014. *Sequence organization in interaction: A primer in conversation analysis* Vol. 1. Cambridge: Cambridge University Press.

Scollon, Ron. 2001. Action and text: Towards an integrated understanding of the place of text in social (inter)action, mediated discourse analysis and the problem of aocial action. In Ruth Wodak & Michael Meyer (eds.), *Methods of critical discourse analysis*, 139–183. London, Thousand Oaks California: Sage.

Shaw, Adrienne. 2017. Encoding and decoding affordances: Stuart Hall and interactive media technologies. *Media, Culture & Society* 39(4), 1–11.

Sinclair, John & Malcolm Coulthard. 1992. Towards an analysis of discourse. In Malcolm Coulthard (ed.), *Advances in spoken discourse analysis*, 1–34. London and New York: Routledge.

De Stefani, Elwys & Lorenzo Mondada. 2014. Reorganizing Mobile Formations: When "guided" participants initiate reorientations in guided tours. *Space and Culture*, 17(2), 157–175.

Tannen, Deborah. 2006. *You're wearing That?: Understanding Mothers and Daughters in Conversation*. New York: Random House.

Thurlow, Crispin & Adam Jaworski. 2011. Banal globalization? Embodied actions and mediated practices in tourists' online photo sharing. In Crispin Thurlow & Kristine Mroczek (eds.), *Digital discourse: Language in the new media*, 220–250. Oxford: Oxford University Press.

Thurlow, Crispin & Adam Jaworski. 2014. "Two hundred ninety-four": Remediation and multimodal performance in tourist placemaking. *Journal of Sociolinguistics* 18(4), 459–494.

Weilenmann, Alexandra. 2003. "I can't talk now, I'm in a fitting room": Formulating availability and location in mobile phone conversations. *Environment and Planning A* 35(9), 1589–1605.

Zouinar, Moustafa & Julia Velkovska. 2017. Talking about talking about things: Image-based topical talk and intimacy in video-mediated family communication. *Pragmatics* 27(3), 387–418.

Rebecca Venema and Katharina Lobinger
8 Visual bonding and intimacy: A repertoire-oriented study of photo-sharing in close personal relationships

1 Introduction

While taking photographs, showing them to, and discussing them with others has always been a means of collaborative meaning-making, of "doing sociality" and of establishing, maintaining, promoting, and performing relationships (Keightley & Pickering 2014; Sarvas & Frohlich 2011), this everyday practice has become an important part of social interaction in digitally networked, mediatized and increasingly visualized societies. Furthermore, visuals in general have become central to conversational, ephemeral and playful communication (Katz & Crocker 2015; Kofoed & Larsen 2016; Kurvinen 2003; Mäkelä et al. 2000; van Dijck 2007; Villi 2015). People do not only talk about images, they also share them to communicate visually, often synchronously – thus bridging geographical distance. All these factors have implications for close personal relationships that are created and maintained in "ongoing conversations" and everyday interactions (Berger & Kellner 1964; Bierhoff & Rohmann 2009; Duck 1990). In this chapter, we therefore investigate the role of visuals and visual communication in interactions between couples and friends.

Research has shown that visual communication and (also analogous forms of) photo-sharing have a variety of social functions in close social relationships. These practices serve, for example, (1) to build, maintain or strengthen social relationships, (2) to create individual or social memory, (3) as an expression of the self, (4) to represent and perform the relationship, and (5) functional purposes (for example when photos are used for the organization and micro-coordination in everyday life, instead of notes; see Kindberg et al. 2005; Ling & Yttri 2002; Van House et al. 2004; Van House et al. 2005; Villi 2015). These general functions remain relatively stable. What has changed, however, are the forms of visual communication and visual interactions, compared to early studies on digital photography and photographic exchange. With networked photography – the convergence of photography with mobile communication and online or social media communication (Rubinstein & Sluis 2008) – pictures can now be shared immediately after capture. This allows for a simultaneity of experience, a "synchronous view" (Villi 2015), visually-mediated co-presence (Villi 2016) and thus the production of affective proximity (Prieto-Blanco 2016; Villi 2012; Villi & Stocchetti 2011).

As pictures can convey emotions more directly and more authentically, this makes them ideal resources for creating connection, intimate communication and "visual intimacy" (Miguel 2016). The increasing synchronicity of visual interactions additionally reduces barriers. Visual communication can thus play a particularly important role in long-distance relationships between romantic partners, but also between friends who live in different cities or countries.

To understand the role of visuals and visual interactions in relationships, we believe that multiple forms of visual communication should be examined against the backdrop of the entire communication repertoire at use. These include the use of different image forms, communicative technologies, and image functions. Previous research on photo-sharing and its communicative uses has primarily focused on selected single devices, platforms, or on specific motifs and photographic genres. These studies provide valuable findings concerning particular forms of sharing, such as publishing images on specific platforms and Social Networking Sites (SNS) (e.g., Bayer et al. 2016; Vainikka, Noppari, & Seppänen, 2017; Vaterlaus et al. 2016; Weilenmann, Hillman & Jungselius, 2013). Others have analyzed the exchange of photographs using certain individual communication technologies, such as mobile phones with cameras or smartphones (e.g., Kindberg et al. 2005; Kurvinen 2003; Villi 2012, 2015). Thus far, however, little is known about how visual communication, photo-sharing and visual practices in general are woven into the complex communication repertoires of people interacting in close relationships.

In what follows, we first discuss the diversity of forms, modes and functions of sharing photographs in close personal relationships. We then explain our in-depth, qualitative cross-media and repertoire-oriented methodological approach for researching visual interactions in relationships. In the results section, we discuss the diverse ways in which images are shared and integrated in communication repertoires and everyday interactions, detailing their specific functions for the maintenance of relationships. Lastly, and based on these findings, we call for further studies on the contexts, meanings and implications of visual interaction in social relationships in contemporary societies.

2 Modes and functions of taking/sharing photographs

There has been a rapid proliferation and diversification of media use in social relationships in current highly mediatized societies and life-worlds. Relationships are established, maintained or even terminated through multiple forms of media, and through mediatized interpersonal communication such as instant messaging, video and voice telephony (see, for example, Caughlin & Sharabi 2013; Gershon 2008; Parks 2017). This diversification also applies to photo-sharing in everyday interactions.

Many recent studies have highlighted the role of photo-sharing as a form of visual texting, chatting or messaging (Bayer et al. 2016; Kofoed & Larsen 2016; Lobinger & Schreiber 2017; Vaterlaus et al. 2016). At the same time, photographs are still used for commemoration, and for creating individual and group memory (Gye 2007). Photo-sharing nowadays encompasses different practices of showing, passing on, sending or publishing pictures and of communicating with one or more co-present or remote communication partners (for an overview see Lobinger & Schreiber 2017). Moreover, people share different kinds of pictures for various purposes using different apps or platforms. People thus actively curate both their image collections and photo-sharing practices, reflecting on aesthetics, audiences and the different affordances of platforms (Schreiber 2017; for an exploratory study on norms and rules of sharing pictures in close social relationships see Venema & Lobinger 2017).

Elsewhere, Lobinger (2016b) distinguished between three different modes of sharing photographs in order to emphasize that the visual object within communication processes can take on very different forms.[1] Pictures can be shared for talking *about* the pictures; for communicating visually *with* them; or for phatic communication – that is, for the sake of creating contact. Villi (2012) described this latter reciprocal form of sharing photos as "visual chit-chat". With this it becomes obvious that even supposedly meaningless or banal pictures can be valuable means of maintaining interpersonal connections over distance. But in order to fully grasp the meaning and relevance of phatic photo-sharing for the relationship, it is important to examine images within practices and social interactions. Certainly, the relational significance of the images cannot be found simply in the image itself.

The first sociological research into everyday photography and its communicative and social uses which included practices of sharing photographs with others dates back to the 1960s. Bourdieu, for example, investigated the practices of amateur photographers and the social uses of photography in France (Bourdieu 1990 [1965]). This analysis points to central functions and uses of photography, such as preserving and "reproducing" significant moments for

---

[1] This is an analytical, ideal-typical systematization in order to underline the different roles of the shared photographic object. It can be assumed that these three modes of sharing pictures occur in mixed forms in everyday practices and interactions.

remembrance in families. Many fundamental insights into the early social functions of sharing pictures are still relevant and valid, despite the many technological transformations in personal photography. Since then, visual research has continuously shown that photos can be very important in social relationships. Linke's (2010, 2011) analysis of the communication repertoires of couples underlines this fact. Even though images and visual communication were not explicitly taken into account in Linke's study, they were found to be an important "identity-forming form" (Linke 2010: 167) and a "subjectively valuable emotional resources" (Linke 2010: 67).

All previous studies provide extremely valuable knowledge regarding practices of photo sharing. However, as already argued, these studies focused on the analysis of specific communication technologies or practices on specific platforms and SNS. The study presented here in turn, focuses on the communication repertoire within a relationship and takes this as a starting point to explore and contextualize the multiple forms, functions and interrelations of visual communication practices.

3 Our study: Visual repertoires in close personal relationships

In light of this previous scholarship, we have been particularly interested in the roles visual communication play in couples' and friends' everyday interactions. We therefore focus here on the relevance of visual communication with respect to other forms of interpersonal interaction, on the functions of visual practices and on how they are integrated into the overall repertoire of everyday interactions. We follow a repertoire-oriented tradition of media and communication research (Bjur et al. 2014; Hasebrink 2015); in other words, we examine visual communication practices in social relationships against the backdrop of the entire communication repertoire, or the so-called "media manifold" (Caughlin & Sharabi 2013; Madianou & Miller 2013) and its complex, multimodal network of mediated and face-to-face interactions (Caughlin & Sharabi 2013; Hasebrink 2015; Licoppe 2004; Taneja et al. 2012). As such, our study does not focus on the use of a single media technology (e.g., the smartphone) or of a single communication application (e.g., WhatsApp) for visual-communicative interaction. This approach allows us to contextualize the visual communication practices and visual interactions, and to acknowledge their specific (situational) functions. Moreover, this approach directs attention to the interrelation of different visual communication and sharing practices. It enables us, for example, to focus on how publishing pictures on Social Networking Sites is also related to more private forms of image exchange, such as those via messenger services. We also consider interrelations and links between mediated visual communication and face-to-face communication.

As previously stated, the empirical focus of our study is on the communication repertoires of couples and close friends. This includes all forms of mediated visual communication (Lobinger 2012; Müller 2003) in respondents' relationships: from interpersonal communication, image-related follow-up communication, to the external representation of the relationship and the performance of the couple and friendship identity. We also consider image handling practices in which the materiality of the image was foregrounded (for example, the exchange/presentation of image objects, the hanging up or destroying of a photograph). As we mentioned earlier, networked photography and photo-sharing are increasingly important in social interactions; however, other types of images (including paintings, drawings, "found" images from media coverage, memes, gifs), "analogue" images and material image objects continue to be relevant and are therefore taken into account.

We conducted 34 qualitative, problem-focused semi-structured single and pair interviews.[2] The communication repertoires of eight couples and the role of visuals and visual interactions in their relationships were examined in eight pair interviews and in 14 individual interviews following the pair interview (one couple separated). In addition, six friendship dyads were examined. Here we interviewed the 12 friends individually. Across all interviews we used several visual methods or visual research techniques (for an overview: Lobinger 2016a). For example, we used participatory visual elicitation, participatory network drawings and printed statements that served as prompts for further evaluation and discussion (for a detailed methodological description see Venema & Lobinger 2017). The use of these visual methods facilitated the representation of visual, non-visual, mediated and non-mediated communication practices and their interplay (Collier 1957; Harper 2002; Hepp, Roitsch & Berg 2016; Lobinger 2016a). Respondents were asked to draw their common communication repertoire (referred to as "communication universe" in the interview). They were then asked to talk about the visual components of their communication repertoires and the functions and meanings of images and visual communication.

---

[2] The pair interviews ranged in length from one to two hours. The individual interviews took about one hour on average, ranging in length from 30 minutes up to two hours. The interviews were conducted between April and June 2015 in a mid-size city in Northern Germany. All interviews were audio-recorded, transcribed verbatim and anonymized by changing all names and places to protect the privacy of participants.

Additionally, photographs were used for visual elicitation. Images with a specific value for the relationship are particularly useful for participatory photo-elicitation (Harper 2002; Kolb 2000; Lapenta 2012; Lobinger 2016a). Therefore, we asked the participants to bring 3–5 photographs that were "meaningful" or "typical" for their relationship and to talk about them in the pair interviews.

Finally, all interviews were analyzed using HyperRESEARCH software to structure and code the data following the logic of qualitative thematic coding (Kuckartz 2014) with a combination of deductively and inductively created codes (Schreier 2014). Summaries of the interviews, analytic memos (Saldaña 2013) and respondents' and dyads' portraits served as first analytical steps. The participants' statements were attributed to main thematic categories deductively derived from the research questions, such as shared visuals, functions of visual practices, and the relevance of visual communication. These deductive thematic categories were then inductively specified, refined and complemented.

4 Findings: Visuals in communication repertoires

Overall, our participants referred to a broad range of motifs and types of pictures in their interactions with partners and friends; these included selfies, photos of landscapes, pets, food, children and friends, screenshots or images they found online. Moreover, the material forms of these photographs were highly diverse. Participants talked about using visual (digital) messaging, but also exchanging and conserving printed photographs – often self-representations as a couple or as friends. They also talked about putting a lot of effort into creating photo-themed gifts and objects, such as analogue photo books, bookmarks or mugs. In reviewing these heterogeneous communication repertoires and different ways of integrating pictures in everyday interactions, we first expand on how communication repertoires and routines of visual practices are established. We go on to discuss the functions of visuals in the relationships, highlighting their particular role in creating intimacy via shared moments and experiences.

4.1 Visuals in communication repertoires

4.1.1 Ritualization

Our results show that visual practices are highly ritualized. Respondents often have the same images in mind when they think of typical images they have taken and shared in their relationship, or when they refer to past conflicts regarding image handling. This ritualization implies that the respondents' routines have become rather "unquestioned", intuitive practices in their everyday lives. For example, Robert (26 years old) only becomes aware during the interview that it seems to be typical for him to document small "achievements" in everyday life with his smartphone and then send them to his girlfriend.

The routines and rituals of visual communication, and what the respondents describe as typical photos taken and shared in their relationship are molded by their overall communication repertoire, and by the established daily routines of interaction. In other words: visual communication practices are structured by personal preferences, (imagined) technological affordances and interpersonal media-selection and matching strategies.

4.1.2 Interpersonal media-selection: Personal preferences and technological affordances

The reasons for using/not using particular apps or Social Networking Sites differ depending on each relationship. For example, participants often mentioned practicality or simplicity of use in particular situations when explaining their switching between different platforms and apps to communicate and share pictures with each other. Moreover, these routines reflect personal preferences and normative attitudes regarding desirable or inappropriate ways of using media. Carsten, for example, refuses to take and remotely share photographs, even characterizing himself as an "anti-photo-person" (Carsten, 34, single interview). He is annoyed by people taking pictures and videos with their phones as he considers media devices and vernacular photography to be disturbing or distracting elements that hinder a direct experience of situations and events. This has important implications for how, when and to what intensity communication takes place in his relationship. His girlfriend Emma (30) has to adapt to his preferred mode of communication. Consequently, they don't reciprocally send photos in their everyday interactions. However, in the interviews it also became obvious that Emma, contrary to her boyfriend, is a highly visual person – a true "pro-photo-person". In fact, with other conversational partners she often shares photographs using a broad set of different technologies and outlets, such as blogs, photo sharing platforms, SNS, and messenger services for synchronous sharing. This example illustrates a general pattern across the interviews: the repertoire of visual communication within the relationship is usually downscaled to the needs and demands of the "less visual" person, while visual practices continue to play an important role in interactions with others.

Thus, on the one hand, repertoires of visual communication seem to reflect participants' personal preferences or subjective "media ideologies" and idioms of practices (Gershon 2010) – their normative views on acceptable media use and acceptable visual practice. On the other hand, communication repertoires and visual communication are also an outcome of interpersonal media selection. They are based on negotiations and the matching of preferences and repertoires with their partners (Höflich 2016: 51–53; Linke 2011). These negotiations are strongly affected by technological affordances of devices at hand, and by the perceived risks and advantages of taking and sharing pictures. This is, for example, the case in Robert and Kerstin's relationship. Both of them refer to Robert's smartphone as a "lame duck", and thus as a major obstacle that hinders their remote photo sharing. Moreover, due to Robert's "slight irrational fear" (Robert, 26, single interview) regarding data security and storage, the couple prefers exchanging digital photographs via a USB flash drive, especially when it comes to more intimate communication. Thus, interpersonal media selection leads to different modes of photo-sharing and to different ways of integrating visuals into interactions.

4.1.3 Modes of photo-sharing: Various ways to share images

Overall, pictures serve an important role in both couples' and friends' interactions. They describe photos as very emotional, playful, humorous and enriching elements of their communication repertoires, and thus as something they would miss in their relationships. However, the ways in which images are shared and integrated in everyday interactions differ drastically. While some respondents describe almost perpetual visual contact through visual messaging and chatting, others rarely send pictures, but rather predominantly share them in co-present, face-to-face interactions to stimulate talk. Emma and Carsten, for example, predominantly collect images they find online (e.g. on Buzzfeed), in order to show them to each other in person. They want to be able to directly observe and "co-experience" the partner's emotions and reactions. As Emma explained: "Because this feeling of sharing is important. That you see it [...]. When I laughed because of a picture, then I want to see that he deems it funny as well and that he is laughing. And I can't see that when I just send it." (Emma, pair interview). What she specifically underlines here is the value of a "real" synchronous gaze – a co-presently shared experience of reception and emotion. Other participants emphasize the strong links between conversations *with* photographs to conversations *about* photographs; quite often photos that were previously shared via Facebook or WhatsApp are taken up again later in face-to-face interactions.

4.2 Visual communication functions

These different ways of integrating pictures in everyday interactions notwithstanding, the overall functions of visuals in friends' and partners' interactions remain rather stable. The respondents specifically and predominantly foreground the use and exchange of images for creating a shared experience or experiencing something together, thus establishing a feeling of connectedness and closeness – be it a mediated quasi-synchronous gaze or the act of seeing together, while partners are physically present in the same place. Moreover, images as digital, but also tangible material objects, are described as valuable emotional resources and means for establishing and communicating a relationship.

4.2.1 Sharing moments and experiences

Visuals allow friends and couples to create and maintain social proximity, and to reassert their mutual bond. In this regard, respondents describe practices of remote photo-sharing as ways of "telling" or showing their everyday, humorous (and serious) experiences, and of keeping significant others informed. Sharing moments and impressions, and thus participating in each other's lives, is an important function of photographs for our respondents. They therefore often underline the specific capacities and benefits of visual communication, such as the emotional surplus values, the instant means of conveying personal experiences, and the ability to share these with the partner or friend. For example, Melanie (22) explained: "In my opinion pictures are there for sharing situations even though your partner is not present, to convey the feeling 'hey, this is just as if you were here right now'." In this way, visual communication seems to decrease social and physical distance between the participants as they allow for a simultaneity of experience and a "synchronous view".

Above all, the interviewees refer to sending a picture as an oftentimes *simple, quick and comfortable way of communicating and interacting*, as Anna exemplarily put it: "Sometimes things are difficult to explain or to summarize. I can give a three hours' detail description of how beautiful the scenery is right now. But through a picture it gets way clearer. Or when I don't have time, I just take a picture and send it." (Anna, 26, single interview). In this quote Anna particularly values general key characteristics of the visual mode. Thanks to their associative and holistic nature, photographs are experienced more intuitively than verbal texts with their linear logic. They can thus convey a certain atmosphere, a specific emotion or spatial relations more directly and effectively (Müller 2003).

Interestingly, however, both friends and couples frequently refer to shared pictures as "nonsense", as content with "no special meaning", while at the same time emphasizing the specific value of these visual "sweet little nothings" (Villi 2012) in their interactions. They refer to sharing selfies as a way of "actually seeing" the partner or friend, and of thus reasserting the relational bond through mediated presence: "when we do not meet and just write, it's just nice to be able to actually see him instead of just reading text messages". Even though a picture does not fully compensate for physical absence "it *creates closeness* – more than if we just communicate via messages" (Marc, 27, single interview). Everyday snapshot photographs and images found online also serve to reconfirm the special bond with a friend or partner. Everyday snapshots are shared in order to directly take up shared memories and situations they experienced together. Alternatively, they are chosen based on the knowledge of a person and, for example, their sense of humor. Here, again, the meaning of the image for the relationship cannot be found by looking at the visual content itself, but by looking at its other functions; namely, to reconfirm a mutual bond, and to maintaining interpersonal connection over distance.

4.2.2 Pictures as (material) emotional resources

For creating intimacy, pictures that "record" important events in the relationship of friends and partners are paramount and become valuable emotional resources. They serve as visual anchors and reference points that stimulate memories and evoke a more detailed and lively re-experience of a situation. In this regard, the respondents particularly underline the materiality of a picture as an important factor.

Speaking of the different visual resources in their relationship, the respondents refer to pictures in various material forms, such as printed, framed photographs, photo books, bookmarks, digitally shared photographs or key fobs. Printed photographs or photo-books allow for occasional "encounters" with them, for example with a quick glance at the wall or in a folder, and can be easily integrated in interactions: "I often come across it and then I look at it. So, these pictures really have a specific importance. Because I printed them out. I think if I had them on the computer, I would not do that." (Johannes, 28, single interview). The prominent position of certain pictures on the walls of living or sleeping rooms significantly supports the function of the visual object as visual anchor. This prominent place could also be a screensaver on a daily used device like the smartphone. But what the respondents foreground is the concreteness, the remaining tangibility of the visual object, that lasts "forever" (Sandra, 54, single interview). Digital visual material, in turn, is often described as being buried in the hard drive-"cemetery", as it is difficult to find. However, our respondents do not delete their digital visual libraries. They keep the entire visual depiction of their lives to enable its potential "browsability". Kerstin (26) for example describes the folder of shared photographs on WhatsApp as a kind of "diary". She sometimes scrolls through it, which enables her to recall and somehow contextualize activities and incidents.

When couples speak about their photos together and the specific contexts in which they were taken, they point to the important role of pictures and their distribution in the initial phase of the relationship. In this early phase, taking and sharing photographs are strong statements of belonging together – this practice serves to establish the relationship, as well as to communicate the establishment and maintenance of the relationship to others. Johannes, for example, described curated photographs, but especially incidental snapshots taken together with his partner, as statements and "proofs" for being a couple and for belonging together. These pictures thus require and show commitment to the relationship which makes them also an intimate and sensitive topic in the early stages. Usually, a first photo-opportunity and thus a true reason for taking a photo is necessary. Kerstin describes how she had taken advantage of the situation that she and her boyfriend dressed up as unicorns. This created a justified photo-opportunity to take the first picture together, enabling her to send it to all her friends and to show them her new boyfriend. Additionally, photographs and their publication were described as *performative acts* to state that a person is "taken." "Guys, that's it. Forget it. It has been settled as you can see" was Emma's implicit message when posting photos of her and Carsten to Facebook (Emma, single interview). Again, we see that taking and sharing photographs serve as strong statements of belonging together and to communicate the relationship to others.

5 Conclusion: Visual bonding and intimacy

In this chapter, we have examined visual practices in the communication repertoires of couples and friends in order to understand the role of visuals and of visual interactions in close personal relationships. This exploratory study points to the importance of visuals and visual interactions for creating, establishing and maintaining close relationships. In fact, visual practices and visual interactions were described as important and beneficial elements of all communication repertoires, despite the form and frequency of these practices being highly heterogeneous. In line with previous research on the social uses of (networked) photography we find that visuals and visual interaction are particularly useful for creating a shared experience and feeling of closeness and that photos serve as important memory objects. Moreover, they also serve functional uses, facilitate playful phatic communication, self-expression and self-representation. The repertoire-oriented approach enabled us to gain insights into the respondents' "media manifolds" and their complex, multimodal network of mediated and face-to-face interactions. Here the respondents specifically underscore the strong links between conversations *with* photographs to conversations *about* photographs. Moreover, the findings underline the need to also look at the material components of images (Gómez-Cruz & Lehmuskallio 2016) as well as the interrelations of digital and analog means of sharing to understand how visuals are integrated into everyday interactions.

Taking up Berger and Kellner's (1964) characterization of pair relationships as "ongoing conversations", serving to confirm and maintain the relationship, we can state that our respondents' conversations with their friends and partners are increasingly saturated with visuals. Overall, these findings clearly contrast mostly critical public discourses on negative implications of changing visual practices for social relationships. These debates predominantly criticize the vast amounts of shared pictures and the prevalence of "nonsense" and "worthless" images, as well as an increasing alienation from "actual reality" and (face-to-face) interactions with partners or friends. These scenarios, however, often lack a differentiated view on the multiple ways in which visuals are captured and used – symbolically and as material objects – in social interactions. As we have shown throughout this chapter, these practices serve important roles within communication repertoires in social relationships. We have illustrated how visuals and visual communication enable doing relationships, bonding, and help create and sustain intimacy. Despite the limiting fact that the study it is based on a small regional sample, it is a vantage point for further studies on the contexts, situational meanings and implications of visual interaction in social relationships.

References

Bayer, Joseph B., Nicole B. Ellison, Sarita Y. Schoenebeck & Emily B. Falk. 2016. Sharing the small moments: Ephemeral social interaction on Snapchat. *Information, Communication & Society* 19(7), 956–977.

Berger, Peter L., & Hansfried Kellner 1964. Marriage and the construction of reality: An exercise in the microsociology of knowledge. Diogenes 12(46), 1–24.

Bierhoff, Hans-Werner & Elke Rohmann. 2009. Persönliche Beziehungen aus sozialpsychologischer Sicht. In Karl Lenz & Frank Nestmann (eds.), *Handbuch Persönliche Beziehungen*, 49–74. Weinheim, München: Juventa.

Bjur, Jakob, Kim Christian Schrøder, Uwe Hasebrink, Cédric Courtois, Hanna Adoni & Hillel Nossek. 2014. Cross-media use: Unfolding complexities in contemporary audiencehood. In Nico Carpentier, Kim Christian Schrøder & Lawrie Hallet (eds.), *Audience transformations. Shifting audience positions in late modernity*, 15–29. London: Routledge.

Bourdieu, Pierre. 1990 [1965]. *Photography. A middle-brow art*. Oxford: Polity Press.

Caughlin, John P. & Liesel L. Sharabi. 2013. A communicative interdependence perspective of close relationships: The connections between mediated and unmediated interactions matter. *Journal of Communication* 63(5), 873–893.

Collier, John. 1957. Photography in anthropology: A report on two experiments. *American Anthropologist* 59(5), 843–859.

Dijck, José van. 2007. *Mediated memories in the digital age*. Standford, CA: Stanford University Press.

Duck, Steve. 1990. Relationships as unfinished business: Out of the frying pan and into the 1990s. *Journal of Social and Personal Relationships* 7(1), 5–28.

Gershon, Ilana. 2008. Email my heart: Remediation and romantic break-ups. *Anthropology Today* 24, 13–15.

Gershon, Ilana. 2010. The breakup 2.0. Disconnecting over new media. Cornell University: Cornell University Press.

Gómez-Cruz, Edgar & Asko Lehmuskallio (eds.). 2016. *Digital photography and everyday life. Empirical studies on material visual practices*. London: Routledge.

Gye, Lisa. 2007. Picture this: The impact of mobile camera phones on personal photographic practices. *Continuum* 21(2), 279–288.

Harper, Douglas. 2002. Talking about pictures: A case for photo elicitation. *Visual Studies* 17(1), 13–26.

Hasebrink, Uwe. 2015. Kommunikationsrepertoires und digitale Offentlichkeiten. In Oliver Hahn, Ralf Hohlfeld, & Thomas Knieper (eds.), *Digitale Offentlichkeit(en)*, 35–49. Konstanz: UVK.

Hepp, Andreas, Cindy Roitsch & Matthias Berg. 2016. Investigating communication networks contextually. Qualitative network analysis as cross-media research. *MedieKultur. Journal of media and communication research* 32(60), 87–106.

Höflich, Joachim R. 2016. *Der Mensch und seine Medien. Mediatisierte interpersonale Kommunikation. Eine Einführung*. Wiesbaden: Springer VS.

Katz, James E. & Elisabeth Thomas Crocker. 2015. Selfies and photo messaging as visual conversation: Reports from the United States, United Kingdom and China. *International Journal of Communication* 9, 1861–1872.

Keightley, Emily & Michael Pickering. 2014. Technologies of memory: Practices of remembering in analogue and digital photography. *New Media & Society* 16(4), 576–593.

Kindberg, Tim, Mirjana Spasojevic, Rowanne Fleck & Abigail Sellen. 2005. I saw this and thought of you: Some social uses of camera phones. In *CHI '05 Extended Abstracts on Human Factors in Computing Systems*, 1545–1548. New York, USA: ACM Press.

Kofoed, Jette & Marlene Larsen. 2016. A snap of intimacy: Photo-sharing practices among young people on social media. *First Monday* 21(11).

Kolb, Bettina. 2000. Involving, sharing, analysing – Potential of the participatory photo interview. *Forum Qualitative Sozialforschung / Forum: Qualitative Social Research* 9 (3). Available: http://www.qualitative-research.net/index.php/fqs/article/view/1155/2564. (28 February, 2019)

Kuckartz, Udo. 2014. *Qualitative Inhaltsanalyse. Methoden, Praxis, Computerunterstützung.* Weinheim: Beltz Juventa.

Kurvinen, Esko. 2003. Only when miss universe snatches me. In *Proceedings of the 2003 International Conference on Designing Pleasurable Products and Interfaces*, 98–102. New York: ACM Press.

Lapenta, Francesco. 2012. Some theoretical and methodological views on photo-elicitation. In Eric Margolis & Luc Pauwels (eds.), *The SAGE Handbook of Visual Research Methods*, 201–213. London: Sage.

Licoppe, Christian. 2004. "Connected" presence: The emergence of a new repertoire for managing social relationships in a changing communication technoscape. *Environment and Planning D: Society and Space* 22(1), 135–156.

Ling, Rich, & Birgitte Yttri. 2002. Hyper-coordination via mobile phones in Norway. In James E. Katz & Mark Aakhus (eds.), *Perpetual contact: Mobile communication, private talk, public performance*, 139–169. Cambridge: Cambridge University Press.

Linke, Christine. 2010. *Medien im Alltag von Paaren. Eine Studie zur Mediatisierung der Kommunikation in Paarbeziehungen.* Wiesbaden: VS Verlag für Sozialwissenschaften.

Linke, Christine. 2011. Being a couple in a media world: The mediatization of everyday communication in couple relationships. *Communications* 36(1), 91–111.

Lobinger, Katharina. 2012. *Visuelle Kommunikationsforschung. Medienbilder als Herausforderung für die Kommunikations-und Medienwissenschaft.* Wiesbaden: Springer VS.

Lobinger, Katharina. 2016a. "Creative" and participatory visual approaches in audience research. In Sebastian Kubitschko & Anne Kaun (eds.), *Innovative methods in media and communication research*, 293–309. London: Palgrave Macmillan.

Lobinger, Katharina. 2016b. Photographs as things – photographs of things. A texto-material perspective on photo-sharing practices. *Information, Communication & Society* 19(4), 475–488.

Lobinger, Katharina & Maria Schreiber. 2017. Photo Sharing – Visuelle Praktiken des Mit-Teilens. In Katharina Lobinger (ed.), *Handbuch Visuelle Kommunikationsforschung*, 1–22. Wiesbaden: Springer Fachmedien.

Madianou, Mirca & Daniel Miller. 2013. Polymedia: Towards a new theory of digital media in interpersonal communication. *International Journal of Cultural Studies* 16(2), 169–187.

Mäkelä, Ann, Verena Giller, Manfred Tscheligi & Reinhard Sefelin. 2000. Joking, storytelling, artsharing, expressing affection. In *Proceedings of the SIGCHI Conference on Human Factors in Computing Systems*, 548–555. New York: ACM Press.

Miguel, Cristina. 2016. Visual intimacy on social media: From selfies to the co-construction of intimacies through shared pictures. *Social Media + Society* 2(2), 1–10.

Müller, Marion G. 2003. *Grundlagen der Visuellen Kommunikation: Theorieansätze und Methoden.* Konstanz: UVK.

Parks, Malcolm R. 2017. Embracing the challenges and opportunities of mixed-media relationships. *Human Communication Research* 43(4), 505–517.

Prieto-Blanco, Patricia. 2016. (Digital) photography, experience and space in transnational families. A case study of Spanish-Irish families living in Ireland. In Asko Lehmuskallio & Edgar Gómez Cruz (eds.), *Digital photography and everyday life*, 122–141. New York: Routledge.

Rubinstein, Daniel & Katrina Sluis. 2008. A life more photographic. *Photographies* 1(1), 9–28.

Saldaña, Johnny. 2013. *The coding manual for qualitative researchers.* London: Sage.

Sarvas, Risto & David M. Frohlich. 2011. *From snapshots to social media – The changing picture of domestic photography*. London: Springer.

Schreiber, Maria. 2017. Audiences, aesthetics and affordances. Analysing practices of visual communication on social media. *Digital Culture and Society* 3(2), 143–163.

Schreier, Margrit. 2014. Qualitative content analysis. In Uwe Flick (ed.), *The SAGE handbook of qualitative data analysis*, 170–183. London: Sage.

Taneja, Harsh, James G. Webster, Edward C. Malthouse & Thomas B. Ksiazek. 2012. Media consumption across platforms: Identifying user-defined repertoires. *New Media & Society* 14(6), 951–968.

Van House, Nancy, Marc Davis, Yuri Takhteyev, Nathan Good, Anita Wilhelm & Megan Finn. 2004. From "what?" to "why?": The social uses of personal photos. Available: http://citeseerx.ist.psu.edu/viewdoc/summary?doi=10.1.1.123.1321 (28 February, 2019)

Van House, Nancy, Marc Davis, Morgan Ames, Megan Finn & Vijay Viswanathan. 2005. The uses of personal networked digital imaging. In *CHI '05 Extended Abstracts on Human Factors in Computing Systems*, 1853–1856. New York: ACM Press.

Vainikka, Eliisa, Elina Noppari, & Janne Seppänen. 2017. Exploring tactics of public intimacy on Instagram. *Participations. Journal of Audience & Reception Studies* 14(1), 108–128.

Vaterlaus, Mitchell J., Kathryn Barnett, Cesia Roche & Jimmy A. Young. 2016. "Snapchat Is more personal": An exploratory study on Snapchat behaviors and young adult interpersonal relationships. *Computers in Human Behavior* 62, 594–601.

Venema, Rebecca & Katharina Lobinger. 2017. "And somehow it ends up on the Internet." Agency, trust and risks in photo-sharing among friends and romantic partners. *First Monday* 22(7).

Villi, Mikko. 2012. Visual chitchat: The use of camera phones in visual interpersonal communication. *Interactions: Studies in Communication & Culture* 3(1), 39–54.

Villi, Mikko. 2015. "Hey, I'm here right now": Camera phone photographs and mediated presence. *Photographies* 8(1), 3–22.

Villi, Mikko. 2016. Photographs of Place in phonespace: Camera phones as a location-aware mobile technology. In Edgar Gómez Cruz & Asko Lehmuskallio (eds.), *Digital photography and everyday life. Empirical studies on material visual practices*, 107–121.

Villi, Mikko & Matteo Stocchetti. 2011. Visual mobile communication, mediated presence and the politics of space. *Visual Studies* 26(2), 102–112.

Weilenmann, Alexandra, Thomas Hillman & Beata Jungselius. 2013. Instagram at the museum: Communicating the museum experience through social photo sharing. *Proceedings of the SIGCHI Conference on Human Factors in Computing Systems*, 1843–1852.

Part 3: **Designing multimodal texts**

Hartmut Stöckl
9 Multimodality and mediality in an image-centric semiosphere – A rationale

1 An image-centric semiosphere

If we interpret Lotman's idea of semiosphere (Lotman, 1990) as the total of a community's semiotic modes, genre repertoires and media, we might safely argue that contemporary communication has been going through a phase of growing image-centricity (Stöckl, Caple & Pflaeging 2020). This is reflected in the common-sense observation that the number of images in popular mass and social media has dramatically increased (52 mill. images per day in Instagram, cf. Caple 2019: 428).

However, the concept of image-centricity set out here comprises two specific notions that focus not on images in isolation as encapsulated in the idea of visual communication (Müller & Geise 2015) but in their multimodal relations to text, i.e. text-image relations (Bateman 2014a), in concrete genres. First, image centricity implies the compositional and perceptual dominance of the image over text on the page or the screen. This entails that layout structures, image size and quality deploy images as perceptual entry points to reading paths and cognitive points of departure for the construal of multimodal meaning. Second, not only are images formally and structurally dominant, they are also semantically central in that they constitute independent nuclei of (story) meaning that can lead a text, become its conceptual core and the object of verbal commentary and interpretation. This notion of image-nuclearity has been developed by Caple (2008, 2013) in relation to news writing and posits that a large, aesthetically pleasing leading image combines with a headline and extended caption to tell an independent story. It can also be seen at work in non-news media such as in popular science writing, advertising or social media posts.

Such a shift in the semiotic landscape towards images as central message components rather than peripheral, negligible illustrations has a number of catalysts. On the one hand, old media development was driven by technological innovations that have facilitated and intensified the production and efficient distribution of high quality images. This has led to a greater reliance on images for the sensorially and experientially rich representation of reality. On the other hand, social media have recently spurred the development of image-centricity as they allow for the easy and intense sharing of pictorial content – still and moving. Share-ability as a functional-technological affordance of social media (cf. Eisenlauer 2016: 443–447) has in turn facilitated a number of sociocommunicative trends (cf. Adami & Jewitt 2016: 265–267). The habitual sharing of visual material promotes re-signification or re-contextualization practices and the emergence of new genres and communicative practices. The logic of sharing offers a huge potential for "self-expression and identity construction" (Adami & Jewitt 2016: 266) as each visual snippet comes as an index of who the sender is socio-culturally and media-aesthetically. But in this interesting mix of public and private text production that social media offer, users also engage in more or less explicit textual evaluation of the "things" they post in the form of visual representations. In this sense image-centric media (old and new) can be seen as particularly potent engines for the manufacture and display of public opinion, which lend themselves to the study of "multi-semiotic affiliative and distancing strategies" (Caple 2019: 444).

The present chapter proposes an explanation of image-centricity as a vital concept in multimodality research (cf. sect. 2) and reflects on its media and genre implications. Rather than see image-centricity as a structural property of text exemplars and genres alone, I suggest that image-centric practices are facilitated and shaped by the functional and relational affordances of media such as printed or online magazines and social media like Twitter and Instagram (cf. sect. 3). It is these medial affordances that allow for "assembling/organizing/designing a plurality of signs in different modes into a particular configuration to form a coherent arrangement" (Kress 2010: 162). Therefore, different types of media may likely produce different types of image-centric genres or practices. The chapter concludes by offering a very brief, rough and ready rationale for studying image-centric media and communication (cf. sect. 4).

2 Image-centricity and text-image relations

The essence of multimodal text and communication is usually seen in "meaning multiplication" (Bateman 2014a: 6) and mode integration within a functional discourse act. This means that text and image for instance both contribute to the overall meaning by forming a structural, discursive and rhetorical whole whose individual semantic contributions cohere (cf. Bateman 2014b) and may be multiplied in the multimodal combination. Such a view generally assumes an equality and balance of modes, which is based on their "mutual elaboration" (Jewitt, Bezemer & O'Halloran 2016: 91) and complementarity or synergy (Royce 1998). Image-centricity, by contrast, implies an imbalance of modes in terms of which of the modes leads the overall message or which of the modes has more "modal intensity" or "weight" (Norris 2014: 90) in the multimodal ensemble. Image-centricity or the reverse case of verbiage-centricity then can be conceptualized as different directionalities of mutual mode elaboration (from image to text or vice versa) or different semantic-functional hierarchies (image superordinate, text subordinate or vice versa). This notion is in fact a rather well-worn one, which in systemic-functional approaches to text-image relations (Martinec & Salway 2005) is captured as relative "status" of the modes, which can be equal or unequal (cf. Figure 9.1). Status in turn derives from Barthes' early ideas on the subject (Barthes 1977 [1964]), which have become known as the terminological pair of "anchorage", and "illustration" for unequal status relations and "relay" for equal ones. Image-centricity, then translates as unequal status relations with language anchoring, i.e. commenting on and explaining a central and leading image in its entirety. In illustration as the verbiage-centric configuration of modes, a superordinate text leads the image(s), which merely elaborate(s) parts of the text (such as emoji in a social media post or a set of illustrative images in a longer feature article).

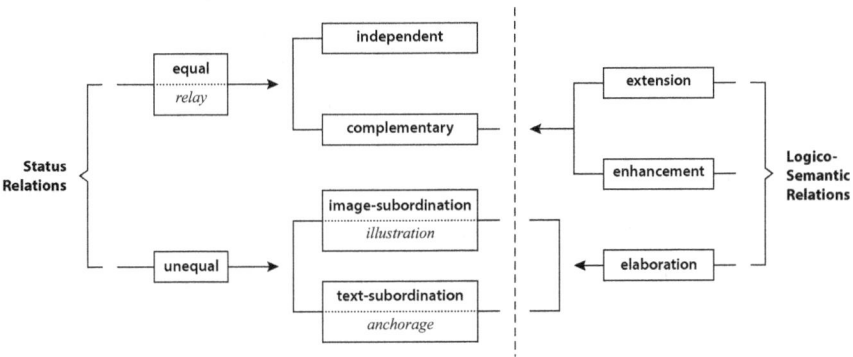

Figure 9.1: A system of status and logico-semantics in text-image relations.

Figures 9.2 and 9.3 provide suitable examples to demonstrate the difference. Both are about popular science content, the first constitutes a self-sufficient "photo of the day" story (cf. Stöckl 2020), which Caple (2008) generally labels "image-nuclear news story"; the latter is a "story intro" (cf. Stöckl 2020) that announces and leads into a story. In terms of the images' perceptual and compositional dominance, both multimodal genres would qualify as image-centric. The viewer cannot but be drawn into the pictorial content and led by it in the overall meaning-making.

However, regarding the semantic centrality of the image, only the text in figure 9.2 is a true case of an image-lead "anchorage", whereas the text in figure 9.3 exemplifies "illustration", i.e. a text leading a subordinate image, which only relates to parts of the text. The "photo of the day" text (Figure 9.2) describes what is in the image and provides related information not depicted in it. Caple (2013: 130–137) has labelled these two functions of accompanying text in image-centric genres "experiential orientation" (*green space nestles between enormous apartment complexes*) and "contextual extension" (*one of the most crowded places on earth, 7 million people living in 427 square miles*). The image is superordinate and leads the text as all info provided in the caption directly relates to, explicates or comments on the image. In the story intro (Figure 9.3) by contrast the text has a leading status as it provides the main information (*indestructible animals survive apocalypse*) and points to an element in the grammatical structure of the statement, which the image visualizes (*these animals*).

Photo of the Day

JULY 14, 2017

DOWN BELOW Green space nestles between enormous apartment complexes in Hong Kong. Hong Kong is one of the most crowded places on earth, with more than 7 million people living in 427 square miles.

PHOTOGRAPH BY ANDY YEUNG, NATIONAL GEOGRAPHIC YOUR SHOT

Figure 9.2: An image-centric story with a nuclear image – National Geographic Online 14-07-2017.

The major semantic descriptors in image-centricity, then are "leading", "superordinate" mode, a "directionality" of multimodal meaning construal from image to text and the idea that one mode functions as a "matrix structure", into which the info provided in the other mode will need to be slotted. An image can lead in the sense of drawing attention to it first and being the cognitive anchor that requires textual specification and commentary. Being the superordinate mode means an image will provide the most general, all-embracing and most newsworthy information of the multimodal ensemble with text merely representing subordinate parts of this message core. Both "leading" and superordinate' entail a directionality of meaning construal with a point of departure located in the central mode. The idea of a matrix mode, finally, suggests that it is the grammar and information design of the central mode that delivers an organizational structure into which elements of the subordinate, peripheral mode must be integrated. In the first sample (cf. Figure 9.2) the caption's lexis slots into the visual structure of the image; in the second sample (cf. Figure 9.3) the image clearly integrates into the sentence structure of the headline.

Figure 9.3: An image-centric story intro with a nuclear text – National Geographic Online 14-07-17.

Mode status in text-image relations has also been linked to logico-semantic relations (cf. Figure 9.1). The general idea posited for image- or text-centricity is mutual mode elaboration, i.e. text (as in Figure 9.2) restating, specifying or generalizing the central image or the image of the animal (as in Figure 9.3) elaborating the headline's message.

Even if status relations are equal, some mode elaboration must be in progress for a multimodal message to be constructed as long as the modes are complementary, i.e. one mode adding info that extends the info of the other ("extension") or qualifies it circumstantially ("enhancement"). Image-centricity – just like complementary, equal text-image relations – most essentially requires elements in both semiotic modes, text and image, that can create inter-semiotic cohesive ties or act as cues for the construal of multimodal coherence. In the absence of explicit links between the modes (inter-semiotic sense relations, e.g. Figure 9.2: *down below, green space, apartment complexes*; deictic elements, e.g. Figure 9.3: *these animals*) such coherence, Bateman (2014b: 157–163) argues, can mainly be derived from discourse semantic and rhetorical relations.

The shift towards image-centricity seems a plausible move to make in present-day media environments of info overload and attention inertia. Essentially it entails a "multimodal nuclearization" (Stöckl 2020), i.e. a consistent combination of a story's informative nucleus in the form of headline or extended caption with a leading and central image. From the point of view of the text producer, dominant and central images increase the visual salience of the message's nucleus of information.

Consequently, the reader will ideally be oriented and attracted to the image and its story-nuclear information. If a medium is generally structured along such image-nuclear messages (as in news-site or social media), it allows faster traversal (cf. Knox 2007: 48) and efficient selectivity for the user. In the long run and extreme case, image-centric media might turn into atomized (Knox 2007: 19) visual tableaus (cf. Twitter walls, Instagram feeds), i.e. image-centric offers of short story nuclei that provide less discursive or argumentative content but a strong technologically motivated option to share, comment on and interactively develop it in "communicative act sequences" (Jucker & Dürscheid 2012).

A theory of image-centricity also confronts problems. They concern the inter-relation between visual dominance and semantic centrality. Following the general dictum that "layout affect(ed) the relationship between image and writing" (Jewitt, Bezemer & O'Halloran 2016: 80), it may be that text-image relations are construed as image-centric even though the images do not provide the nucleus of information. In other words, where language and text are supposed to be subordinated and led by an image, it may after all be the little language there is that has the most semantic impact. Generally, there may be an apparent rift between deployed, structural status relations and reconstructed or inferred ones. This means that any analysis would have to be sensitive to both the typology and descriptive categories of text-image relations as well as the semiotic work "these relationships are intended to do" (Bateman 2014a: 47).

3 Image-centric (genre) practices and medial differences

3.1 Functional and relational affordances of media

It is my general assumption here that image-centric practices are diverse and may crucially be determined by the affordances of the medium used. This would entail that image-centricity materializing in the mainstream mass media magazine or newspaper (e.g. a multimodal feature article or news report) differs from the one in new/social media like Instagram and Twitter (e.g. posts). These prototypical examples will serve here as representing old-style printed media and computer mediated communication (CMC), respectively. The envisaged enterprise of teasing out likely tendencies in the ways image-centric practices are used and will develop from underlying medial affordances – both technological/functional as well as situational/relational – is fraught with difficulties. This is because, first, changes in the design and affordances of CMC are happening swiftly and lead to a great diversification and mixing of available formats and signing/interacting options.

Generalizations about such a "moving target" (Locher 2014: 557) are inherently difficult and cannot but simplify things that are more complex in reality. Second, we must be cautious not to endorse a crude technological determinism (cf. Page et al. 2014: 15) by assuming that features of the medium directly produce and correlate with social-semiotic practices. The more adequate view would see image-centric genre practices as shaped by medial factors and, as a result, as medially predisposed to perform certain communicative tasks more effectively than others. Ultimately, however, what users really do with available affordances of a medium is influenced by a whole host of situational factors and personal/institutional preferences. The argument developed here seeks to determine the scope of image-centric design options in relation to aspects of the medium and the communicative situation.

Placing text-image relations in the context of media development is one little step towards answering the "call for an incorporation of (...) multi-modality in the CMC research toolkit" (Locher 2014: 563 – referring to Thurlow & Mroczek 2011: ix/xxv). Based on the idea of technological/functional and relational affordances of media (cf. Eisenlauer 2016: 444), Herring (2007) has developed a classification scheme for CMC that is based on medial and situational factors. I will draw on a majority of these factors in order to first compare old mass/print media to new/social media. Notable medial and situational differences will then be used to sketch ways in which image-centric (genre) practices are likely to diverge in both media.

3.2 Medial and situational factors – print vs. social media

(1) Synchronicity as a hallmark of much CMC is clearly afforded by social media even though platforms do not totally rely on real-time "communicative act sequences" (Jucker & Dürscheid 2012: 46). Social media have generally increased the potential rapidity of the interaction, in turn producing ever bigger streams of "data", which pose questions to a *persistence* of the text archives (cf. Page et al 2014: 18). In any case, social media outperform old media in terms of speed and recency of information, whereas the material persistence still seems responsible for a credibility bonus of print. *(2) Message transmission* and *participation structure* characterize social media as tools that allow users to form large groups which collaboratively and interactively communicate and share messages in all directions and group constellations (one-to-one, one-to-many, many-to-many). The dialogic and co- constructed nature of social media communication contrasts starkly with the essentially unidirectional mass communication of magazines and newspapers. A high degree of intertextuality, mutual thematic responsivity and general media convergence are facilitated by social media. In terms of *(3) message size*, an odd paradox emerges: while text size is restricted in some social media (e.g. Twitter) and generally tends towards brevity in collapsed contexts (Wesch 2009), the participation structure allows for the potentially endless exchange of communicative act sequences and sharing of exported media fragments. What's more, embedded audio and video files extend the size of the messages despite textual limitations. Printed media, on the other hand have always battled with constraints on message size but have offered writers formatted spaces to systematically and explicitly develop their ideas on a given subject in the quietude of asynchronous writing. Local brevity, easy multimodal expendability and message interactivity in social media contrast with sizeable, elaborate and monologic messages in old/print media.

In Herring's framework (Herring 2007), medium is most closely characterized by the two factors *(4) channel* and *message format*. The first relates to the semiotic modes used in the communication; the second one to publishing architectures such as layouts, and templates (cf. Page et al 2014: 16–28). In terms of modes, print is infinitely poorer than social media as the latter essentially allows for most modes and their flexible manipulation – in this sense, we can speak of media richness (Kaplan & Haenlein 2009). As for message formats, both media face their own constraints: print media favour spatial order, thematic sectioning and textual/genre closure, while social media have been shown to favour recency and ranking of information as well as temporal/linear interactive sequences and a blurring/mixing of formats (Page et al. 2014: 17). *(5) Privacy settings, anonymity,* and *participant characteristics* all relate to the user's display and "self-disclosure" (Page et al. 2014: 13) of his socio-cultural status to co-communicators. Whereas anonymous printed mass media communication caters its strategically selected content to targeted socio-demographic groups, social media users can negotiate to whom they want to be visible (cf. semi-public, semi-private), and how much of their identity (cf. profiles) they like to disclose. Self-disclosure in old style, mainstream mass media interestingly concerns stances taken and evaluations made in relation to story content, which may be expressive of media ideologies. Finally, *(6) purpose, topic, tone* and *norms* – all situational factors – primarily describe content aspects. Much variation seems possible here and the criteria seem less suited to teasing out medial differences, however, some valid generalizations can be made. Magazines and newspapers mainly *relate* or *explain* (topical) information, whereas Twitter and Instagram predominantly *share, re-contextualize* and *comment* on such information.

The topic-diversity on social media and its mash-up potential is virtually infinite; mass/print media usually focus on certain neatly delineated special interest subjects (e.g. politics, sports, cooking) and structure these systematically. The tone as set by the linguistic/visual choices can differ greatly in both types of media, however, interactive, dialogue-oriented CMC tends to be more informal, fragmented and less elaborate/explicit than printed prose. While it is the users in social media that can re-negotiate their own communicative practices, these are set by institutions and policed by style guides in classic print media, only to be overturned in times of strategic, re-positioning or re-launching make-overs.

3.3 Types of image-centricity in different media – hypotheses

What follows from these media-differentiating observations for likely trends in the multimodal design of image-centric genres? Reconnecting to the framework set out above I will sketch five hypotheses. First, image-centric practices in social media will be more versatile and changeable than in old media owing to the collaborative sharing of material that originates from a mix of other media and is selected by diverse users with multiple semiotic tastes and communicative experiences. Classic magazines and newspapers, on the other hand, will develop more stable, media-distinct image-centric practices that can be linked to the careful planning of professional authors and inert institutional norms. Transmission and participation structure also predispose new-media image-centricity to operate in shared but implicit or collapsed contexts, whereas old-media image-centricity must explicate contexts more closely.

Second, the richness of semiotic modes in social media will favour a generally stronger dominance and centrality of the images in its multimodal practices. Image-type diversity will be higher than in old media, where certain genres have been shown to favour fixed image-types (Stöckl & Pflaeging 2018: 117–119). Also, the heavy sharing of visual material from all kinds of media increases this diversity and makes the selected image/video the nucleus of the post, which encourages short verbal commentaries in potentially long communicative act sequences. In contrast to social media, the message formats of old media allow for flexible layouts and varying image-size; they also allocate sufficient space for longer captions or accompanying text as part of a whole genre convention.

Third, privacy settings and anonymity but also the general social purpose of social media will lead to image-centric practices where images primarily serve to mediate aspects of the users' everyday experiences to be commented on in the verbal texts of the posts. Rather than come inscribed with strategic evaluative stances, the images and their cumulative choice are indexical of the tastes, habits and preferences of the users. By posting and sharing visual material they disclose aspects of their personality and can use their image-choices – just like the settings of their profiles and anonymity – for a more or less subtle impression management. Image-centricity in old media strategically selects images for their evaluative stance in relation to particular stories, which can be reinforced or commented on in captions and accompanying text. So rather than stand for themselves as reality/media fragments, old-media images serve to inscribe views of media institutions in a market of social groups and corresponding opinions.

Fourth, image-centric practices in new/social media will be crucially shaped by an availability of modal richness (cf. above) on the one hand and locally restricted linguistic message size such as in tweets, for instance, on the other. This means that text-image relations in social media focus on the central image as a deliberately selected and re-contextualized visual with strong self-sufficiency. Verbal commentary must consequently be oriented towards re-signifying practices, which develop in the course of interactive and mutually responsive co-constructing meaning-making in the form of communicative act sequences. In old media, by contrast, modal poverty is offset by the classic extended caption or any accompanying text directly relating to the image in an act of systematically explaining and extending the pictorial context and tying the text-image relation into the thematic structure of an entire text/genre. More specifically, then, old-media image-centricity must be prone to prioritize experiential orientation, whereas social media are likely to predominantly engage in contextual extension in the way of an evaluative commentary.

Fifth, given that social media's message formats favour recency, ranking, interactivity and content mixing, the content continuity of its image-centric practices will tend to be low as compared with old media. User communities quickly move from one topical subject to the next hardly elaborating and systematizing content (the platforms might do post-hoc). Old media's technological and situational publishing framework by comparison supports the consistent elaboration of one topic over a longer time and in structural depth and detail.

4 Conclusions – implications for multimodal research

Based on an explanation of image-centricity as a hallmark of current mediascapes, this brief chapter has set out a differential portrait of old and new/social media comparing their potential for different types of image-centricity. In accounts of differences between older forms of social media (e.g. SMS/1984) and more recent ones (e.g. Twitter/2006, Instagram/2010) scholars have cautioned against overemphasizing the novelty of CMC-formats and their linguistic/semiotic features (Locher 2014: 561). Herring (2013) has used the term "familiar" to describe phenomena in new/social media that are not genuinely new but were already applied in older media. Image-centricity clearly appears to be one such long-familiar phenomenon, which perhaps is being "reconfigured" (cf. Herring 2013) in social media. Medial traits that have facilitated such a reconfiguration would seem to be the easy share-ability of convergent media content and its resignification through posting as well as the co-constructed, collaborative nature of meaning-making with its fast turnover of messages and quick recycling of existing patterns. If we were to posit image-centricity as a multimodal universal, we could argue that recent media development has merely intensified it and diversified its practices. Genuinely new or "emergent" (cf. Herring 2013) image-centric practices, on the other hand, seem rare and are only likely to develop based on new technological affordances, primarily those that derive from software or platform architecture, such as new image-making technology or easier ways of superimposing text on an image or inserting new audio in film. Emojis appear to be a genuinely new/emergent semiotic mode and come as the most prototypical manifestation of what Herring & Dainas (2017) call "graphicons". Technological affordances of new/social media have made the integration of these schematized, pictographic icons into keyboard-to-screen writing effortless, and thus a new multimodal practice started to develop. While not necessarily leading to image-centricity as discussed here, it will most certainly increase the complementarity of text and image as emojis take over numerous functions in relation to text (cf. Herring & Dainas 2017). The first part of the present book thus rightly puts emoji use centre-stage.

To conclude, we might ask which directions multimodal research into different forms of image-centricity could profitably take. Based on the hypotheses about differences in old- and new/social-media forms of image centricity, it will be useful to look at:
1) change vs. stability of image-centric practices in one medium over time
2) image-type diversity
3) layout-patterns in text-image relations
4) evaluative stances taken or impression management through image selection
5) re-signifying/re-contextualizing practices
6) distribution and linguistic realization of experiential orientation and contextual extension in captions/posts
7) story development or unfolding of communicative act sequences with regard to thematic continuity

Whatever the focus, the present chapter suggests a multimodal research agenda that links concrete practices such as image-centric patterns to medial and situational characteristics and looks at the practices as emerging from and being shaped by them. Stöckl and Pflaeging 2018 propose and illustrate an integrated toolkit for multimodal analysis, which takes a potentially wide perspective and includes:
1) profiles of genres (or practices) typical in one medium or communicative form,
2) their prototypical layout- and thematic structures
3) image-types and their repertoires
4) systematic relations between genre types and image-types (allowing statements about "illustration intensity" and "illustration diversity")
5) text-image relations (for a detailed toolkit, cf. Stöckl 2020)

References

Adami, Elisabetta & Carey Jewitt. 2016. Special Issue: Social media and the visual. *Visual Communication* 15(3), 263–270.
Barthes, Roland. 1977 (1964). The rhetoric of the image. In *Image, Music, Text*, 32–51. London: Fontana.
Bateman, John A. 2014a. *Text and image: A Critical introduction to the visual/verbal divide*. London: Routledge.
Bateman, John A. 2014b. Multimodal coherence research and its applications. In Helmut Gruber & Gisela Redeker (eds.), *Pragmatics of discourse coherence: Theories and applications*, 145–175. Amsterdam: Benjamins.
Caple, Helen. 2019. "Lucy says she is a Labradoodle": How the dogs-of-Instagram reveal voter preferences. *Social Semiotics* 29(4), 427–447.
Caple, Helen. 2013. *Photojournalism: A social semioticapproach*. Basingstoke & New York: Palgrave Macmillan.
Caple, Helen. 2008. Intermodal relations in image-nuclear news stories. In Len Unsworth (ed.), *Multimodal semiotics. Functional analysis in the contexts of education*, 125–138. London: Continuum.
Eisenlauer, Volker. 2016. Facebook als multimodaler Gesamttext. In Nina-Maria Klug & Hartmut Stöckl (eds.), *Handbuch Sprache im multimodalen Kontext*, 437–454. Berlin & Boston: de Gruyter.
Herring, Susan C. 2013. Discourse in web 2.0: Familiar, reconfigured, and emergent. In Deborah Tannen & Anna Marie Trester (eds.), *Georgetown University Round Table on Languages and Linguistics 2011: Discourse 2.0: Language and New Media*, 1–25. Washington, DC: Georgetown University Press.
Herring, Susan C. 2007. A faceted classification scheme for computer-mediated discourse. *language@internet4* (www.languageatinternet.de)
Herring, Susan C. & Ashley Dainas. 2017. "Nice picture comment!" Graphicons in Facebook comment threads. *Proceedings of the Fiftieth Hawaii International Conference on System Sciences (HICSS-50)*. Los Alamitos, CA: IEEE.
Jewitt, Carey, Jeff Bezemer & Kay O'Halloran. 2016. *Introducing multimodality*. London & New York: Routledge.
Jucker, Andreas H. & Christa Dürscheid. 2012. The linguistics of keyboard-to-screen communication: A new terminological framework. *Linguistik Online* 56(6/12), 39–64.
Kaplan, Andreas M. & Michael Haenlein. 2009. Users of the world unite! The challenges and opportunities of social media. *Business Horizons*, 53, 59–68.
Knox, John. 2007. Visual-verbal communication on online newspaper homepages. *Visual Communication*, 6(1), 19–53.
Kress, Gunther. 2010. *A social semiotic approach to contemporary communication*. London & New York: Routledge.
Locher, Miriam. 2014. Electronic discourse. In Klaus P. Schneider & Anne Barron (eds.), *Pragmatics of Discourse*, 555–581. Berlin/Boston: de Gruyter.
Lotman, Yuri. 1990. Über die Semiosphäre. *Zeitschrift für Semiotik* 12(4). 287–305.
Martinec, Radan & Andrew Salway. 2005. A system for image-text relations in new (and old) media. *Visual Communication* 4(3), 337–371.

Müller, Marion G. & Stephanie Geise. 2015. *Grundlagen der Visuellen Kommunikation*. Konstanz: UVK.

Norris, Sigrid. 2014. Modal density and modal configurations. In Carey Jewitt (ed.), *The Routledge Handbook of Multimodal Analysis*, 86–99. London & New York: Routledge.

Page, Ruth, David Barton, Johann W. Unger & Michele Zappavigna. 2014. *Researching language and social media. A student guide*. London & New York: Routledge.

Royce, Terry D. 1998. Synergy on the page: Exploring intersemiotic complementarity in page-based multimodal text. *JASFL Occasional Papers* 1(1), 25–48.

Stöckl, Hartmut. 2020. Image-Centricity – When visuals take centre stage. Analyses and interpretations of a current (news) media practice. In Hartmut Stöckl, Helen Caple & Jana Pflaeging (eds.), *Shifts toward image-centricity in contemporary multimodal practices*, 19–41. New York: Routledge.

Stöckl, Hartmut, Helen Caple & Jana Pflaeging (eds.). 2020. *Shifts toward image-centricity in contemporary multimodal practices*. New York: Routledge.

Stöckl, Hartmut & Jana Pflaeging. 2018. Populärwissenschaftliche Magazine der Geisteswissenschaften als Gegenstand der medienvergleichenden und multimodalen Textlinguistik. In Martin Luginbühl & Juliane Schröter (eds.), *Geisteswissenschaften und Öffentlichkeit – linguistisch betrachtet*, 107–138. Bern: Lang.

Thurlow, Crispin & Kristine Mroczek. 2011. Introduction: Fresh perspectives on new media sociolinguistics. In Crispin Thurlow and Kristine Mroczek (eds.), *Digital discourse: Language in the new media*, xix–xxiv. Oxford: Oxford University Press.

Wesch, Michael. 2009. YouTube and you: Experiences of self-awareness in the context collapse of the recording webcam. *Explorations in Media Ecology* 8(2), 19–34.

Lara Portmann
10 Designing "good taste": A social semiotic analysis of corporate Instagram practices

1 Introduction

Food is an essential part of life. It is also a well-known site where judgements about 'good taste' are employed for boundary-marking and class status maintenance. Today, much of this plays out through social media, where food is one of the most popular topics (Hu, Manikonda & Kambhampati 2014). With its strong emphasis on images, the photo-sharing platform Instagram is a perfect example of this practice. Food itself is, of course, a multisensory phenomenon and therefore inherently multimodal. Eating is rarely just about gustatory taste: the look, smell, and texture of a dish are often equally important. In a broader sense, as Bourdieu (1984: 5) famously notes, taste and notions of "good taste" are matters of social distinction and status, taking shape through the "primacy of forms over function, of manner over matter". It is with this in mind that this chapter presents a social semiotic analysis of the corporate uses of Instagram by Switzerland's two major supermarket chains, *Coop* (www.instagram.com/coop.ch/) and *Migros* (www.instagram.com/migros/). In the context of a larger study (Portmann 2018), my objective in this chapter is two-fold. First, I document the on-the-ground, everyday ways these corporations visualize and construct the social meanings of food/eating, with a view to how otherwise privileged foodways may be normalized (cf. Mapes 2018). As such, I seek to address how social media – for all their claims to participatory democracy (e.g. Loader & Mercea 2011) – effectively reinforce social hierarchies of taste. Second, and along these lines, my analysis speaks to the way in which the social construction of elite status is an inherently multimodal endeavour, following the work of Thurlow & Jaworski (e.g. 2017). In this regard, I am interested in the "division of labour" (van Leeuwen 2008; Kress 2010) between different semiotic modes in Instagram posts, and the role played by visual resources – most obviously the photos – in avowing or disavowing privilege.

2 Visualizing food and 'good taste'

As sustenance, food is quite literally essential. We all eat, often without giving much thought to the matter. Yet the consumption of food is also socially meaningful. Food itself is a key site of identity construction, implicated in discourses of, for instance, race, gender, and class (e.g. Bradley 2016). Existing at the intersection of discourse, materiality, and power (Frye & Bruner 2012), even the most mundane food choices that we make when shopping, cooking, or eating are always linked to money, taste and, ultimately, social class. Bourdieu (1984) famously discusses food and eating as a key site for the production of distinction; a place where judgements about "good taste" are made in the construction and maintenance of class privilege/inequality. Evidently, judgements of "good taste" not only surface when we consume food but also – or perhaps especially – when we communicate with and about food. As Thurlow (2019) demonstrates, contemporary class formations continue to be organized around some extremely lavish but exploitative foodways. Having said which, Mapes (2018) also shows how relatively elite ways of eating are nowadays often obscured through the disavowal of privilege and under the guise of their simplicity, locality and/or low-brow origins.

Food photography in particular is both subject to reflecting cultural discourses (Matalon-Degni 2010) and part of contemporary public displays of social prestige (McDonnell 2016). While visual representations of food have long been a popular subject in art, it is in the 1990s that contemporary (and often commercial) food photography surfaced, alongside a significant rise in food magazines and advertising (Dejmanee 2015). In this regard, food photographer Helen Ventura Thompson credits editor and food stylist Donna Hay as responsible for the changing aesthetics of food photography and food photography's subsequent rise in popularity. Hay's use of shallow depth of field both brought about a new way of depicting food and "gave consumers the idea that anyone can make good food".[1] Her photographic style also placed an almost obsessive emphasis on food itself, something still prevalent in contemporary 'food porn' photography (cf. McDonnell 2016). While food photography may at times serve functional purposes, many of the images we encounter on social media platforms appear to be a way in which everyday commodities are aestheticized and used to mark social distinction. Indeed, McDonnell (2016: 239) calls such digital

---

[1] Source: *The history of food photography: Donna Hay.* Retrieved from https://web.archive.org/web/20160614222831/http://helengraceventurathompson.com/blog/historyoffoodphotography/?p=40 (accessed August 3, 2019)

displays of food the contemporary "conspicuous consumption of food". "For the twenty-first century *nouveau riche*", McDonnell (2016: 241) writes, "publicly sharing photographs of aestheticized food enables the public demonstration of social prestige, the participation in high cultural capital, as a form of conspicuous consumption". Importantly, though, it is not the "super rich" but rather the aspiring classes who engage most in these practices. In this sense, the display of food choices through food photography allows one to express not just cultural capital but also one's aspirations and one's social trajectory (McDonnell 2016: 241).

Through its discursive framing and enactment, food accrues cultural value and can therefore be employed to maintain and assert class status. As such, institutions which feed and control everyday discourses of food are powerful also in shaping the social order. One obvious example are supermarkets, which, as Thompson (2012: 58) points out, sell not just fish, meat and vegetables but also stories (see also Dixon 2007). In other words, corporate chains like *Coop* and *Migros* not only hold significant power over what products people can access, but, through their marketing and branding activities, they also furnish people with cultural narratives and lifestyles (or ways of living). In short, I suggest that the Instagram posts discussed here may well be driven by obvious profit-generating goals, but they also have cultural repercussions.

3 The corporate uses of Instagram

The study presented here is based on data drawn from Instagram, a social media platform that is strongly associated with food and the food industry – so much so that it is even credited with being responsible for raising both the price of avocados and the value of Starbucks shares.[2] This, of course, brings us to the question of corporations and their use of social media technologies, which is far from straightforward. Social media platforms are a key site where the line between the corporate and the rest of our lives is strategically blurred, and where "'humble and mundane' mechanisms" are employed to exert social control (Thurlow 2013: 235). As such, social media platforms like Instagram simultaneously blur and reinforce boundaries between, say, the public and the private, but also the corporate and the social. With regard to Instagram, corporate

---

[2] Source: *How social media influences food trends*. Retrieved from https://www.aljazeera.com/programmes/countingthecost/2017/05/social-media-influences-food-trends-170528085240437.html (accessed August 3, 2019).

social media use is still not well researched. While there has been a recent surge in social semiotic analyses of Instagram (e.g. Tiidenberg 2015; Zappavigna 2016; Duguay 2017), much of this research has focussed on its private uses. By contrast, little attention has been paid to its strategic uses by corporations and institutions (see Mapes, in press, for a recent exception however). And while business and marketing studies do offer many descriptive accounts of how corporations use Instagram (e.g. Zhu & Chen 2015; Godey et al. 2016; Che, Cheung & Thadani 2017), such studies generally offer little critical reflection. With regard to Instagram in general, several scholars observe that it reinforces dominant discourses (e.g. Tiidenberg 2015; Carah & Shaul 2016; Duguay 2017). In particular, Duguay (2017: 99) points out that the sociotechnical affordances of Instagram encourage users to create and share images that "symbolically reference upper class lifestyles", through which mundane pictures of everyday life can be transformed into status symbols.

Against this backdrop, I am interested in how corporate Instagram practices around food are implicated in the visual production – hence visualization – of taste and/as social status. To engage this topic, my social semiotic analysis is guided by the following inter-related research questions:
1. How do *Coop* and *Migros* visually depict food and foodways in their Instagram posts; how do these visualizations inscribe notions of "good taste"?
2. How do these visual-discursive practices and the corporate uses of Instagram thereby work to (re)produce or normalise class privilege/inequality?

The Swiss retail market is somewhat unusual, characterised as it is by a well-entrenched duopoly (Coll 2016). Overall, the price range of *Coop* and *Migros* is similar and they address a similar domestic market. Both corporations are quite active and popular on Instagram, which currently places them among the top ten Swiss Instagram users that post images of food.[3] As part of my larger study (Portmann 2018), I have collected a randomised sample of 75 *Coop* posts and 75 *Migros* posts that these corporations have published on their Instagram profile in 2017–2018. I also collected a randomised sample of user-created content posted under the hashtags #MeinCoop and #Migroschind, although these are not discussed here. Since my primary interest in the current chapter is the visualization of food itself, I focus on just those official posts which depict food. Ultimately, this leaves me with a subset of 113 Instagram posts. The methods I use for analysing this material are visual content analysis (e.g. Bell 2001) and

---

[3] Source: *Most popular Instagram accounts worldwide*. Retrieved from https://likeometer.ch/ (accessed August 3, 2019)

social semiotics (e.g. Kress & van Leeuwen 2001; 2006). Following the lead of Thurlow, Aiello & Portmann (2019), the combination of these two methods enables me to offer an initial quantitative-descriptive perspective on the data and then a more qualitative-interpretive one which highlights the 'inner workings' of the photos themselves – most notably, their design and compositional meanings.

4 Descriptive results: Food as unmarked and decontextualised

My overall content analysis comprises 46 different variables that address the images, the captions, and the comments of these Instagram posts (Portmann 2018). In the present chapter, however, I focus on the quantitative results of only ten variables, which are presented in Table 10.1. Given that I did not find any striking differences between the Instagram posts of *Coop* and *Migros*, in Tables 10.2 and 10.3 I have consolidated the results for ease of reading.

Table 10.1: Key content analytic variables.

Variable	Description
1. (Extra)ordinariness	Whether the food depicted is familiar/ordinary or exotic/extraordinary
2. Presentation of food	Whether the food depicted is presented in a casual fashion or in a neat/intricately arranged manner
3. Packaging	Whether packaging is visible, and whether it is presented neatly (e.g. closed) or not (e.g. ripped open)
4. Labels	Brands/labels visible in image
5. Background surface	Texture of the background surface (e.g. wood, marble, etc.)
6. Tableware	Type of tableware that is visible (plastic/non-plastic)
7. Setting	Setting depicted in photograph (e.g. kitchen, dining room, etc.)
8. Presence of people	How many people are visible
9. Background	How much background detail is visible
10. Representation	Whether the image is a narrative or a conceptual image (cf. Kress & van Leeuwen, 2006)

Table 10.2: Food and food presentation in *Coop* and *Migros* posts.

Variable	N=113
(Extra)ordinariness	
Extraordinary/exotic food	37%
Ordinary/familiar food	56%
Not determinable	7%
Presentation of food	
Neat	43%
Casual	40%
Not determinable	16%
Packaging	
None/not visible	60%
Visible, neat	39%
Visible, messy	1%
Labels	
None	59%
High-end (e.g. Sélection)	9%
Budget (e.g. Prix Garantie)	–
Mid-range (e.g. M-Classic)	5%
Health/lifestyle (e.g. Naturaline)	19%
Ethical (e.g. Max Havelaar)	–
Local (e.g. TerraSuisse)	–
Several labels	2%
Other	6%
Tableware	
None	30%
Plastic/packaging itself	20%
"Proper" tableware	49%
Background surface	
Nice wood	33%
Cheap wood	23%
Marble	15%
Paper	4%
Tablecloth	17%
Plastic	2%
Other	6%

Note: Numbers may not add up to 100% due to rounding.

On this basis, I offer an overview of the kinds of foods that these Instagram posts depict as well as the concrete ways in which the foods are presented.

The results of my content analysis show that, for the most part (56%), the food and foodways depicted (and promoted) by *Coop* and *Migros* are rather ordinary and mundane. Foods are styled almost equally often as either casual or neat (40% and 43%, respectively), and there is no predominance of high-end labels. As far as labels go, budget lines are noticeably absent and the stores' high-end ranges – *Fine Food* (*Coop*) and *Sélection* (*Migros*) – are not featured more than any other food. Indeed, the most frequently shown labels are those denoting organic and "healthy lifestyle" lines (19%). This might not be an innocent choice, however. While *Fine Food* and *Sélection* overtly display prestige, the privilege associated with organic and "healthy lifestyle" foods is more subtle, allowing its eaters to foreground altruistic goals rather than luxury (cf. Johnston & Baumann 2010). And, with the exception of the budget and mid-range products, all these labels of course entail an increase in price.

What is also interesting to observe from Table 10.2 is the immediate setting in which foods are placed. 49% of the posts show food that is served with proper tableware, while only 20% of these posts show food that is served in its original packaging or with plastic tableware. This relative absence of 'non-standard' eating is noteworthy. Bieling (2018), for example, identifies the practice of repurposing food packaging as an eating utensil as a strategy that consumers can employ on Instagram to defy common eating norms and speak back to discourses of "proper" eating. While food packaging is visible in 40% of the posts from *Coop* and *Migros*, it is almost always depicted in a neat and tidy manner (39%), as if it were there simply for pointing to the specific product featured. Thus, rather than denoting an environment where unconventional eating practices may take place, *Coop* and *Migros* seem to establish a cultural space where only 'correct' eating norms are observed.

Finally, Table 10.2 also reveals the surfaces on which dishes are presented; these are made of various materials but rarely cheap ones. In the *Coop* and *Migros* posts, the surfaces shown are often made of high-quality wood (33%), covered with a tablecloth (17%), or made of marble (15%). Only 23% of these images feature cheap wooden surfaces, and even fewer show plastic (2%) or paper (4%) surfaces. Ultimately, the foods depicted are not particularly spectacular. The setting in which they are placed, however, seems more interesting and we begin to see how food is elevated in the way it is framed by props and surfaces. In this regard, I turn next to Table 10.3.

Table 10.3: Visualized settings in *Coop* and *Migros* posts.

Variable	N=113
Setting	
Kitchen	1%
Dinner table	2%
Other, inside	6%
Other, outside	8%
Not determinable	83%
Presence of people	
None	86%
Single person	11%
Pair	–
Small group (<10 people)	3%
Large group (>10 people)	–
Background	
No/hardly any details visible	88%
Some details visible	11%
Details visible	1%
Representation	
Narrative image	1%
Conceptual image	99%

Note: Numbers may not add up to 100% due to rounding.

Table 10.3 shows an overview of the broader setting in which foods are placed, listing the results for the variables *setting, presence of people, background* and *representation*. Once again, the numbers are revealing. To start, 83% of the images do not show a clearly discernible setting, and only 14% of them depict a person (or even just the hands of a person). Indeed, in most images (88%) hardly any background detail is given; this makes it almost impossible to determine when, where, or by whom the food is supposedly made and/or consumed. We cannot tell whether these eating practices take place in a student flat, the kitchen of a middle-class family, or a working-class family's dining room. These are de-contextualised representations, typical examples of what Kress & van Leeuwen (2006: 45–113) call *conceptual* images; that is, images which do not reflect something actually happening in the world (a "social action") but rather an abstract idea (a "social construct"). Conceptual images represent participants or objects "in terms of their more generalized and more or less stable and timeless essence" (Kress & van Leeuwen 2006: 79), which makes them particularly suitable for conveying ideological concepts. What Table 10.3 thus shows is that, in order to understand how these Instagram posts work, we need to look beyond *what* is shown and consider *how* it is shown.

5 Interpretive results: Visual materialities and modalities

In the following sections, I provide a closer analysis of individual Instagram posts which are indicative of some of the key design strategies or compositional meanings at work. Specifically, I focus on two visual-discursive tactics – materiality and modality – used often by *Coop* and *Migros* for aestheticizing otherwise quite ordinary foods.

5.1 Materiality: Elevated settings

As the results of my content analysis show, most of the foods featured in these Instagram posts are rather mundane. What is interesting, however, are the props used to establish the contexts of eating. Recall from above that in most of the Instagram posts a broader setting is seldom discernible. What we do see, though, is the surface on which the foods are laid out. Here, materiality plays an important role in creating a generic yet distinguished setting. Quite often, the choice of background leads to an interesting contrast between the food that is shown and the material setting in which this food is placed, as exemplified by Figure 10.1.[4] In this particular case, a simple dish of microwaved spaghetti has been placed neatly on a black cloth against a white, marbled surface. The food has been transferred from its plastic container onto a proper plate; it is also served with a fork whose ornamental design is reminiscent of antique silverware. Through the simple choice of background and the addition of a few props, this simple dish is reframed as something more special, more stylish. Ordinary food is thereby elevated. This is contrary to the ways Mapes (2018) shows otherwise elite food being styled as simple and low-brow, although in both cases food is being used as a resource for the performance of status.

---

[4] The visual extracts used in Figures 10.1 to 10.7 are from publically available Instagram posts and used fairly for the purposes of scholarly comment and critique. All the figures are also made available in colour here: http://discourse.ch/goodtaste2020.pdf

Figure 10.1: Example of an elevated setting.

In much the same vein, Figure 10.2 offers another example of how the materiality of props works in these Instagram posts.

Here, we see coffee – French press coffee, as the caption specifies – that has been served in clean, white coffee cups. Saucers have been used, and the milk has been served in a matching little milk jug. In the background, just out of focus, some white tulips are discernible. Everything is placed on a wooden table, whose textured surface alludes to a rustic-chic interior, all very reminiscent of the fashionable visual-material rhetoric of locality which Aiello & Dickinson (2014) find in their study of rebranded Starbucks stores.

Social semioticians note that meaning making never happens solely through what is said or shown, but also through what is left out (cf. Hodge & Kress 1988: 263–268). Choices in representation are an act of negation, and hence "only meaningful in relation to the fuller structure of what is chosen and what is rejected" (Hodge & Kress 1988: 263). It is surely no coincidence that this surface and exactly these props have been chosen for the photograph in Figure 10.2. Indeed, it is when thinking about what else the photographer might have chosen that we come to better understand the effect of this setting. What if these cups were not perfectly clean and polished but showed signs of usage? What if there was no dedicated milk jug on the table but simply an opened carton of milk? What if this was placed on a plastic picnic table rather than the wooden table

10 Designing "good taste" — 213

Figure 10.2: Example of props and materiality.

that we see here? What if the tulips were the more common red or yellow tulips instead of white ones? Or what if they were plastic tulips? The choices that have been made in the production of this photograph all indicate a particular attention to detail and harmony, both notions which Daloz (2013: 103–105) identifies as signs of distinction.

In a similar albeit slightly less obvious way, the same strategy is also used in Figure 10.3.

In this case, we see yoghurt served with fresh figs in a glass bowl. An unopened yoghurt pot has been placed next to this bowl, perhaps to clarify what product is actually being promoted. What is striking about this Instagram post is, again, the emphasis placed on the specific container in which this yoghurt is served. Just as the milk in Figure 10.2 had been transferred from a carton into a dedicated milk jug, here the yoghurt has been transferred from its original plastic container into a glass bowl. Once again, a shift from cheap eating practices to not necessarily high-end but still more fancy ones is accomplished. In both cases, this change is achieved through the simple addition of a few props that function as shorthand to connote the "nature of [the] activities" (Machin 2004: 322) that we see in these images. As Machin (2004) points out, props index types rather than concrete identities or settings. Similarly, the props used in Figures 10.1, 10.2 and 10.3 operate not through concrete representations of experiences but by activating

Figure 10.3: Example of container materiality.

clichéd connotations. Essentially, the meaning that is created here is based on the provenance (Kress & van Leeuwen 2001: 10) of these materialities. It relies less on the concrete bodily experience of the materials and more on knowing where the signs come from; that is, on the kinds of circumstances that are connoted through, for instance, marble, glass dishes or textured wood.

From these three examples it is apparent that, while the foods and foodways depicted may be unspectacular, the way they are presented is not. (Again, the comparison with Mapes 2018 is telling.) These simple foods are elevated through the deployment of artefacts that have a certain materiality. Of course, any visual-material props do not actually change the gustatory quality of the food; they do however confer symbolic status on the products and, by association, on the people who consume them. It is in this way that marketers strategically work to 'stylize' customers as elite (Thurlow & Jaworski 2006) while also schooling them in the ways of good taste as well as aspirational status (Thurlow & Jaworski 2017). Such carefully assembled settings also imply a willingness to spend time on food and eating. In this sense, these elevated settings also function to mark one's ability to engage in the kind of conspicuous leisure Veblen (2007[1899]) so famously wrote about. The foods and foodways depicted are framed as an occasion for entertainment and pleasure. This is something I will now consider in more detail with reference to modality.

5.2 Modality: Food as sensory pleasure

Nowadays, when digital media have made images of food ubiquitous and pervasive (Rousseau 2012), images like the ones posted on the Instagram profiles of *Coop* and *Migros* are arguably in the service of entertainment (Ketchum 2005). Used as a means for expressing and generating cultural capital, these images showcase desirable foods in order to elicit symbolic and sensory pleasure (cf. McDonnell 2016). It is exactly this aspect of food as sensory pleasure that *Coop* and *Migros* exploit. Indeed, the two corporations construct the social meaning of food not so much as sustenance but rather as a site of pleasure. Many of the images in *Coop*'s and *Migros*' Instagram posts are designed in such a way that they follow what Kress & van Leeuwen (2006: 165) call a "sensory coding orientation". It is thus through their modality that these images cue sensory meaning potentials.

Modality is a term that originally comes from linguistics and refers to the reliability or "truth value" of a statement. Social semioticians understand that such appeals to truth can be expressed not only through explicit linguistic markers but also through other means, such as hedging or intonation (Hodge & Kress 1988: 121). What is more, modality can be expressed in other semiotic modes such as in visual images (Hodge & Kress 1988: 121–161; see also Kress & van Leeuwen, 2006: 154–174); in other words, images likewise make claims about their verisimilitude. Kress & van Leeuwen (2006) offer a classification of four different kinds of visual modality or "coding orientations": naturalistic modality, sensory modality, abstract modality, and scientific/technological modality. Of these, naturalistic modality is perhaps easiest to understand: it is judged by how much an image resembles something in real life, achieved by, for example, colour saturation and hue. By contrast, sensory modality orients not to how realistic a representation is but to the effect of (dis)pleasure that it elicits. Images with sensory modality often appear slightly more than real, for instance through highly saturated colours. In this sense, "vibrant reds, soothing blues, and so on" (Kress & van Leeuwen 2006: 165) are typical for images with sensory coding orientation. In contrast to this, images with abstract or scientific/technological modality may appear less than real, reducing objects and people to lines, as is often the case in scientific diagrams or modern art.

Modality, understood thus, is a key tactic by which *Coop* and *Migros* elevate foods and, thereby, give primacy to the form of foods and eating practices over their alimentary function (cf. Bourdieu 1984). Take for example the image in Figure 10.4. As the comments of users @rabigoncalves and @it_lele_zh indicate, there is something about the image in Figure 10.4 that immediately makes us think about the sensory act of eating these popsicles. Their comments read

Figure 10.4: Example of colour and sensory modality.

"hmm <black heart>" and "Mmmmh <black heart>", alluding to a gustatory savouring of the food that is shown.[5] As a direct representational strategy, fresh fruits are used as props, linking the representation with gustatory experiences. There is, however, more at work here than just what is shown. Through the use of colour, this image foregrounds sensory meaning potentials, prompting viewers to assess it based not only on how realistically it represents the world, but rather in terms of the pleasure experienced in looking at the photo.

Colour plays an important role in cultural life. Despite often lacking the vocabulary to express how we make sense of it, we constantly use colour to communicate (cf. Kress & van Leeuwen 2002). In Figure 10.4, two aspects of colour are particularly striking. Firstly, the red of the popsicles is highly saturated. As Machin (2007: 70–71) notes, saturation can make a colour "emotionally intense, bold, and engaging" and is typical for images with sensory modality. Essentially, what we have in Figure 10.4 is exactly the kind of "vibrant red" Kress & van Leeuwen (2006: 165) refer to in speaking about modality. It is this which gives

---

[5] Throughout this chapter, I transcribe emojis based on their Unicode common locale data repository (CLDR) short name; see https://unicode.org/emoji/charts/emoji-list.html (accessed August 3, 2019)

the image its 'tangible', sensory qualities. Secondly, the red used in Figure 10.4 also shows a deliberate use of colour modulation. We see not just a flat, single shade of red in this image; rather it is possible to discern several different shades of red. High colour modulation such as this can connote variety, realness, and richness (Machin 2007: 77). This might indicate a naturalistic coding orientation but depending on how much colour differentiation there is in a representation, it may also make the image feel "hyper real", thus indicating a sensory coding orientation (Kress & van Leeuwen 2006: 158). In Figure 10.4, this impression of 'hyper realness' is further emphasised by the sharpness of the image and the amount of detail that is thus rendered visible.

In regard to visible details, we can, for example, make out individual ice crystals on the two popsicles at the top of the image just as it is possible to detect the tiny velvet hairs on some of the raspberries. Overall, the combination of high colour saturation, high colour modulation, and the sharpness of the image create an impression of vibrancy and richness that is almost too real and which points to a sensory coding orientation. Through this change in modality, the food itself is framed as being no longer about its factual qualities, such as, for instance, its nutritional value or its price; rather, the image constructs an eating experience that foregrounds first and foremost pleasure and enjoyment.

Colour is, of course, not the only semiotic resource that can be used to mark sensory modality. In the Instagram posts of *Coop* and *Migros*, sensory modality is also often invoked through texture, as exemplified by Figure 10.5.

Notice how again, many of the user comments on this post entail an emotional if not visceral response to this picture: @ciellenoire for instance says, "this is exactly what meat should look like <drooling face>", while @ramona_roggli writes "looks tasty <smiling face with smiling eyes> <face savoring food>". The negative reaction that this Instagram post elicits from user @isyspepito, who uses an angry-faced and four nauseated emojis to express disgust, is also expressed through an affective response. Once again, the colour saturation of the photograph featured in this post is relatively high. What is most striking about this image, however, is its attention to detail and texture. As Aiello (2018) observes, the strategic use of texture lends itself particularly well to foregrounding experiential meaning potentials; that is, meanings which are rooted in our actual, physical experience of the world. Emphasis on texture thus invokes the sensory or "emplaced, embodied and overall phenomenological qualities of given representational resources" (Aiello & Pauwels 2014: 282). In Figure 10.5, texture is foregrounded through the skilled use of focus and lighting: we can clearly see the muscle fibres of the cooked meat, the individual peppercorns on its crust, and we can even perceive a few of the tiny scratches on the bones of this lamb shank. The amount of detail visible makes the image appear vivid – pointing

Figure 10.5: Example of texture and sensory modality.

again to a sensory coding orientation which cues viewers to assess the image on the basis of (dis)pleasure.

Lastly, Figure 10.6 serves as an example for how depth of field as well as composition can be deployed to create a 'hyper-real', sensory image. Through the extreme close-up and the shallow depth of field used in this image, we are able to make out the individual bubbles of foam that are forming; as such, viewers are encouraged to let their gaze linger on this focal point. The composition of the image further reinforces this effect: cup, filter, coffee, and foam all form concentric circles that draw the gaze to the middle of the image, while the stream of water functions as a vector or reading path guiding viewers to the same point. This image thus tells us that "there is nothing but this moment, right here, *this food*" (McDonnell 2016: 262, emphasis in original). Together, these different semiotic resources create a multisensory experience which transforms something as ordinary as filter coffee into something beautiful, teasing, and delightful. Essentially, what images like the ones in Figures 10.4, 10.5 and 10.6 do is draw the viewer's attention to and *into* the image. Such particular use of composition, framing, and depth of field are typical of what McDonnell (2016) identifies as the aesthetic conventions of so-called food porn. As McDonnell shows, not only do these conventions frame food as an object of pleasure, but the overall

Figure 10.6: Example of depth of field/composition and sensory modality.

activity of creating, sharing, and viewing photographs of aestheticized food can also be understood as a contemporary expression of cultural capital.

To sum up, by emphasising the sensory qualities of foods, eating is constructed as a foodway which foregrounds pleasure and entertainment. Colour, texture, composition and depth of field are used to mark the sensory modality of these images, inviting people to read them not in terms of their factual 'realness' but with regard to their effectiveness in eliciting pleasure, judged by "the truth of feeling" (Machin 2007: 59). As a result, food is framed not simply as sustenance. This emphasis of form over function, argues Bourdieu (1984: 374), is central to the production of distinction and privilege; it is the privileged who can afford to disregard the "taste for necessity", looking instead at food as something more decidedly affective and aesthetic.

6 Designing (and democratising) "good taste"

Through the strategic use of materiality and modality, *Coop* and *Migros* manage to elevate the relatively simple, mundane foods featured in their Instagram posts; as such, they effectively "confer aesthetic status on objects that are banal"

(Bourdieu 1984: 5). By deploying specific materialities, the two grocery chains can frame ordinary foods as more elite. Material attributes like wood or marble surfaces, or the use of fabric napkins and nice tableware work to connote an elegant, sophisticated setting. How and where becomes more important than what is actually eaten. By emphasising the sensory qualities of these foods, in particular through the use of colour, texture, composition, and depth of field, these two supermarkets can furthermore frame food and eating as something that is concerned with pleasure and entertainment rather than sustenance and nutrition. These Instagram posts employ a sensory coding orientation that cues us to evaluating them on the basis of the affective pleasure that we derive from them rather than on the basis of their functional value. So, through both materiality and modality, these foods are presented to us as part of a more distinguished lifestyle that emphasises *how* food is eaten over *what* is eaten. What we see, then, is a typical reproduction of Bourdieu's (1984) distinction between upper and lower class tastes in modern form. Food is here not a source of nutrients but of entertainment and pleasure. These supermarkets thus convert everyday commodities into symbolic objects (Bourdieu 1993): the limited commercial value of these foods is transformed into more extensive cultural value, and the images as such become a means for performing elite lifestyles (Thurlow & Jaworski 2017; see also Mapes 2018).

And yet, these two grocery chains are not aiming to address a distinguished elite but, above all, the average Swiss consumer. I want to close by offering one example of how *Coop* and *Migros* achieve this by multimodally re-contextualising "good taste" as something domestic and, thus, egalitarian. It is important to remember that my objective in the larger project (Portmann 2018) was to document the semiotic division of labour across a range of resources; the focus in this chapter on visual resources (i.e. photos) is a matter of analytic convenience and space limitation. Notwithstanding, Figure 10.7 and Extract 10.1 illustrate how hashtags are used by *Coop* and *Migros* to explicitly present otherwise quite privileged food/foodways as ordinary and accessible.

> Extract 10.1: Caption used in Figure 10.7
> Wir wünschen euch einen guten Start in den Tag! Danke @_prilapo_ für das tolle Frühstücksbild #MeinCoop #Gipfeli #Croissants #Zmorge #Breakfast #<croissant>
>
> *We wish you a good start to the day! Thank you @_prilapo_ for the great breakfast image #MeinCoop #Croissant #Croissants [English in original] #Breakfast #Breakfast [English in original] #<croissant>*

Despite the highly stylised nature of the image used in Figure 10.7, the hashtags that *Coop* chose for categorising this Instagram post are, next to their branded

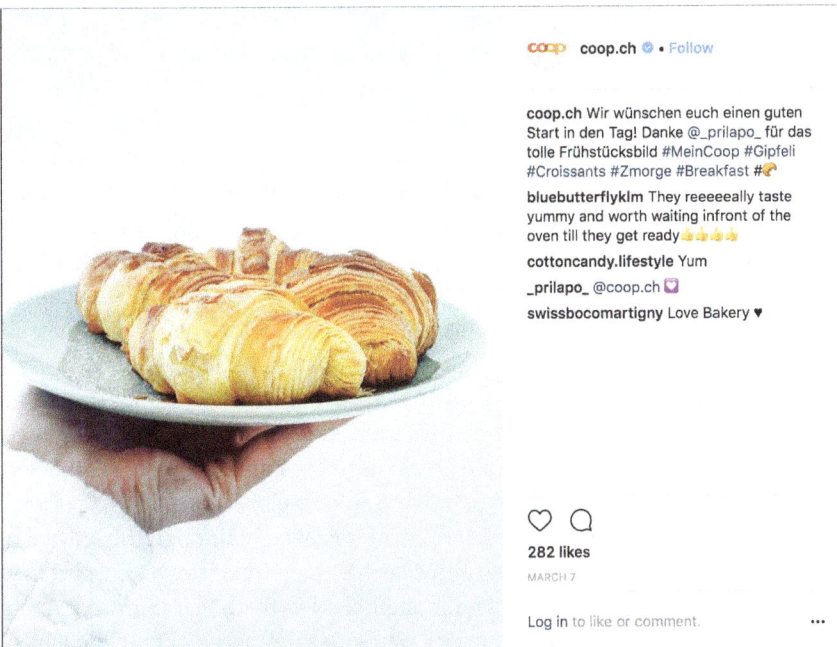

Figure 10.7: Example of banal hashtags vs. elite food.

hashtag #MeinCoop, the humble terms "breakfast" and "croissant". Both are written out in both Swiss German and English; *croissant* is also listed a third time in the casual form of just a croissant emoji. These simple hashtags do two things. On the one hand, they fulfil a representational function (cf. Zappavigna 2015), simply documenting what we see in the visual content of this post. After all, this is an image of croissants, and croissants are typically eaten for breakfast. Next to this, however, these hashtags also function as an "evaluative metacomment" (Zappavigna 2015) that is used to re-contextualise this stylised depiction of food as ordinary and casual. Especially when one thinks about the potential other choices that *Coop* could have made, it becomes clear that by choosing these unspectacular and casual terms as hashtags, *Coop* can signal that their posts are to be situated not in contemporary foodie culture but rather in the realm of everyday eating: this is not #Instafood, this is simply #Zmorge. Despite the gesture of servitude that we see in the image in Figure 10.7 – an exemplary case of the "visible-invisible labour" that Thurlow & Jaworski (2013) find to be typical of symbolic performances of eliteness – we are told that this is nothing but ordinary breakfast. Through this juxtaposition between image and caption, elite eating is effectively re-contextualised as a simple feat, accessible for anyone. By framing these foods as both extraordinary, sensual experiences *and* simple, everyday foods, privilege can be constructed and at the same time obscured and rendered invisible.

A key aspect of social media platforms is their (apparent) openness and inclusivity. However, several scholars note that while Instagram may seem egalitarian, the platform as such actually reinforces hegemonic discourses (e.g. Tiidenberg 2015; Duguay, 2017; Carah & Shaul 2016). This is also the case with *Coop*'s and *Migros*' use of Instagram. Through the discursive control that they can exert on Instagram, these corporations have considerable power in shaping discourses of food, taste and, ultimately, class. Corporations like *Coop* and *Migros* do not just sell us particular foods but also particular (elite) lifestyles. These Instagram posts aestheticize banal foods, thus transforming everyday goods into symbolic objects that can be used to do status work (cf. Bourdieu 1993). Next to this, my analysis also shows that elite status is an inherently multimodal phenomenon. Often, several modes are employed together to perform privilege (e.g. Thurlow & Jaworski 2017), and it is exactly through this interplay of different modes that privilege can be at the same time avowed and disavowed. It is perhaps not surprising but nonetheless striking that in my data, distinction and privilege are constructed in particular through less tangible means such as colour or modality, while modes that are often claimed to be more explicit, such as written language, are used to re-contextualise these posts as domestic and banal. Thus, while privilege is constructed through intangible semiotic resources, (seemingly) unambiguous representational means are used to then anchor privilege as accessible and democratic. What we see here, then, is evidence of a growing aestheticization or "fashioning" of banal goods, where the economic and the symbolic are "interlaced and interarticulated" (Lash & Urry 1994: 64) – rendered possible through a clever interlacing of linguistic and visual discourse.

References

Aiello, Giorgia. 2018. Losing to gain: Balancing style and texture in the Starbucks logo. In Christian Mosbæk Johannessen & Theo van Leeuwen (eds.), *The materiality of writing: A trace-making perspective*, 195–210. New York: Routledge.

Aiello, Giorgia & Greg Dickinson. 2014. Beyond authenticity: A visual-material analysis of locality in the global redesign of Starbucks stores. *Visual Communication*, 13(3), 303–321.

Aiello, Giorgia & Pauwels, Luc. 2014. Special issue: Difference and globalization. *Visual Communication*, 13(3), 275–285.

Bell, Philip. 2001. Content analysis of visual images. In Theo van Leeuwen & Carey Jewitt (eds.), *Handbook of visual analysis*, 10–34. Los Angeles, CA: Sage.

Bieling, Simon. 2018. *Konsum zeigen: Die neue Öffentlichkeit von Konsumprodukten auf Flickr, Instagram und Tumblr*. Bielefeld: Transcript Verlag.
Bourdieu, Pierre. 1984. *Distinction: A social critique of the judgement of taste*. Cambridge, MA: Harvard University Press.
Bourdieu, Pierre. 1993. *The field of cultural production: Essays on art and literature*, In Randal Johnson (ed.). Cambridge, UK: Polity Press.
Bradley, Peri. 2016. Introduction. In Peri Bradley (ed.), *Food, media & contemporary culture: The edible image*, 1–5. Basingstoke: Palgrave Macmillan.
Bruno Godey, Aikaterini Manthiou, Daniele Pederzoli, Joonas Rokka, Gaetano Aiello, Raffaele Donvito & Rahul Singh. 2016. Social media marketing efforts of luxury brands: Influence on brand equity and consumer behavior. *Journal of Business Research*, 69, 5833–5841.
Carah, Nicholas & Michelle Shaul. 2016. Brands and Instagram: Point, tap, swipe, glance. *Mobile Media & Communication*, 4(1), 69–84.
Che, Jasmine W.S., Christy Cheung & Dimple R. Thadani. 2017. *Consumer purchase decision in Instagram stores: The role of consumer trust*. Paper presented at the 50th Hawaii International Conference on System Sciences.
Coll, Sami. 2016. Discipline and reward: The surveillance of consumers through loyalty cards. *Geschichte und Gesellschaft* 42(1), 113–143.
Daloz, Jean-Pascal. 2013. *Rethinking social distinction*. Basingstoke: Palgrave-Macmillan.
Dejmanee, Tisha. 2015. "Food porn" as postfeminist play: Digital femininity and the female body on food blogs. *Television & New Media*, 17(5), 429–448.
Dixon, Jane. 2007. Supermarkets as new food authorities. In David Burch & Geoffrey Lawrence (eds.), *Supermarkets and agri-food supply chains: Transformations in the production and consumption of foods*, 29–50. Cheltenham: Edward Elgar Publishing.
Duguay, Stefanie. 2017. *Identity modulation in networked publics: Queer women's participation and representation on Tinder, Instagram, and Vine*. PhD thesis, Queensland University of Technology.
Frye, Joshua J. & Michael S. Bruner. 2012. Introduction. In Joshua J. Frye & Michael S. Bruner (eds.), *The rhetoric of food: Discourse, materiality, and power*, 1–6. New York: Routledge.
Hodge, Robert & Gunther Kress. 1988. *Social semiotics*. Malden, MA: Polity Press.
Hu, Yuheng, Lydia Manikonda & Subbarao Kambhampati. 2014. What we Instagram: A first analysis of Instagram photo content and user types. In *Proceedings of the Eighth International AAAI Conference on Weblogs and Social Media*, 595–598. Ann Arbor, MI: AAAI Press.
Johnston, Josée & Shyon Baumann. 2010. *Foodies: Democracy and distinction in the gourmet foodscape*. New York: Taylor & Francis.
Ketchum, Cheri. 2005. The essence of cooking shows: How the food network constructs consumer fantasies. *Journal of Communication Inquiry*, 29(3), 217–234.
Kress, Gunther. 2010. *Multimodality: A social semiotic approach to contemporary communication*. London: Routledge.
Kress, Gunther & Theo van Leeuwen. 2001. *Multimodal discourse: The modes and media of contemporary communication*. London: Arnold.
Kress, Gunther & Theo van Leeuwen. 2002. Colour as a semiotic mode: Notes for a grammar of colour. *Visual Communication*, 1(3), 343–368.
Kress, Gunther & Theo van Leeuwen. 2006. *Reading images: The grammar of visual design*. 2nd edn. London: Routledge.
Lash, Scott & John Urry. 1994. *Economies of signs and space*. London: Sage Publications.

Loader, Brian D. & Dan Mercea. 2011. Networking democracy? Social media innovations and participatory politics. *Information, Communication & Society*, 14(6), 757–769.

Machin, David. 2004. Building the world's visual language: The increasing global importance of image banks in corporate media. *Visual Communication*, 3(3), 316–336.

Machin, David. 2007. *Introduction to multimodal analysis*. London: Hodder Education.

Mapes, Gwynne. 2018. (De)constructing distinction: Class inequality and elite authenticity in mediatized food discourse. *Journal of Sociolinguistics* 22(3), 265–287.

Mapes, Gwynne. In press. Mediatizing the fashionable eater: Orders of elitist stancetaking in 'throwback Thursday' Instagram posts. In *(Dis)avowing distinction: Elite authenticity and class inequality in food discourse*. London and New York: Oxford University Press.

Matalon-Degni, Francine. 2010. Trends in food photography. *Gastronomica*, 10(3), 70–83.

McDonnell, Erin Metz. 2016. Food porn: The conspicuous consumption of food in the age of digital reproduction. In Peri Bradley (ed.), *Food, media & contemporary culture: The edible image*, 239–265. Basingstoke: Palgrave Macmillan.

Portmann, Lara. 2018. *Mundane distinction: The production of status and privilege in corporate social media – a social semiotic analysis*. MA thesis, University of Bern.

Rousseau, Signe. 2012. *Food and social media: You are what you tweet*. Lanham, MD: AltaMira Press.

Thompson, John. 2012. "Food Talk": Bridging power in a globalizing world. In Joshua J. Frye & Michael S. Bruner (eds.), *The rhetoric of food: Discourse, materiality, and power*, 58–70. New York: Routledge.

Thurlow, Crispin. 2013. Fakebook: Synthetic media, pseudo-sociality, and the rhetorics of Web 2.0. In Deborah Tannen & Anna M. Trester (eds.), *Discourse 2.0: Language and new media*, 225–249. Washington, WA: Georgetown University Press.

Thurlow, Crispin. 2019. Expanding our sociolinguistic horizons? Geographical thinking and the articulatory potential of commodity chain analysis. *Journal of Sociolinguistics*. doi.org/10.1111/josl.12388

Thurlow, Crispin, Giorgia Aiello & Lara Portmann. 2019. Visualizing teens and technology: A social semiotic analysis of stock photography and news media imagery. *New Media & Society*. doi.org/10.1177/1461444819867318

Thurlow, Crispin & Adam Jaworski. 2006. The alchemy of the upwardly mobile: Symbolic capital and the stylization of elites in frequent-flyer programmes. *Discourse & Society*, 17(1), 131–167.

Thurlow, Crispin & Adam Jaworski. 2013. Visible-invisible: The social semiotics of labour in luxury tourism. In Thomas Birtchnell & Javier Caletrío (eds.), *Elite mobilities*, 176–193. London: Routledge.

Thurlow, Crispin & Adam Jaworski. 2017. The discursive production and maintenance of class privilege: Permeable geographies, slippery rhetorics. *Discourse & Society*, 28(5), 535–558.

Tiidenberg, Katrin. 2015. Odes to heteronormativity: Presentations of femininity in Russian-speaking pregnant women's Instagram accounts. *International Journal of Communication*, 9, 1746–1758.

Van Leeuwen, Theo. 2008. *Discourse and practice: New tools for critical discourse analysis*. Oxford: Oxford University Press.

Veblen, Thorstein. 2007 [1899]. *The theory of the leisure class*. Oxford: Oxford University Press.

Zappavigna, Michele. 2015. Searchable talk: The linguistic functions of hashtags. *Social Semiotics*, 25(3), 274–291.
Zappavigna, Michele. 2016. Social media photography: Construing subjectivity in Instagram images. *Visual Communication* 15(3), 271–292.
Zhu, Yu-Qian, & Houn-Gee Chen. 2015. Social media and human need satisfaction: Implications for social media marketing. *Business Horizons*, 58, 335–345.

Jana Pflaeging

11 Diachronic perspectives on viral online genres: From images to words, from lists to stories

Is it just me or has the Internet been consumed by lists? Every day I see more and more lists of things, most of which are absurd, humorous, and arbitrarily numbered. Like, 14 Interesting Facts You Did Now Know About Pizza. Usually said list is paired with an intriguing photo and I just can't help myself-I have to click on the link and spend time scrolling through a list of stuff I don't really need to know.   (Kinser 2013, 26 Dec)

1 Introduction: The rise of the listicle

October 24, 2014. Late afternoon. If I logged onto my Facebook now, I would probably be looking at: Updates from Friends who share moments of awkwardness and awe. Pointers to new postings from groups and pages I follow. Explorations of memories made. Invitations to events yet to come. More groups to join, more Friends to find. However, it is not only personal occurrences and private oddities that are shared. Scrolling down my Facebook timeline, I am also likely to encounter something like this:

Listicle-posts that reveal to us *24 Cartoon Doppelgangers Spotted In Real Life* (see Figure 11.1). We are also reminded of *23 (Somewhat) Shameful Things That Happen When You Live Alone*. We may dream about *34 Isolated Houses* that are *As Far Away From Busy As You Can Get*. And we may drool over *The 30 Teeniest Tiniest Puppies Being Adorably Teeny Tiny*. It is items that beg for a click, hyperlinked baits that drag Facebook users off their social networking sites to external web spaces, such as *distractify.com*, that promise to make "wasting time [...] more than just a waste of time" (Distractify 2018).

By the click of a button, we find distraction from the sobriety and banality of everyday life in historic "conflicts in which the greatest among us fight the unimaginable": *The 16 Greatest Battles Fought By The Most Courageous Cats Of Our Time* (see Figure 11.2). A scroll down the page successively uncovers 16 list items, each composed of a typographically marked headline, an animated gif-image at the center with a note on its source, and a short caption: Cats competing with a lizard, a slice of ham, a toy, a string-on-sheets, and a paper bag, and the list continues until we reach the bottom of the page where more multimodal "baits" are waiting.

https://doi.org/10.1515/9781501510113-012

Figure 11.1: *Listicle*-post which appeared on a Facebook timeline in October 2014.

As documented in the epigraphic quote above, list-patterns like that in Figure 11.2 had gained considerable prominence by 2013. Blogger Kinser noticed "more and more lists of things", and outlines recurring communicative patterns. He also expects his readership to immediately comprehend the example he gives. All these aspects indicate that Kinser and his audience had begun to accumulate *genre* knowledge about such lists due to their frequent encounter of them.

In essence, *genres* are "bundles of strategies for achieving particular communicative aims in particular ways" (Bateman et al. 2017: 131). They are marked out due to a reoccurrence of similar communicative choices, hence patterns, and are typically described with respect to several analytical levels. In many linguistic and multimodal approaches to genre (cf. Stöckl 2015: 62ff.), these levels broadly classify as communicative situation/setting, multimodal text structure and textual function.

Often times, genres acquire specific names, i.e. *genre labels*, by which they are identifiable within a community. The existence of such genre labels is a strong indicator of the fact that recurrent communicative patterns have become more stable and more widely shared by members of a community. This phenomenon can be observed with lists such as those described above.

Less than four years after Kinser's blog post, not only the salience of the list-pattern itself but also the increasingly common genre label *listicle* prompted its inclusion in the *Oxford English Dictionary* (OED Online, s.v. "listicle, n.").[1]

---

[1] In Pflaeging (2015), I referred to the same communicative phenomenon as *listsite*, among others drawing on a quote by web user Milo Grika who states in June 2014: "Buzzfeed and Distractify are List of X sites that are basically the same probably feed off each other, and

11 Diachronic perspectives on viral online genres — 229

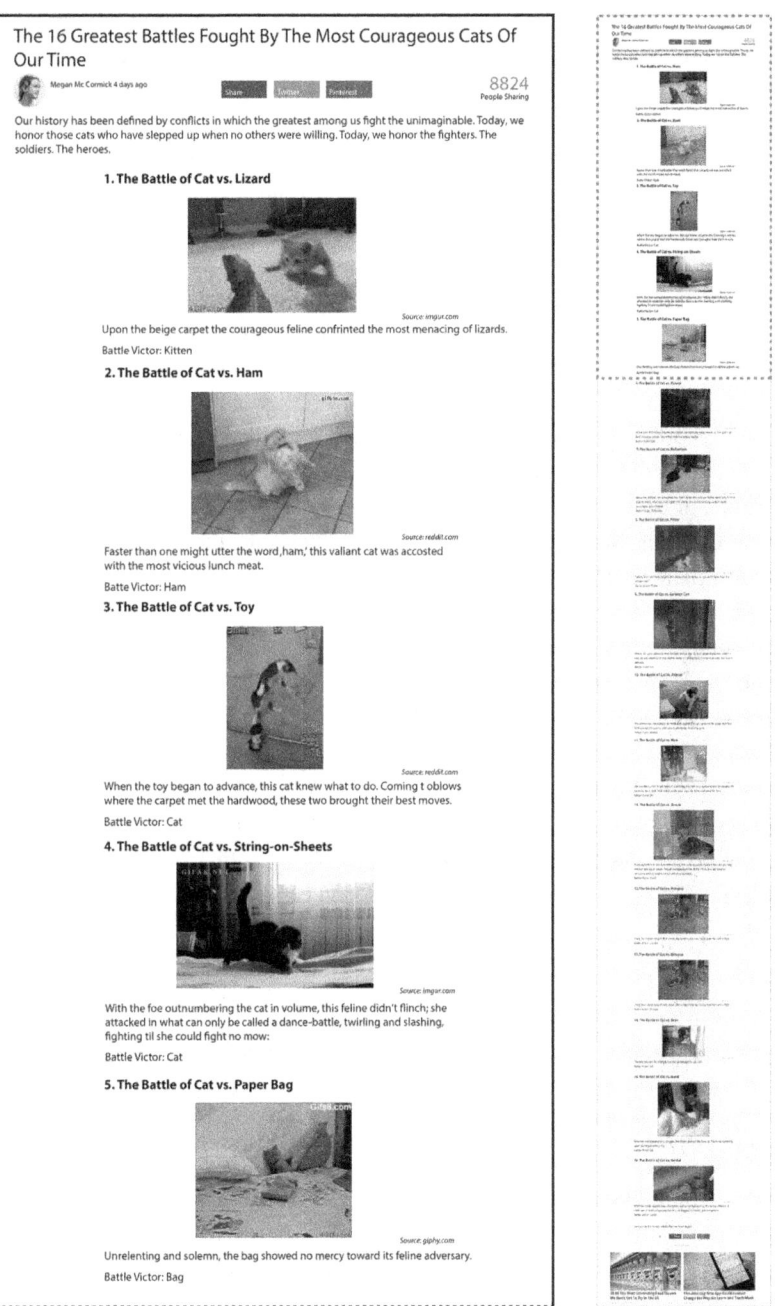

Figure 11.2: Top Section of a *Distractify*-listicle, as published in October 2014.

Listicles, another blogger argues in October 2015, "have become all the rage and entire websites have surfaced which dedicated [*sic!*] themselves to nothing other than creating high quality listicles" (Vegibit 2014).[2]

Among these websites are *Distractify.com* and other viral content providers such as *Buzzfeed, Up-worthy, Viralnova* or *IWasteSoMuchTime.com* (see Figure 11.3). They put on display content that proves "sticky" in that it lures as many visitors as possible to their sites to "[keep] them there indefinitely in ways that best benefit the site's analytics" (Jenkins et al. 2013: 6).[3]

The time that users spend on these websites and the page impressions they create correlate directly with the value of advertising spaces (Jenkins et al. 2013: 6). As can be seen in Figure 11.3, individual listicles integrate a considerable number of advertising spaces, in the form of banner or sidebar ads (Cook 2006: 224). In order to generate profit from such listicles, content providers constantly aim at feeding multimodal texts onto Facebook that are meant to attract large groups of users and achieve virality.

These users, however, ideally do not feel talked into *sharing* what they consumed with their Facebook Friends but see a different – social – value in it. In a participatory networked culture (Jenkins 2009), countless items on a Facebook timeline compete for a user's attention and appreciation. If a *listicle* is to spread virally on the Web, it seems of crucial importance that Facebook users perceive a high degree of *share-worthiness* (Pflaeging 2015: 158) or *worthiness-of-curation* (see below).[4]

Listicles, which embed advertising genres to a considerable extent and, what is more, are offered frequently in similar communicative contexts, need to show a certain degree of variation and innovation to retain attractiveness, as findings from advertising research suggest (Cook 2006: 224). At the same time, a certain degree of stability is required to make *listicles* recognisable and bind "customers" (Adamzik 2012: 135). However, since online audiences are characterized by a high

---

really, just take the junk lists that people email around to each other and write an article around it." Given the currency the term has gained both through several dictionary entries and on the Web in general, I give preference to *listicle* in my chapter here.

2 The article, tellingly entitled "14 Steps To Write A Great Listicle," does not bear a time stamp. By means of the Internet Archive's *Wayback Machine*, it was possible to trace back its publication to "prior to 29 September 2014," when it was first crawled by the *Wayback Machine*.

3 Such websites have been described as *walled gardens*, in which visitors wander from one flower to another (Dworschak 2010: 177, qtd. in Runkehl 2012: 15).

4 See Pflaeging (2015: 159–160) for an earlier (and slightly more elaborate) account of the concept *worthy- of-curation* and *capable-of-curation*, which I labelled *share-worthiness* and *share-ability* at the time.

11 Diachronic perspectives on viral online genres — 231

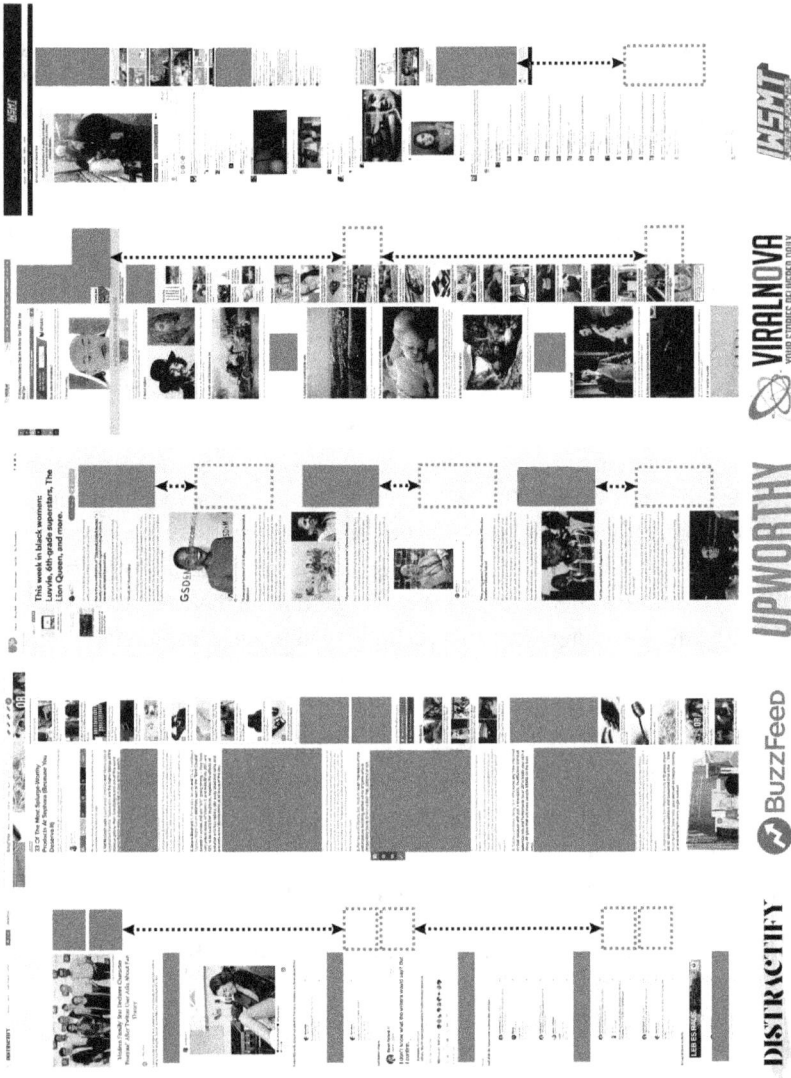

Figure 11.3: Spatially-fixed and moveable advertisements on the web pages of several viral content-providing websites, as captured in 2017.

"level of indeterminacy" (Varis & Blommaert 2014: 18) and recipient's feedback is delayed (cf. Bell 1991: 70), professional content providers need to anticipate their audience's expectations.

With this paper, I seek to provide a deeper insight into the complex interrelationship between conviviality, virality and genre by the example of the *listicle* and its development over time. My particular interest is how the need for conviviality between users of social networking sites is commercially exploited by professional content providers, who seek to achieve viral spreads of the content they create to increase the value of advertising spaces on their sites. For this reason, I investigate what communicative choices are made by content providers when anticipating their audience's expectations with regard to designing *listicles* and how they develop diachronically.

Pursuing this aim requires a diachronic approach to viral online genres. In order to frame my argumentation, I first introduce the notions of *conviviality* and *virality* and relate them to *genre (expectations)* (Section 2). I will use this section to already present my empirical findings with regard to the communicative situation and textual function of the genre since they showed a high degree of pattern stability over time and were in line with general assumptions about the mechanisms of viral online communication. In this sense, my study of two sets of 50 exemplars of the genre *listicle* (later *storicle*) sampled from distractify.com in 2014 and 2017 may add further detail to the complex interrelation between conviviality, virality and genre. Resulting from this section, I will specify my research questions with regard to the multimodal structure of the genre. Subsequently, I offer a brief outline of data and method (Section 3) and present the results of my empirical investigations into the development of the multimodal structure of *listicles* (later *storicle*) (Section 4). Finally, I provide a short conclusion (Section 5).

2 Sticky patterns and social buttons: Conviviality, virality and genre expectations

Of the 3.5 billion Internet users worldwide, almost 60 percent were active Facebook users in 2017. In 2014, an average U.S. Facebook user had 350 Friends (Edison Research 2014) and spent about 42 minutes on the site (eMarketer 2015) to update their status, send private messages, or react to other users' posts (Pew Research Center 2014). Such practices are part of social networking, which constitutes "the backbone of social media sites" (Lerman & Jones 2007: n. p.; qtd. in Müller 2012: 51). It serves to form and maintain social networks (boyd & Ellison 2008: 210; Deumert 2014: fn1).

Much of this hinges on a human need for "phatic communion" (Varis & Blommaert 2014: 2, in ref. to Malinowski 1923 (1936), see also Radovanovic & Ragnedda 2012: 11–12; Jakobson 1960), which is a type of communicative exchange which "'serves to establish bonds of personal union between people brought together by the need of companionship'" (Malinowski 1923 (1936), qtd. in Varis & Blommart 2014: 2). While phatic communion allows for a social construction of identity in active "processes of [...] commonality, connectedness and groupness" (Leppänen et al. 2014: 112–113), the emerging social networks are not characterized by "deeply shared values and functions [...] but by loose bonds of shared, even if superficial interest" (Varis & Blommart 2014: 7). As a result, online communication among such groups does usually not require extensive and deep conversation, but rather what Varis & Blommaert (2014: 17) call *conviviality*, "a level of social intercourse by largely 'phatic' and 'polite' engagement. Aquaintances are not there to be 'loved', they are to be 'liked'."

The importance of phatic communion on social networking sites is likely to have prompted the introduction of "social buttons" (Gerlitz & Helmond 2013: 4), i.e. *share*- and *like*-buttons, to Facebook timelines and other external websites in 2009 (cf. Pflaeging 2015: 159–160). Due to such buttons, users have become increasingly capable of content *curation* (Pflaeging 2015; cf. PewInternet 2013). Multimodal texts that prove socially significant and are thus regarded as *worthy-of-curation* are shared with a user's circle of Facebook Friends and beyond. This process has also been referred to as *entextualization* (Leppänen et al. 2014: 113; Androutsopoulos 2014: 8). The concept allows for "explaining how in social media activities discourse material originating elsewhere gets lifted out of its original context and is repositioned and remodified as a meaningful element in a new context" (Leppänen et al. 2014: 116).

Web infrastuctures, esp. those of social networking sites, have become increasingly *capable-of-curation*. The fact that content can be shared by a mere "push of a button" facilitates *virality*, here understood as a "social information flow process where many people *simultaneously* forward a specific information item over a short period of time" (Nahon & Hemsley 2013: 6, original emphasis).

Drawing on Facebook's potential for curation, viral content providers aim to *profit* from web users who seek distraction in social interaction online. As professional content providers, they offer multimodal texts that are likely to be considered worthy-of-curation by participants, who then "mobilize" (Leppänen et al. 2014: 132) them in processes of socialising and identity work (Page 2014: 47). This translates into a complex participation framework (Goffman 1981) that shifts dynamically with regard to communicative situation and the textual functions or intentions of different groups of participants.

In that sense, viral online communication interrelates and oscillates between two perspectives: the more global and essentially commercial perspective of professional providers of (meant to go) viral content on the one side, and the more local and essentially phatic perspective of "regular" users of social networking sites.

These assumptions are supported by the results of my diachronic analyses. In the following, I characterize Distractify's communicative practices in 2014 and 2017 with regard to communicative situation and textual function. Here, my analyses indicated a high amount of stability in communicative choices when seen in a diachronic light. Thus, I will abstract away from the individual time cuts and present two distinct phases of viral online communication, by the example of *Distractify*, their Facebook audience and their Friends.

In a 1st phase of text production and reception, when *listicle*-exemplars are created and put on display, commercial success appears to be central to Distractify's communicative intentions. This success is based on an exploitation of a Facebook user's readiness to curate whatever seems worthy-of-curation. It seems plausible, however, that any commercial interests should reside in the background from a recipient's viewpoint. This seems to explain why professional writers such as *Mark Pygas, Rob Fee, Pinar, Alex Scola*, both in 2014 and 2017, use pseudonyms and snapshot-like photographs that evoke connotations of casuality and informality (see Figures 11.2 and 11.4). At the same time, 2014-*listicles* strive to fulfill an appellative function by means of degree adverbs that challenge a recipient's prior experiences by implying that they are about to witness something *absolutely, extremely, unbelievably adorable* if they just clicked to see for themselves.

In a 2nd phase, Facebook users select and distribute listicles among their social networks. In doing so, they move on from their role as recipients. However, since they merely forward texts they did not produce themselves, the term *curator* seems more apt to describe their participant role. Instead of an appellative and informative or referential function that featured prominently in the 1st phase, the potential for phatic communication is now foregrounded when Facebook users curate *40 Powerful Photos of Love And Its Many Beautiful Forms* to wallow collectively in feelings of friendship and belongingness.

These findings also attest to the crucial importance of the communicative choices made when designing multimodal texts in an endeavor to achieve virality, an issue that has rarely been addressed in virality research (Tan et al. 2014) but is of particular interest to multimodalists. Thus, it is worthwhile to reflect once more on the particular circumstances of viral text production and relate them to the concept of *genre* and *genre expectations*.

Not only is it the fact that Distractify writers purposefully craft listicles with the intention to achieve their viral distribution (cf. Heimbach et al. 2015: 40). As with similar forms of journalistic and commercial mass media communication, Distractify needs to compensate for what Bell called "delayed feedback" (Bell 1991: 70) from a necessarily imaginary audience. Professional content providers learn about any success in achieving virality only after a multimodal text is distributed among members of its target audience. Since "post and pray" (Jenkins et al. 2013: 195) is not an option, strategies such as intentional "overproduction" (Jenkins et al. 2013: 196) are pursued. In 2014, *Distractify* shared listicles onto Facebook at a regular interval of 15 minutes. Facebook shares, likes and comments were then monitored, and genre exemplars that users did not approve of were instantly taken off the platform (see Pflaeging 2015: 163).

Also, professional content providers anticipate their audience's *genre expectations*. This notion is inextricably linked to the ethno-methodological branch of genres studies, where *genres* have also been conceptualized as prototypically organized "socio-cognitive devices for sense-making" (Lomborg 2014: 45; Sandig 2000) that participants draw on both in text production and reception (see Luginbühl 2014; Schildhauer 2016; Pflaeging 2017). In that sense, genres function as frames of reference on whose grounds situated use is made sense of, and pattern conformity and divergence are noticed. In case of viral online communication, whose similarity to advertising discourse has been pointed to above, it seems advisable to partly refrain from established patterns to ensure ongoing attractiveness. Contrary to advertisements, however, phenomena of pattern change in viral online communication seem to be conditioned by retaining a potential for phatic communion and hence conviviality.

In light of the interrelations between conviviality, virality, and genre (expectations), and my findings with regard to communicative situation and textual function, the following research questions have guided the remaining part of this paper:
- Focussing on the analytical level multimodal structure, what phenomena of pattern stability and change over time can be described for *listicle* as an online genre whose exemplars are designed to attract user attention and to spread virally on the Web?
- What possible explanations for any phenomena of pattern stability and change can be given?

I now introduce my data, present my findings and discuss them.

3 Research design

The data for the present study was collected in 2014 and 2017. The first time cut resulted from an initially casual observation, similar to the one voiced in the epigraph to this article. Guided by the assumption that ad-incorporating genres need to change rapidly so that they retain their attractiveness, I opted for collecting further data relatively shortly after the first sample.

The first *listicle*-corpus was established in October 2014. I sampled 50 genre exemplars from *distractify.com* by eliciting each exemplar that appeared as I scrolled down the main page. The second corpus was established in March 2017 by pursuing the same strategy while ensuring the same sample size.

As indicated above, my theoretical-methodological toolkit is inspired by established frameworks for multimodal genre description (esp. Stöckl 2016, see also Adamzik 2016). As suggested above (in ref. to Stöckl 2015), many approaches to (multimodal) genre analysis give emphasis to a description of a genre's communicative setting (i.e. features of the communicative context, incl. participant constellations, see Goffman 1981), its textual function (i.e. the intentions with which texts are produced and the overall communicative use to which they are put), and its multimodal structure (esp. layout structure/composition of the page space, as well as rhetorical relations between layout elements, see Bateman 2008, any indicators of a more general rhetorical "logic" and, more specifically, its general choice of topic and patterns of topical unfolding). With regard to these three prominent analytical dimensions, I have carried out qualitative analyses and some explorative quantifications.

In the subsequent section, I focus particularly on prominent shifts and changes in terms of multimodal structure, as I have already addressed the considerable extent of pattern stability with respect to communicative situation and textual function.

4 Diachronic perspectives on the genre *listicle* (later *storicle*)

4.1 2014: Image-centric listicles

In 2014, the page layout of *listicles* is typically sub-divided into three sections: a *header area*, a *main body* of the page, which accommodates 20 list items on average, and a *footer area*. In all instances, the *header area* gives the headline of the listicle, information on the author (in form of a name/pseudonym and an avatar image) and the publication time (following the pattern ... *hours/days ago*). Furthermore, it typically provides a lead-in to the list to follow. The *footer area* is regularly composed of a number of hyper-linked teasers to further *listicle*-exemplars. Both sections employ a large number of social buttons that allow for sharing onto *Facebook*, *Twitter*, and *Pinterest*. Also, list items feature the same share-buttons that appear as the cursor hovers over the image. Thus, there is a high degree of curate-ability strategically built into the page by means of hyperlinks.

In addition, it seems relevant to explore the multimodal means with which users ought to be *persuaded* to curate. A closer look at the language use in the headlines of 2014-listicles reveals that the personal deictic *you*, which enables direct reader address, is used in 20% of the headlines. Furthermore, headlines contain 11.26 word-forms on average (with a standard deviation of $\sigma = 2.16$) and are long enough to sell the gist of what to expect straight away. In order to increase legibility and ensure quick and effective perception, all words of a headline consistently begin with upper case letters, a typographical style called *start case* (cf. White 1992: 26). Numerals are given in 62% of the corpus texts; essentially, they seem to allow for estimating the (short amount of) time users will need to browse through the listicle at hand.

The *list items* are typically multimodal clusters with short stretches of language framing a perceptually dominant and rhetorically central illustration. It seems that the advantages of the visual mode for quick and direct perception are used to keep the information flowing and a users' attention high. A large amount of the 1006 illustrations included in the 50 texts I coded are snapshot-like photographs and animated gifs that revolve around topics such as LIFESTYLE & CULTURE (e.g., *26 Of The Best Halloween Movies Of All Time (And What To Drink While Watching Them)*, ART & DESIGN (e.g., *20 DIY Projects To Help Game of Thrones Fans Survive The Winter*), or ANIMALS (e.g., *28 Photos That Prove Owls Are The Most Magnificent Birds In The Animal Kingdom*).

As the example given in Figure 11.2 suggests, all of these visuals are sourced from web sites all over the Internet, an intertextual quality of *listicles* that is closely tied to the textual logic typically construed in 2014. Listicles seem to follow a *list-logic*; that is, a concept or conceptual frame triggered in a listicle headline is elaborated on in image-centric list items that present instantiations or sub-types of said frame (cf. Figure 11.2). Accordingly, 2014-listicles show a low degree of narrativity, that is, a lack of central dynamic narrative cues such as character development, spatio-temporal development or an unfolding of action including cause-effect relationships between narrative events.

In sum, the multimodal design of 2014-listicles with their clearly structured layout space and attention-grabbing image-centric list items promises easy and quick consumption. It anticipates new kinds of digital visual literacies, in particular scrolling, which are likely to have evolved through frequent interaction on other image-heavy microblogging media such as Tumblr or Instagram. Social buttons facilitate viral distribution of contents and the broad, but positive choice of topics cater to users' needs for conviviality.

4.2 2017: Language-centric storicles

My analysis of the 2017-data, and comparison to the 2014-data suggests a high degree of pattern stability in terms of the basic composition of the page space. Genre exemplars continue to feature a *footer area* with links to further texts of a similar kind, and a *header area* that provides a headline (composed from $\bar{x}$ = 11.14 word-forms, σ = 1.8, similar to 2014), the author's photograph and name/pseudonym as well as a time stamp. Furthermore, a large teaser image is now incorporated into the *header area* of all 2017-texts (see Figure 11.4). It seems plausible that this pattern emerged to compensate for a generally image-deprived main body of the page. It is this section of 2017-texts, more precisely the strategies for organizing the page space structurally and rhetorically, which shows the highest degree of pattern change. A mean average of 4.3 illustrations (cf. $\bar{x}$ = 22 illustrations in 2014) and 554.23 word-forms (cf. $\bar{x}$ = 14 word-forms in 2014) are used per main section, which amounts to 129 word-forms per illustration. These figures attest to a considerable shift in how extensively the resources of image and language are drawn on in composing the 2017-texts.

It is worth to note that the shift from image- to language-centricity can mainly be attributed to an abundant embedding of stretches of Twitter discourse into the page space of 2017 genre exemplars (cf. Figure 11.4). In fact, only 45% of the linguistic material integrated into the main sections of texts has been authored by Distractify-staff. The compositional structure of tweets, however, remains intact; rectangular frames identify embedded tweets as self-contained layout components. Due to such noticeable indexes to what could be seen as a different kind of virtual materiality, the dense intertextual ties inscribed into 2017-corpus texts become much more apparent than with embedded images in 2014-listicles. However, these findings not only indicate that embedded tweets *originate* on web platforms other than distractify.com; they also suggest that they are drawn from self-contained strands of Twitter discourse that revolves around a singular social occurrence that is worthy of being reported on and whose communicative locus is either offline, online, or has come to oscillate between both discursive spheres. More importantly, however, it is on web platforms other than Distractify.com where the worthiness of reporting on a respective event is constructed. Distractify-authors rather act as narrators, who select tweets, establish coherence, comment, provide an emotional stance, and conclude. What is reported on follows a *story-logic*, with a temporal (and partly spatial) unfolding of action, cause-effect relations between different sections of a plot, climactic structures and very often a resolution or evaluation stage at the end.

What had been labelled *list area* does not anymore live up to its name: Only three of the 2017-corpus texts draw on a *list-logic* as the main strategy to

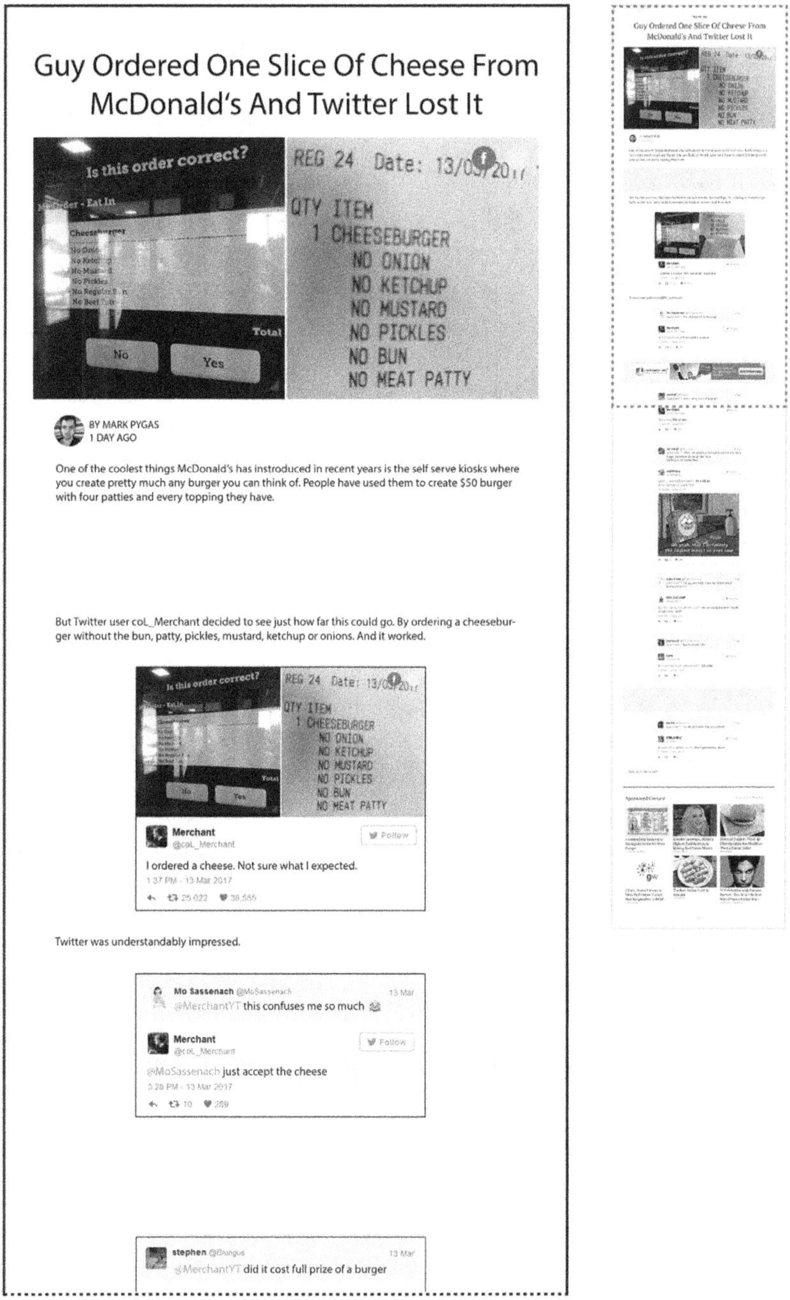

11 Diachronic perspectives on viral online genres — **239**

Figure 11.4: Top Section of a *Distractify*-storicle, as publ. in March 2017.

structure and rhetorically organize the body section of the page space, that is, integrate enumeration and image-centric list items; all other sample texts have abandoned this pattern. Consequently, the genre *listicle* ought to be relabeled as *storicle*. Such developments are also reflected in a re-design of headlines. In 2014-listicles, 88.5% of the headlines were composed of complex noun phrases with quantifiers, pre-modifying adjective phrases that typically comprise degree adverbs and simple adjectives (see, e.g., Burton-Roberts 1998: 62–65, 160), and prepositional phrases, appositive or *-ing* participle clauses as post-modifiers (see, e.g., Burton-Roberts 1998: 166–168; Greenbaum & Quirk 2002: 50): *25 Of The Most Bizarre Superstitions From Around The World*, *23 (Somewhat) Shameful Things That Happen When You Live Alone*, or *The 30 Teeniest Tiniest Puppies Being Adorably Teeny Tiny*. By 2017, the complex noun phrase-pattern has given way to a considerable number of finite clauses that present a narrative event in a nutshell: *This Teen Made A Hilarious Escape Video After She Was 'Trapped' In Her Own Bedroom*, *This Rescue Pup Faceplanted During A Dog Show And We Couldn't Love Him More*, or *Guy Ordered One Slice Of Cheese From McDonald's And Twitter Lost It*. In many cases, the headlines call up two incompatible frames or scripts (see, e.g., Brown & Yule 1983 for an overview) whose incongruencies participants seek to resolve.

In sum, the basic composition of the page space in the 2017-examples remained stable in comparison to the 2014-examples. Yet, in 2017, large images are used in the header section, possibly to entice users to scroll further down; the main body typically features only few images. It still draws on compositional clusters, i.e. short stretches of language given in text frames, when embedding a large number of tweets, a practice user will be well familiar with from (soft) news media sites. Also, there is a noticeable shift from a list-logic to a story-logic and content providers act as narrators, who present stories that appeal to their users' desire for conviviality and thus potentially become viral.

5 Conclusion: From images to words, from lists to stories

The main aim of this chapter was to explore the interrelations between conviviality, virality and genre through a diachronic study of the virality-ensuring practices of Distractify's content providers. I suggested two fundamental trends in the development of the *listicle*-genre: from images to words, and from lists to stories.

In 2014, the page space of the *listicle* typically integrates a considerable amount of illustrations, that is, mainly photographs and animated gifs. They usually form the rhetorical nucleus of structurally prominent list items. By 2017, the main body of *listicles* has been visibly reorganized. The semiotic resources of the verbal mode are employed to a greater extent, which is largely due to embedded tweets.

The 2014-corpus texts reiterate a *list-logic* by presenting a certain number of instantiations or sub-types of a conceptual hyper(o)nym; only few narrative cues are detectable in 2014-sample texts. By 2017, the degree of narrativity integrated into the page space of corpus texts has increased. Texts typically revolve around a social occurrence that is worthwhile to report on and instantiate an overarching *story-logic*. Distractify-authors have emerged as narrators who select, re-arrange, and comment on episodes of social interaction. Not the least, these observations prompt a relabeling of *listicles* as *storicles*.

These findings attest to the fact that *listicles* (or *storicles*) changed considerably with respect to text producers' communicative choices made in designing the multimodal structure of 2014- and 2017-texts. This raises the question of what explanations can be given as to why these differences occur. Furthermore, and perhaps more importantly, I shall consider the question of why diachronic changes in the multimodal page spaces took place to the extent they did.

As indicated above, the shift towards language-centricity in 2017-storicles largely results from an extensive embedding of Twitter discourse. Tweets deal with singular social occurrences that are addressed, for instance, in evaluative or anecdotal meta-commentaries. Language shows communicative advantages over generally more ambiguous images in meeting the demands of voicing an opinion or telling an anecdote. Also, given the thematic specificity and the pace at which exchanges on social media platforms often progress, participants might not seek to complement a quick tweet with an image for reasons of time and availability.

In the light of more global trends towards *visualizing (in) the new media* and *image-centricity* in general (Stöckl et al. fc.) the shift from image-centricity to language-centricity in contemporary viral online genres may seem counterintuitive at first sight. Given that multimodal texts investigated are typically interspersed by adverts, this move becomes plausible. Once established, and with reference to what he calls the principle of reversal, Cook (2006: 224) argues that "many features [...] typical of ads [...] are liable to be replaced by their opposite". The motivation behind this, he explains further, is to "[defeat] expectation and [arrest] attention". Due to the strong commercial function of viral online genres, this principle of reversal seems to apply to the development of listicles/storicles as well. Thus, if gaining a Facebook audience's attention and initiating viral spreads requires a shift from image to language, then this shift is likely to happen.

However, the implementation of this principle of reversal in the case of viral online communication does not seem to mean avant-gardist experiments. As my study suggests, the situational settings and participant constellations show a high degree of stability. Also, both in 2014 and 2017 the same set of textual functions and a dynamic shift from informative and appellative functions to phatic intentions have been attested – be it on the basis of appealing images, positive topics, or narrative discourse structures. In fact, research on viral marketing strategies has shown that achieving virality hinges on a high degree of emotionality of the message (see Dobele et al. 2007; Berger & Milkman 2010, 2012; Heimbach et al. 2015).

In a constantly-changing and fast-paced online world, Distractify will continue to "[draw] over 30 million people away from something boring (like waiting for the bus), tedious (like doing homework) or pointless (like every conference call) [...]" (Distractify 2018). And in this endeavour they are likely to explore new strategies for reinventing their listicles or storicles' multimodal page spaces – while ensuring their potential for conviviality, connectedness, and groupness.

References

Adamzik, Kirsten. 2012. Werbekommunikation textlinguistisch. In Nina Janich (ed.), *Handbuch Werbekommunikation: Sprachwissenschaftliche und interdisziplinäre Zugänge*, 123–142. Tübingen: Francke Verlag.
Adamzik, Kirsten. 2016. *Textlinguistik: Grundlagen, Kontroversen, Perspektiven*. Berlin/Boston: Mouton de Gruyter.
Androutsopoulos, Jannis. 2014. Moments of sharing: Entextualization and linguistic repertoire in social networking. *Journal of Pragmatics* 73, 4–18.
Bateman, John A. 2008. *Multimodality: A foundation for the systematic analysis of multimodal documents*. Basingstoke: Palgrave Macmillan.
Bateman, John A., Janina Wildfeuer & Tuomo Hiippala. 2017. *Multimodality: Foundations, research and analysis. A problem-oriented introduction*. Berlin/Boston: Mouton de Gruyter.
Bell, Allan. 1991. Audience accommodation in the mass media. In Howard Giles, Justine Coupland & Nikolas Coupland (eds.), *Contexts of accommodation: Developments in applied sociolinguistics*, 69–102. Cambridge: Cambridge University Press.
Berger, Jonah & Katherine L. Milkman. 2010. Virality: What gets shared and why. In Margaret C. Campbell, Jeff Inman & Rik Pieters (ed.), *Advances in consumer research*, 118–121. Duluth: Association for Consumer Research.
Berger, Jonah & Katherine L. Milkman. 2012. What makes online content viral? *Journal of Marketing Research* 49 (2), 192–205.
Boyd, Danah, & Nicole Ellison. (2008). *Social Network Sites Definition, History, and Scholarship*. Journal of Computer-Mediated Communication, 13, 210–230.
Brown, Gillian & George Yule. 1983. *Discourse analysis*. Cambridge: Cambridge University Press.

Burton-Roberts, Noel. 1998. *Analysing sentences: An introduction to English syntax*. London: Longman.
Cook, Guy. 2006. *The discourse of advertising*. London: Routledge.
Deumert, Ana. 2014. The Performance of a ludic self on social network(ing) sites. In Philip Seargeant & Caroline Tagg (eds.), *The language of social media: Identity and community on the internet*, 23–44. Basingstoke: Palgrave Macmillan.
Distractify. 2018. http://www.distractify.com/about (3 March, 2018.)
Dobele, Angela, Adam Lindgreen, Michael Beverland, Joëlle Vanhamme & Robert van Wijk. 2007. Why Pass on Viral Messages? Because They Connect Emotionally. *Business Horizons* 50. 291–304.
Edison Research. 2014. The infinite dial 2014. http://www.edisonresearch.com/wp-content/up loads/2014/03/The-Infinite-Dial-2014-from-Edison-Research-and-Triton-Digital.pdf (24 November, 2018.)
eMarketer. 2015. Average daily time spent with selected social networks among internet users in the United States as of November 2014, by age (in minutes). *Statista – The Statistics Portal*. Available: http://www.statista.com/statistics/368698/us-user-daily-minutes-social-network-by-age (28 February, 2019)
Gerlitz, Carolin & Anne Helmond. 2013. The like economy: Social buttons and the data-intensive web. *New Media & Society* 15(8), 1348–1365.
Goffman, Erving. 1981. *Forms of talk*. Philadelphia: University of Pennsylvania Press.
Greenbaum, Sidney & Gerald Nelson. 2002. An introduction to English grammar. London: Longman.
Heimbach, Irina, Benjamin Schiller, Thorsten Strufe & Oliver Hinz. 2015. Content virality on online social networks: Empirical evidence from Twitter, Facebook, and Google+ on German news websites. In *HT 15, September 1–4, 2015, Guzelyurt, Northern Cyrpus*, 39–47.
Jakobson, Roman. 1960. Closing statement: Linguistics and poetics. In Thomas A. Sebeok (ed.), *Style in language*, 350–377. Cambridge: Massachusetts Institute of Technology.
Jenkins, Henry. 2009. *Confronting the challenges of participatory culture: Media education for the 21st century*. Cambridge: Massachusetts Institute of Technology.
Jenkins, Henry, Sam Ford & Joshua Green. 2013. *Spreadable media: Creating value and meaning in a networked culture*. New York: New York University Press.
Kinser. 2013, 26 Dec. http://tllsga.org/making-a-list-checking-it-twice (1 September, 2015.)
Leppänen, Sirpa, Samu Kytölä, Henna Jousmäki, Saija Peuronen & Elina Westinen. 2014. Entextualization and resemiotization as resources for identification in social media. In Philip Seargeant & Caroline Tagg (eds.), *The language of social media: Identity and community on the internet*, 112–136. Basingstoke: Palgrave Macmillan.
Lerman, Kristina & Laurie Jones (2007): *Social Browsing on Flickr*. In: Proceedings of the 1st International Conference on Weblogs and Social Media.
Lomborg, Stine. 2014. Social media, social genres: Making sense of the ordinary. New York/ London: Routledge.
Luginbühl, Martin. 2014. *Medienkultur und Medienlinguistik: Komparative Textsortengeschichte(n) der amerikanischen "CBS Evening News" und der Schweizer "Tagesschau"*. Bern: Peter Lang.
Malinowski, Bronislaw. 1923/1936. *The problem of meaning in primitive languages*. In Charles K. Ogden & Ivor A. Richards (eds). The Meaning of Meaning, 296–336. London: Kegan Paul.

Müller, Christina Margrit. 2012. Kommunikation im Bild: Notizen in Fotocommunities. In Torsten Siever & Peter Schlobinski (eds.), *Web 2.0. Entwicklungen zum III. Workshop zur linguistischen Internetforschung*, 49–72. Frankfurt am Main: Peter Lang.

Nahon, Karine & Jeff Hemsley. 2013. *Going viral*. Hoboken: Wiley.

Page, Ruth. 2014. Hoaxes, hacking and humour. Analysing impersonated identity on social networking sites. In Philip Seargeant & Caroline Tagg (eds.), *The language of social media: Identity and community on the internet*, 46–64. Basingstoke: Palgrave Macmillan.

PewInternet. 2013. Additional analysis: Pew Research Center's internet and American life project. *PewInternet.org*. Available: http://www.pewinternet.org/2013/10/28/additional-analysis/#curators (28 February, 2019)

Pew Research Center. 2014. Typical daily activities of Facebook users in the United States in 2013. *Statista – The Statistics Portal*. https://www.statista.com/statistics/192716/typical-daily-facebook-activities-of-us-users/ (01 August, 2019.)

Pflaeging, Jana. 2015. "Things that Matter, Pass them on": ListSite as viral online genre. *10plus1: Living Linguistics* 1, 156–182.

Pflaeging, Jana. 2017. Tracing the narrativity of National Geographic feature articles in the light of evolving media landscapes. *Discourse, Context & Media* 20(4), 248–261.

Radovanovic, Danica & Massimo Ragnedda. 2012. Small talk in the digital age: Making sense of phatic posts. *2nd Workshop on Making Sense of Microposts*, 10–13.

Runkehl, Jens. 2012. Vom Web 1.0 zum Web 2.0. In Torsten Siever & Peter Schlobinski (eds.), *Web 2.0. Entwicklungen zum III. Workshop zur linguistischen Internetforschung*, 9–24. Frankfurt/Main: Peter Lang.

Sandig, Barbara. 2000. Text als prototypisches Konstrukt. In Martina Mangasser-Wahl (ed.), *Prototypentheorie in der Linguistik: Anwendungsbeispiele – Methodenreflexion – Perspektiven*, 93–112. Tübingen: Stauffenburg.

Schildhauer, Peter. 2016. *The personal weblog. A linguistic history*. Frankfurt am Main: Peter Lang.

Stöckl, Hartmut. 2015. From text linguistics to multimodality. Reflections on definitions, transcription, and analysis. In Janina Wildfeuer (ed.), *Building bridges for multimodal research. International perspectives on theories and practices of multimodal analysis*, 51–75. Frankfurt/Main: Peter Lang.

Stöckl, Hartmut. 2016. Multimodalität. Semiotische und textlinguistische Grundlagen. In Nina-Maria Klug & Hartmut Stöckl (eds.), *Handbuch Sprache im multimodalen Kontext*, 3–35. Berlin: de Gruyter.

Stöckl, Hartmut, Helen Caple & Jana Pflaeging (eds.). forthcoming. *Shifts towards image-centricity in contemporary multimodal practices*. London/New York: Routledge.

Tan, Chenhao, Lillian Lee & Bo Pang. 2014. The effect of wording on message propagation. Topic- and author-controlled natural experiments on Twitter. Available: https://chenhaot.com/pubs/wording-effects-message-propagation.pdf (28 February, 2019).

Varis, Piia & Jan Blommaert. 2014. Conviviality and collectives on social media: Virality, memes and new social structures. *Tilburg Papers in Cultural Studies* 108, 1–21.

Vegibit. 2014. 14 Steps to write a great listicle. Available: https://vegibit.com/how-to-write-a-listicle/ (28 February, 2019)

White, Alex 1992. *Type in Use: Effective Typography for Electronic Publishing*. Design Press.

Dorothee Meer and Katharina Staubach

12 Social media influencers' advertising targeted at teenagers: The multimodal constitution of credibility

1 Introduction

While some studies have outlined similarities between youth language and advertising language (cf. Buschmann 1994: 219; Ehrhardt 2007: 253ff.; Homann 2006: 56ff.), Efing indicates that the few studies based on empirical evidence conclude that youth language is rarely used in advertisements. Furthermore, if it is used, it is usually with great caution (cf. Efing 2012: 172). The question arises, then, that if teenagers are rarely targeted by advertisements using youth language, what other strategies are employed to address young consumers? Arguably, one explanation can be found in the work of Baacke and Lauffer (1994: 97), whose study of commercial youth magazines emphasizes that in the magazine BRAVO there is a high percentage of advertising, that is not clearly separated from the editorial content. Similarly, Katheder (2008: 52) not only confirms this assumption with regards to BRAVO, but also coins a term to reflect the pervasion of youth magazines by unmarked product placement: osmotic advertising. Of course, this term refers to the biological notion of osmosis (i.e. the unconscious absorption of information). Following Katheder, we suggest that in the context of social media influencer advertising, teenagers are not primarily addressed in "traditional" ways – e.g., by using youth language in print ads –, but are rather to a large extent addressed through the implicit means of unmarked product placement. This hypothesis is confirmed by empirical work done by Dreyer et al. (2014), who, in their study of websites for 7–11-year-olds, routinely observe the unmarked linkage of advertising and non-advertising content (ibid.: 114ff.). Thus, on the back of this introductory discussion, we set out to address the following, two-fold question: How do implicit advertisements in social media influencer advertising for teenagers work, and to what extent does this kind of interactive, multimodal communication (cf. Herring 2016: 398f.) produce a higher rate of acceptance, or for that matter, a higher level of credibility than traditional advertising formats?

We have shown elsewhere that the relevance of implicit or osmotic advertising is by no means restricted to the realm of print, but that this way of addressing consumers has grown enormously under the conditions of hypermedial communication (cf. Kelly-Holmes 2016; Meer 2018; Meer & Staubach in prep.).[1] So-called haul videos on YouTube may be regarded as prototypical examples of interactive, multimodal formats using implicit advertising strategies. In these videos, social media influencers – who are primarily young women, and more or less the same age as their addressees – present their latest cosmetic or clothing purchases which are introduced with product names and prices and/or are *used* in front of the camera (cf. Harnish & Bridges 2016: 113). In our chapter here, we examine on a video called "XXL HAUL + MEGA VERLOSUNG" (hereafter XXL HAUL) produced by German YouTuber Dagi Bee and uploaded onto YouTube in 2016.[2]

In the next section, we start by focusing on multimodal strategies or practices used by influencers for addressing XXL HAUL's (mostly female) teenage audience. Using a fine-grained analysis (cf. Keating 2016: 258), we are specifically interested in the visual construction of a common or shared space. In the section which follows, we offer further evidence with the help of a more detailed analysis of the haul at hand. Finally, we demonstrate how para-social techniques, thanks to their multimodal, visual and digitally mediated integration, constitute a *sine qua non* for the credibility of social media influencer advertising. Before moving on, however, we want quickly to clarify our approach to multimodality. Following Stöckl (2016; see also the current volume), we define multimodality as, on the one hand, different semiotic modalities (in the sense of "codes") like language, image, music, noise, which are relevant to the haul being analyzed. Following Deppermann and Schmitt (2007), however, we also consider interactively relevant communicative resources such as glance, gesture, object presentation and object manipulation as well as technologically constructed aspects of the communication space constructed by the camera. Through our analysis, it should become clear that all these different semiotic resources – these different modes and media for communicating visually – are decisive in the success of social media influencer's advertising.

---

[1] In this context, the JIM survey, which conducts interviews with 1.200 German teenagers every year about media usage and free time behavior, underlines that the use of digital media has become a daily habit of teenagers. Nearly every teenager (97%) possesses a smartphone used most often for connecting to the internet (cf. JIM survey 2017: 26–27). Besides communication, entertainment activities (consuming images, music, and videos) are among the online activities teenagers pursue most often (ibid.: 31).

[2] See Dagi Bee: "XXL HAUL + MEGA VERLOSUNG" (09/16/2016) Available: https://www.youtube.com/watch?v=xsdP9JDW5ug (28 February, 2019)

2 The para-social and multimodal construction of credibility

Despite there being no feasible means for users to directly influence the course of haul videos, there are multiple implicit and explicit communicative acts which suggest otherwise. Using various para-social techniques (e.g. Horton & Wohl 1956; Horton & Strauss 1957), speakers across different media formats generate the impression that they are in face-to-face interactions with other users (cf. Meer 2018a; Tolson 2010: 279, Frobenius 2014: 61). These phenomena are realized multimodally, and in particular, visually. While the use of multimodal and predominantly visual resources to address media users para-socially is not unique to digital media (cf. Burger & Luginbühl 2014: 418–420), the parasocial connection between media agents such as YouTubers has nonetheless increased with contemporary social/digital media; among other reasons, the reception situation of users has been significantly individualized through the extensive equipment of teenagers with web-enabled devices (again, see endnote 1). Young people can therefore decide relatively autonomously (i.e. independently from adults) when and where they use which format and how they want to react to it.[3]

The established context of free, autonomous digital media access allows social media influencers to create the impression that their audience is directly involved in the making of a "haul". For example, in XXL HAUL, a seemingly "bad" start is not edited out but deliberately maintained and commented on with irony by using an old test pattern from German public service broadcasting. Consider the following extract from the transcript (min 0:00 – 0:10).[4]

---

[3] This model of individualized communication with web-enabled devices is significantly different from traditional situations of reception – say, in front of the TV in the living room.
[4] The transcript of the verbal-linguistic elements of the video was written in accordance with the conventions of GAT 2 and is, moreover, oriented towards the extended freeze variant to capture the multimodality of the haul at hand. The numbers in the left column relate to the respective "turn construction unit" (TCU), which can, in singular instances, also span two lines. The freeze represents the movement relevant for the given TCU. If several movements are relevant, several freezes have been included in the transcript. The arrow above the verbal transcript indicates at which point of the TCU the freeze was shot.

01	HEI leute-
hi guys-
02	und GANZ herzlich willkommen zu einem NEUen video von mir.
and a warm welcome to a new video of mine

03	und in DIEsem video wird es (.) mal (.)
and in this video I will do

03	wieder (.) einen (.) HA:::UL geben;
a haul once again
[Dagi Bee intonates the word "HA:::UL" in a singsong intonation.]

```
04    OH- wow- nein? ?hm?hm; ?hm?hm;
      oh wow- no ?hm?hm; ?hm?hm
```

(On-screen display) Freeze with a residual image and the corresponding disturbance tone.

In this extract, and as we say, Dagi Bee pointedly does not erase the "production mistakes" (e.g. by using the technological possibilities of a retrospective cut); as such, the impression is created that viewers are present at the time of filming (Frobenius 2014: 68).

Importantly, we are less concerned with the construction of *authenticity* (as "realness"; cf. Tolson 2010), but rather with the multimodal – and in particular visual construction – of *credibility*. The difference between these two dimensions is a matter of perspective. Authenticity, as Deppermann (2000) explains in the context of his study about teenage skaters, is tied to the moral claims individuals use to explicitly present themselves as "real" and to distance themselves from other "non-authentic" lifestyles. Such attitudes or aspirations are not found in the beauty formats relevant here; social media influencers like Dagi Bee almost never refer to "authenticity" (or "realness"), but rather operate at the level of the visual – that is, with what can actually be seen by viewers. Consequently, it is credibility that is most relevant for Dagi Bee's videos, because of the style-oriented offers she makes her viewers. These predominantly serve as multimodal, rapport-building acts, which frame Dagi Bee as a credible friend giving advice on one's outer appearance.

Thus, we are most concerned with how Dagi Bee, by using para-interactive means, succeeds in creating credibility with/for her fans. Having said which, we do not wish to deny that authenticity and credibility may, in principle, be connected. Nonetheless, hauls are not concerned with the necessarily moral question of authenticity or trueness, but merely with the question of how effective social media influencers' fashion tips actually are with teenage viewers.

3 Para-sociality and multimodality in social media influencer advertising

Elsewhere we have pointed out that Dagi Bee, in the context of her make-up tutorials, establishes a "trickster identity" (Meer 2018: 216–221). By this, and following Lévi-Strauss's (1955) concept of myth, we mean a narratively and interactively-constructed identity which enables subjects to oscillate between two incompatible poles. The "charm" of such an identity construction is that remnants of the opposite pole always remain (cf. Lévi-Strauss 1955: 441), allowing the subject to retain a high degree of flexibility. What is remarkable about Dagi Bee's identity construction in her make-up tutorials (between 2011 and 2016) is how she stages herself as a successful YouTube star and beauty expert, and simultaneously as a "normal" teenager. While her beauty expertise certainly gives her credibility, it is her peer status which creates a different, no less important sort of credibility: that of a friend or older sister.

The 2016 XXL HAUL video differs in two ways from Dagi Bee's earlier beauty tutorials: on the one hand, she has inevitably aged, thereby threatening her status as a peer. And on the other hand, the haul text-type does not presuppose any special expertise. Perhaps, then, hauls are especially apt for focusing on the fun of shopping and outer appearances, rendering it possible to forget the increasing age difference with her viewers.[5] There are indeed remnants of her star identity to be found in the haul; for example, she advertises her tour through Germany (min 0:18) and does not merely present the clothes she bought on her bed but also adds shots of her posing as a model in a situation resembling a studio

---

5 This assumption is supported by the fact that Dagi Bee has, besides hauls and "private" videos, increasingly staged herself as a fashion star and model in videos of her traveling the world and in 2014 launched her second channel "BE a BEE".

shooting. However, Dagi Bee's predominant role in this haul is that of a peer who has just returned from a shopping trip. Therefore, we focus next on how Dagi Bee strengthens her "peer" credibility by using mediated (i.e. technological) and multimodal resources.

3.1 The staging of a shared space

From a linguistic perspective, it might seem intuitive to approach the construction of commonalities between Dagi Bee and her fans by referring to the variety of youth styles she employs. However, by looking at the material offered in the haul itself, it becomes apparent that linguistic style is not the most important feature (cf. Norris 2004: 3). As Tolson (2010) has noted, and as we have also observed in our data, most beauty content is shot in the bedrooms of the influencers. Although this might be due in part to the conditions of production which are available, the stability of this spatial variable cannot be explained by this alone. The bedroom setting is maintained even when the influencers, as a result of success and age, no longer physically reside in their teenage homes. This can be explained by the high credibility value of this arrangement, which can be seen in Figure 6 (see also Tolson 2010: 280).

Thus, the fact that Dagi Bee invites her fans into her home, and even into her room and "onto her bed" alludes not only to the common everyday practices of teenage girls hanging out with their friends, but also creates a situation which is experienced as credible by virtue of its intimacy. This is underlined by the fact that the color composition, lighting and design of the chosen scene bears all visual trademarks of a stereotypical, teenage girl's bedroom.

This sense of intimacy and credibility becomes more relevant if one also considers the typical context of viewing for teenage YouTube users. The prototypical place for personalized use of modern media is no longer the family living-room but, as stated above, the bed in a teenager's private bedroom where devices are often held on laps (cf. Meer 2018). This therefore evidences a visually-produced "spatial symmetry" between influencer and viewer who effectively sit opposite each other on a bed, looking at each other directly (see Kress & van Leeuwen 2006: 114 on demand images; also Jewitt & Oyama 2001: 145). From a para-social perspective, this kind of visual directness shores up the sense of contact, heightening the credibility of Dagi Bee and the viewing experience.

The following extracts from XXL HAUL (min 3:16 – 3:22) feature Dagi Bee presenting a newly-purchased long "unisex T-shirt" while standing on her bed with bare legs. These show how the aforementioned symmetry does not merely "frame" the setting, but is a permanent part of the para-interactional construction of an all-too familiar situation.

01   ich zeig euch mal (.) wie lang dieses (.) OBERteil ist-
     i'll show you how long this shirt is
     [Dagi Bee stands up, looking into the camera from below.]

02   ich hab auch ne (.) HOSe an;
     i'm also waering pants;
     [Dagi Bee kneels onto her bed.]
03   und es würde mir theoretisch bi:s (--)
     and it would theoretically be

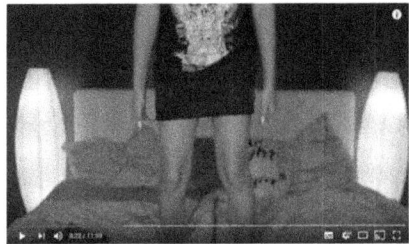

```
            |
03     HIERhin gehen;
       up to here;
```

First, by means of camera perspective, the scene is para-socially constructed in a way which leads viewers to the impression that they are sitting directly in front of Dagi Bee while she pulls down the T-shirt, steps onto the bed and shows the viewers the length of the T-shirt. She makes use of gestural as well as linguistic resources to convey a concrete impression of the T-shirt when she marks its lower rim with her hands while at the same time uttering the words "up to here" (l. 3).[6] The impression of unmediated presence is visually achieved by the specific use of the camera as a digitally mediated resource for clarifying the process and its point-of-view; allowing viewers only to see the legs on the bed it seems as though they are seated directly in front of Dagi Bee. Apart from this multimodal staging of para-social presence, this scene additionally invokes a practice which is highly popular among young girls; namely, that of showing each other new clothes by trying them on and presenting each of their new acquisitions. This, too, supports the seemingly unmediated presence of viewers, who in reality exist behind smartphones or tablets. However, it is not only the practice of trying on clothes that is central to XXL HAUL. Additionally, Dagi Bee introduces a problem-situation which is typical of the viewers' ages (min 0:40):

> WEIL- ich hab meinen kleiderschrank so un(.)FASSbar ausgemistet, und ich DACHte so, NO? ich hab einfach NICHTS MEHR DRIN- ich muss einfach ma wieder SHOPpen gehen.
>
> *Because I mucked out my wardrobe so unbelievably, and I thought like, no? i simply had nothing left – I just have to go shopping again.*

---

6 Stukenbrock (2010) has shown that the deictically used expression *so* (like, in our example, the deictic "here") only generates meaning in its multimodal context and in association with a corresponding gesture, which once again underlines the need for an analysis which into account multimodal resources.

Here, too, the verbal integration of the visually presented clothes into the users' social sphere constitutes a performance of credibility. Furthermore, Dagi Bee's comment here serves to stylistically mark the situation as youthful – using linguistic resources, she frames the haul as belonging to her fans' lifeworlds. For example, she comments – using several English words (marked by italics here) – on a sweater by saying "I totally celebrated" (min 2:05; Ger. "feier" – see endnote 7) or assessing a T-shirt as "super *nice*" (min 1:49), "really *nice*" (min 4:49) and "completely *deep and gothic*" (min 1:26). Likewise, by describing another T-shirt as "a bit of *crop*, but not too *crop*" (min 2:32), but also by means of discourse markers such as "no idea" (min 1:28) and "is not a thing" (min 3:58) and by addressing users directly with "isn't it hot?" (min 4:45), the overall exchange is framed verbally as a youthful (and female) one. Thus, Dagi Bee linguistically, testifies to her status as a peer – and thus to her credibility.

As a next step, we analyze two concrete para-social practices Dagi Bee applies to stage the exchange as "unmediated" and, thus, to frame it as credible.

3.2 The visual, para-social production of credibility

3.2.1 The visual embedding of verbal forms

Because verbal forms of para-social behavior have been covered extensively in the literature (e.g. Burger & Luginbühl 2014; Deppermann & Schmidt 2016; Meer 2018), we do not address them in much depth here. Rather, we aim to show that the majority of verbal forms of para-social address are made relevant in combination with other modalities and resources. However, it is important to note the high concentration of para-social verbal expressions typically found in YouTube videos. In XXL HAUL, for example, there are on average about two explicitly verbal para-social addresses to users per minute. Typical examples are salutations and farewell expressions (all translated here) like "Hey, guys, and a really warm welcome to my new video" (min 0:01), grammatically integrated para-social constructions such as "many will say" (min 10:41) or independent constructions like "in any case, keep in touch" (min 0:54). The function of these constructions can be interpreted as a first indication of the value of a seemingly unmediated contact between influencer and viewer.

While we find multiple deictic-referential elements in the verbal forms of para-social activity whose objects (in their de-contextualized forms) are not straightforward (e.g., "is this what they're called," min 4:28; and cf. Stukenbrock 2015: 13–18), we are not concerned with differentiating between separate deictic modes of occurrence here. Rather we are interested in the function of deictic references with different modalities and expressive resources for the construction of a common or shared space. Thus, we take into account everything which occurs simultaneously with the verbal utterances. For example, consider the following extract (min 11:53 – 11:57), in which Dagi Bee bids her fans farewell:

01 ich wünsch euch einen GANZ wunderschönen tag-
    have a very wonderful day-
    [Dagi Bee looks into the camera and points at it with her open hands.]

02 und wir sehen uns bald WIEder und, (.)
    and see you soon and

03 bis dann,
    so long

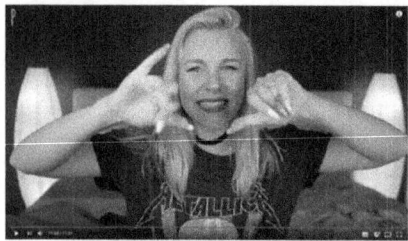

```
                    |
04      tschüssi:::?
        bye:::
        [Dagi Bee looks into the camera, smiles, waves with both hands and finally covers
        the camera with both hands.]
```

If we were to examine only the verbal aspects of this farewell sequence, we would probably conclude that the speech act is successful: the viewers have been directly addressed and there are elements of youth language, at least in the final "bye". However, the orienting of this farewell specifically to teenagers only becomes entirely clear if one additionally takes into account the visuality of the influencer's facial expression and gestures, both of which serve an interpersonal meta-function (Kress & van Leeuwen 2006: 114). The sweeping gesture preceding the verbal utterances (l. 01) along with the blown kisses (l. 02) and subsequent waving occur simultaneously with Dagi Bee's smile (l. 04); it all makes the staging of the farewell ceremony visible. At the same time, it is only the visually-perceptible friendliness of the farewell which supports its interpretation as somehow distinctively youthful. Dagi Bee's verbal utterances do not always (or usually) precede her glances and gestures; as such, they should not be interpreted merely as additional multimodal amplifications of what is said, but must be understood as a complex integration and intertwining of different modalities.

3.2.2 The multimodal construction of a sensory experience

Dagi Bee's glance behavior is an important aspect to her para-social construction of a digitally mediated space shared with viewers. The influencer's glance or the change of direction of her view from the presented objects to the teenage viewers (and vice versa) in XXL HAUL clearly contributes to her audience's impression that they are examining the purchases together with here – in the same room. For example:

01 |
    SO.
    alright

           | |
02   fangen wir ma   an mit dem ERSTen teil;
     let's start   *with the first piece*

Note here the change of direction in Dagi Bee's gaze, which can be observed from shot 01 to shot 02. This is typical of this particular haul. Dagi Bee first looks at the presented object and then at the camera; for viewers (as *interactive participants*; Kress & van Leeuwen 2006: 114) this creates the impression that they are being looked at directly. Therefore, her glance creates a certain visual closeness, serving as a kind of *demand image* (Kress & van Leeuwen 2006: 121). Furthermore, the continuous switching back and forth of Dagi Bee's gaze between viewers and presented objects leads to viewers likewise concentrating on the purchases (Keating 2016: 263). Additionally, while the use of the camera as a (para-social) resource leads viewers to believe Dagi Bee is looking directly at them, there is another effect: given the limitations of the camera's perspective, viewers must also experience Dagi Bee's glance shifting to her purchases as a result of their own change of focus. This experiential potential is reinforced by the aforementioned spatial symmetry, in which the users sit "opposite" Dagi Bee on their own beds, with their web-enabled terminal devices directly in front of them.

We turn now to the presented objects as multimodal resources for visually producing credibility. Specifically, we analyze an extract (min 5:07–5:20) where Dagi Bee temporarily presents the advertised object in front of a neutral wall (cf. section 3.3). In spite of this more-or-less "professional" location (reminiscent of a fashion studio), Dagi Bee focuses on the tactile quality of the sweater using body orientation, gestures, and facial expressions. She thus multimodally contextualizes the sensory experience of wearing the presented object as tactile and personal.

01   Und ich hab mir einen so KUSCHligen (.) SCHÖnen (.) pullover bestellt;
      and i have ordered such a cuddly beautiful pullover for myself

02   DER is von der marke:: free people;
      it is by the brand free people

```
03    auf jeden fall- seht euch mal den KRAgen an-
      definitely look at the collar
04    und oh mein gott LEUte-
      and oh my god guys
```

```
05    am liebsten würd ich darin (.) EINgehen und darin sterben.
      wished i could perish and die in it
06    es ist (.) SO weich;
      it is so soft
```

The expressive framing of the object presentation in this sequence gives the impression that users are sitting directly in front of Dagi Bee, intimately following the tactile delight triggered by her purchase. Beyond the nonverbal cues of body orientation (ll. 02, 03, 05), gesture (l. 03) and facial expression (ll. 01, 05) – all of which are realized visually – the vocal stress on "cuddly beautiful" (l. 01), "guys" (l. 04), "perish" (l. 05) and "so soft" (l. 06) also underline the sensory experience of the purchase/product. Thus, the visual presentation of cuddling with the presented object in the shots (corresponding to lines 2 and 5) translates the influencer's tactile experience into the realm of visual perception for the viewers, rendering it empathetically comprehensible.

In the same vein, the sensory experience shared between influencer and viewers is also accomplished through object manipulation, as we show in the following XXL HAUL extract (min 1:09–1:17) with more details from the blouse presentation introduced above.

07   ähm ist halt ein BLUse bluse stoff;
     well it's just a blouse blouse fabric

08   aber die is irgendwie son bisschen stretchy;
     but it is somehow a little stretchy
     [Dagi Bee alternately looks into the camera and at the blouse in her hands, stretching the fabric.]

09   das is so VOLL- (2.0)
     this is so (2.0)

10   ANders;
     different

11   ich kann das gar nich so beschreiben;
     i can't really describe it

After the blouse has been introduced against the backdrop of the neutral wall, Dagi Bee is then free to experience its tactile quality also by manipulating it. The blouse is first characterized verbally as "blouse fabric" (German "bluse stoff" is probably meant to be Blusenstoff). While looking at the users, Dagi Bee then (l. 08) attempts one more verbal characterization ("But it is somehow a little stretchy"), but at the same time visually demonstrating the material qualities of the fabric by repeatedly stretching it. Terminating yet another attempt of verbal classification ("this is so"; l. 09), she invites her viewers to visually "experience" the "stretchy quality of the blouse" by stretching the fabric for two seconds. She conclusively confirms the dominance of visual qualities over verbal ones by using the qualification "different" before making explicit her inability to put things into words: "I can't really describe it" (cf. Weidner 2017: 28).

As the entire XXL HAUL video is highly multimodal, its para-social character, too, can be understood as semiotically complex: by purposefully using the camera as an expressive resource, directly looking at the viewers, and presenting objects to them as well as staging their use, Dagi Bee makes it possible for her viewers to imagine themselves sitting in the same room as their YouTube star. Furthermore, both the camera and the use of Web 2.0 affordances enable Dagi Bee to realize not only visual and acoustic sense perceptions, but also to visually and audibly convey tactile experiences (cf. Holly & Jäger 2012: 153).

3.3 The social media influencer as trickster

Based on what we have established so far concerning the specific objects integrated into the haul (e.g. T-shirts, sweat shirts, blouses, shorts, glasses, and jackets), it is fair to conclude that the visual presentation of these objects is integrated into a conversation-like exchange with teenagers, one that is framed multimodally as friendly and intimate. The impression of an unmediated exchange hinges on para-social forms of addressing viewers multimodally. The para-social framing is, at the same time, a premise for viewers to experience the whole exchange as credible. This begs the question, why is a haul like the one analyzed here not primarily a form of friendly exchange?

First of all, the sheer number of products Dagi Bee presents establishes her to be a well-financed YouTube star, not a peer. Second, she introduces almost every product by mentioning the name of the brand before presenting it in use (i.e., being worn). She also only ever evaluates products positively, celebrating them (recall German "feiern"[7]) and finding them "nice", all of which marks the presentation as typical advertising discourse (cf. Stöckl 2012: 255; Janich 2012: 218f.). On the other hand, the haul fulfills precisely that function which distinguishes digital influencer advertisement from traditional forms of print advertisement: its goal is for the product presentation to remain unobtrusive as advertising but rather to appear as a natural part of the lifeworld of the influencer.

Additionally, the implicit or osmotic advertising in Dagi Bee's haul becomes obvious in the extracts we analyze: those in which the YouTuber reveals her role as a *trickster*, leaving the friendly setting of her room in order to present the products in front of a neutral grey wall. By leaving her bedside, Dagi Bee also leaves behind the mythologized 'pole' or identity of peer, instead framing herself as professional by presenting the pullover in poses resembling those of fashion models. Viewers are thus confronted with a rather professional, much less amateur setting, technologically mediated through the techniques of cutting and point-of-view shots. This setting can, of course, be easily left behind again with the next cut. Indeed, the switching back and forth between the two identity poles of *peer/friend/older sister* and *model/expert* is managed smoothly thanks to the technical affordances of the media; it also constitutes a decisive part of the credibility of the haul.

The relevance of the trickster identity for social media influencer advertising has already been described by Tolson (2010: 286), albeit from a different

---

[7] The expression "feiern" (*celebrate*) is a teenage slang word which stems from rap culture and signifies enthusiastic support or appreciation.

perspective. He notes that the advising function of digital formats should not hide the fact that influencers such as Dagi Bee pursue genuinely egoistic purposes with their videos – in other words, for the purposes of self-promotion. This means that forms of implicit advertising are in these text genres by no means limited to the presented products, but are always made potentially relatable for targeted viewers as well. In this regard, an interesting, explicit intersection between the spheres of product placement and self-promotion is also evident in the XXL HAUL video. In our final extract (5:30 and 7:48), Dagi Bee draws an iPhone to give away to one of her fans. The raffle is connected to the product placement of the app *Stylefruits*, which is displayed and demonstrated:

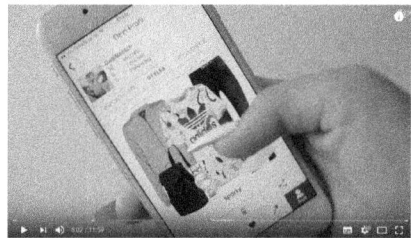

By using this app, users can combine virtual outfits to form a collage with pictures of the respective clothes. To take part in the raffle, viewers are asked to create an outfit of their own under the keyword "Dagi Contest", using a T-shirt from Dagi Bee's merchandise store as the starting point. The best outfit is to be chosen by Dagi Bee herself and rewarded with an iPhone.

Here it becomes especially apparent how the advertising function of this sequence is subordinated to the context of the raffle. The sequence is not about presenting the preferences of a certain product (cf. Stöckl 2012: 255), as described above, but viewers are integrated into a process of interaction and thereby contribute to the promotion of the product themselves. Key here is that this process is not openly discernible; rather, it is staged as a part of Dagi Bee's own fan maintenance (the title "Dagi Contest" already hints at the fact that the users can outwardly enact themselves as "Dagi fans" with this keyword; cf. Meer 2018). On the other hand, the display of a personal outfit can be understood as an important part of teenage identity work, as clothes have become an important form of identity expression and teenage identity work in modern society (cf. Staubach 2017; Staubach 2018).

This moment can again be linked to para-sociality, since Dagi Bee's direct addressing of her viewers is particularly apparent, as seen in the following extract:

|

01 und zwar kennt ihr sehr wahrscheinlich das proBLEM;
    you probably all know the problem

|

02 euer Kleiderschank ist VOLL;
    your wardrobe is full

|

03 ihr habt aber keine AHnung;
    but you have no idea

12 Social media influencers' advertising targeted at teenagers — 265

04 wozu ihr DIEse schuhe, DIEses top, DIEse hose, DIEses kleid;
   how to combine these shoes this top these trousers, this dress

05 alles miteinander KOMbinieren könnt;
   everything can be combined together

06 Aber (.)
   but
07 DA habe ich jetzt eine kleine hilfe für euch;
   i have a little help for you

In this sequence, Dagi Bee constructs some another credible frame for the advertisement by tying it to an everyday problem with which her viewers are supposedly familiar. The combination of the visually discernable glance and the direct verbal address ("you probably all know the problem") together with the shared experience constitutes a common space for interaction; this is perpetuated by the frequent use of generalized "you" address forms ("your wardrobe is full" "but you have no idea") (Forbenius 2014: 61). Immediately following the introduction of this problem, the trickster becomes apparent, however. Dagi Bee continues to address the viewers directly, presenting a proposed solution for the problem: she introduces the app *Stylefruits* for finding the right outfit. After having advertised the app in an implicit way by also making it visually experiential, she uses this message to tie the advertisement of her own products and her self-promotion to it.

4 Conclusion

In this chapter we have focused on a haul video, showing how credibility is constructed multimodally (and predominantly visually) in digital media (beauty) formats on YouTube. This is achieved by the fact that YouTubers who are roughly the same age as their addressees encounter the latter in their digitally mediated lifeworld as slightly older advisors, a role they take on using para-social practices. The product advertisement is integrated into this advising role in a way which makes it potentially experienced as "amicable advice" rather than as a conventional advertisement. What is crucial in this context is that the social media influencers present themselves as both friends who are roughly the same age, and also as experts. It is often assumed that it is the communicative construction of authenticity which is at the center of things, but we argue here that it is in fact the credibility of the recommendations.

Credibility is to a large degree supported by the multimodal (specifically, visual) construction of a common space in which influencers and viewers seem to be tangibly co-present. This impression is primarily created materially as well as by addressing viewers, which, on the para-social level, generates the impression of a friendly exchange about fashion amongst peers. This should not hide the fact, however, that the spoken verbal elements must always be examined in their multimodal contexts. In the haul analyzed here, it is primarily the combination of verbal resources with visually emobodied resources such as object presentation, object manipulation, glance, and gestures which is of crucial importance to the construction of credibility. Beside her para-social strategies, the credibility of Dagi Bee's recommendations is also – and to a large degree – shaped by her role as a trickster figure. Ultimately, her teenage fans/viewers are inclined to believe her recommendations because they experience her, on the one hand, as a trustworthy peer of roughly the same age, and on the other hand, as an expert in the field of fashion.

References

Baacke, Dieter & Jürgen Lauffer. 1994. *Nicht nur schöner Schein. Kinder- und Jugendzeitschriften in Deutschland: Übersicht und Empfehlungen*. Bielefeld: GMK.

Burger, Harald & Martin Luginbühl. 2014. *Mediensprache. Eine Einführung in Sprache und Kommunikationsformen der Massenmedien*. Berlin/Boston: De Gruyter.

Buschmann, Matthias. 1994. Zur „Jugendsprache" in der Werbung. *Muttersprache* 104, 219–231.

Deppermann, Arnulf. 2000. Authentizitätsrhetorik. Sprachliche Verfahren der Unterscheidung von „echten" und „unechten" Mitgliedern sozialer Kategorien. In Wolfgang Eßbach (ed.), *wir/ihr/sie. Identität und Alterität in Theorie und Methode*, 261–282. Würzburg: Ergon.

Deppermann, Arnulf & Reinhold Schmitt. 2007. Koordination. Zur Begründung eines neuen Forschungsgegenstands. In Reinhold Schmitt (ed.), *Koordination. Analysen zur multimodalen Interaktion*, 15–54. Tübingen: Narr.

Dreyer, Stephan, Claudia Lampert & Anne Schulze. 2014. *Kinder- und Onlinewerbung Erscheinungsformen von Werbung im Internet, ihre Wahrnehmung durch Kinder und ihr regulatorischer Kontext*. Leipzig: Vistas Verlag.

Efing, Christian. 2012. Werbekommunikation varietätenlinguistisch. In Nina Janich (ed.), *Handbuch Werbekommunikation. Sprachwissenschaftliche und interdisziplinäre Zugänge*, 161–178. Tübingen: A. Francke.

Ehrhardt, Claus. 2007. Himmlisch hip – teuflisch hot. Jugendsprache in der deutschen und der italienischen Werbekommunikation. In Eva Neuland (ed.): *Jugendsprachen: mehrsprachig – kontrastiv – interkulturell*, 251–266. Frankfurt am M.: Peter Lang Verlag.

Feierabend, Sabine, Theresa Plankenhorn & Thomas Rathgeb. 2017. *JIM-Studie – Jugend, Information, (Multi-)Media. Basisstudie zum Medienumgang 12–19-jähriger in Deutschland*. Stuttgart: MPFS. Available: www.mpfs.de/fileadmin/files/Studien/JIM/2017/JIM_2017.pdf (28 February, 2019)

Frobenius, Maximiliane. 2014. Audience Design in monologues: How vloggers involve their viewers. *Journal of Pragmatics* 72, 59–72.

Harnish, Richard J. & Robert K. Bridget. 2016. Mall Haul Videos: Self-Presentational Motives and the Role of Self-Monitoring. *Psychologie & Marketing* 33/2, 113–124.

Herring, Susan C. 2016. New frontiers in interactive multimodal communication. In Alexandra Georgakopoulou & Tereza Spilioti (eds.), *The Routledge Handbook of Language and Digital Communication*, 398–402. London/New York: Routledge.

Holly, Werner & Ludwig Jäger. 2011. Transkriptionstheoretische Medienanalyse. Vom Anderslesbar-Machen durch intermediale Bezugnahmepraktiken. In Jan Georg Schneider & Hartmut Stöckl (eds.), *Medientheorien und Multimodalität. Ein TV-Werbespot – Sieben methodische Beschreibungsansätze*, 151–168. Köln: Herbert von Harlem Verlag.

Homann, Meike. 2006. *Zielgruppe Jugend im Fokus der Werbung. Verbale und visuelle Kodierungsstrategien jugendgerichteter Anzeigenwerbung in England, Deutschland und Spanien*. Hamburg: Verlag Dr. Kovac.

Horton, Donald & R. Richard Wohl. 1956. Mass communication and para/social interaction. Observations on intimacy at a distance. *Psychiatry* 19, 215–229.

Horton, Donald & Anselm Strauss. 1957. Interaction in Audience-Participation Shows. *The American Journal of Sociology* 62(6/1957), 579–587.

Janich, Nina. 2012. Werbekommunikation pragmatisch. In Nina Janich (ed.), *Handbuch Werbekommunikation. Sprachwissenschaftliche und interdisziplinäre Zugänge*, 213–228. Tübingen: A. Francke.

Jewitt, Carey & Rumiko Oyama. 2001. Visual meaning. A social semiotic approach. In Theo van Leeuwen & Carey Jewitt (eds.), *Handbook of visual analysis*, 134–156. London: SAGE-Publications.

Katheder, Doris. 2008. *Mädchenbilder in deutschen Jugendzeitschriften der Gegenwart. Beiträge zur Medienpädagogik*. Wiesbaden: VS Verlag für Sozialwissenschaften.

Keating, Elisabeth. 2016. The role of the body and the space in digital multimodality. In Alexandra Georgakopoulou & Tereza Spilioti (eds.): *The Routledge handbook of language and digital communication*, 259–272. London/New York: Routledge.

Kelly-Holmes, Helen. 2016. Digital advertising. In Alexandra Georgakopoulou & Tereza Spilioti (eds.), *The Routledge handbook of language and digital communication*, 212–225. London/New York: Routledge.

Kress, Gunther & Theo van Leeuwen. 2006. *Reading images. The grammar of visual design*. Second edn. London/New York: Routledge.

Lévi-Strauss, Claude. 1955. The structural study of myth. *Journal of American Folklore* 68, 428–444.

Meer, Dorothee. 2018. Dagi Bee und die Bewerbung von Jugendlichen: aktuelle Entwicklungen im Bereich der Hypermedien am Beispiel der Textsorte „Tutorial". In Sascha Michel & Steffen Pappert (eds.), *Multimodale Kommunikation im öffentlichen Räumen. Kommunikationsformen und Textsorten zwischen Tradition und Innovation*, 201–230. Stuttgart: ibidem.

Meer, Dorothee. 2018. „Liebe dagi bee du bist wunder wunder hübsch 😊😊😊😊😊" – Identitätskonstruktionen in Kommentaren Jugendlicher zu Videos auf YouTube. In Eva Neuland, Benjamin Könning & Elisa Wessels (eds.), *Jugendliche im Gespräch: Forschungskonzepte, Methoden und Anwendungsfelder aus der Werkstatt der empirischen Sprachforschung*, 299–328. Frankfurt: Lang Verlag.

Meer, Dorothee & Katharina Staubach. In prep. *Coole Starlooks – „Modestrecken" in der BRAVO. Eine textsemiotische Annäherung an Identitätsangebote für Jugendliche*.

Norris, Sigrid. 2004. *Analyzing multimodal interaction: A methodological framework*. London: Routledge.

Staubach, Katharina. 2017. Multimodale Sehflächen lesen. Eine semiotische Analyse jugendlicher Bekleidung. *Zeitschrift für Angewandte Linguistik* 66, 31–58.

Staubach, Katharina. 2018. Was verraten Jugendliche über ihre Kleidung? Ergebnisse einer Interview- und Gruppendiskussionsstudie. In Eva Neuland, Benjamin Könning & Elisa Wessels (eds.), *Jugendliche im Gespräch: Forschungskonzepte, Methoden und Anwendungsfelder aus der Werkstatt der empirischen Sprachforschung*, 151–174. Frankfurt: Lang Verlag.

Stöckl, Hartmut. 2012. Werbekommunikation semiotisch. In Janich Nina (ed.), *Handbuch Werbekommunikation. Sprachwissenschaftliche und interdisziplinäre Zugänge*, 243–262. Tübingen: A. Francke.

Stöckl, Hartmut. 2016. Multimodalität – Semiotische und textlinguistische Grundlagen. Nina Klug & Hartmut Stöckl (eds.), *Handbuch Sprache im multimodalen Kontext*, 3–35. Berlin/Boston: De Gruyter.

Schneider, Jan Georg & Hartmut Stöckl (eds.). 2011. *Medientheorien und Multimodalität. Ein TV-Werbespot – Sieben methodische Beschreibungsansätze*. Köln: Herbert von Harlem Verlag.

Stukenbrock, Anja. 2009. Herausforderungen der multimodalen Transkription. Methodische und theoretische Überlegungen aus der wissenschaftlichen Praxis. In Karin Birkner & Anja Stukenbrock (eds.), *Die Arbeit mit Transkripten in Fortbildung, Lehre und Forschung*, 144–69. Mannheim: Verlag für Gesprächsforschung.

Stukenbrock, Anja. 2010. Überlegungen zu einem multimodalen Verständnis der gesprochenen Sprache am Beispiel deiktischer Verwendungsweisen des Ausdrucks so. In *InLiSt – Interaction and Linguistic Structures* 47. http://www.inlist.uni-bayreuth.de/issues/47/InLiSt47.pdf (28. February, 2019).

Stukenbrock, Anja. 2015. *Deixis in der face-to-face-Interaktion*. Berlin: De Gruyter.

Tolson, Andrew. 2010. A new authenticity? Communicative practices on YouTube. *Critical Discourse* Studies 7(4), 277–289.

Weidner, Beate. 2017. Zwischen Information und Unterhaltung: Multimodale Verfahren des Bewertens im Koch-TV. *Gesprächsforschung – Online-Zeitschrift zur verbalen Interaktion* 18 (2017), 1–33.

Index

aestheticization 222
aesthetics 109, 115, 117, 121, 125
affect 217, 219–220
affordances 173, 177–178, 190, 195
alphabet 70, 72, 75
ambiguity 126, 160, 162, 164
annotation 90, 101
attention 152–153, 164–165

blogging 107, 111, 120
bonding 181–182

camera 152, 154, 159–160, 163–166
camera action 140
capable-of-curation 7
class 204, 222
colour 216–217, 219–220, 222
communication repertoires 172, 174–175, 176–178, 181–182
communicative situation 2, 6–10
composition 218–220
computer-mediated communication 99
consumption 204–205
content analysis 50, 206
context analysis 89–98
contextual extension 192, 199
conviviality 6–7, 9, 11, 14, 16
corporate social media 206
corpus 81–82, 84, 87, 89, 93–94, 96, 98–99
corpus linguistics 89, 100
credibility 245–246, 249–252, 254, 258, 262, 268
cross-media research 172
cultural capital 205, 215, 219

deixis 144, 146
design 207, 211, 219–222
digital discourse 45, 47–48, 52–53, 57
digital influencer advertising 262
digital media 47, 52
digital photography 7, 22, 25
digital video 36
discourse studies 108

distinction 203–204, 213, 219–220, 222
"domain of scrutiny" 146

embodiment 23
emoji 45–46, 49–57, 60–61, 65–74
emotion 66–67
environment 152–153, 164, 166
Ethnomethodological Conversation Analysis (EMCA) 136
evaluation 153, 158–160, 162–163
experiential meaning potential 217
experiential orientation 192, 199
expression 255, 261

Facebook 10
facecam 132, 134, 142, 144
femininity 108–111, 125
food 203–211, 215–222
food photography 204–205
foodways 203–204, 206, 209, 214, 219–220

gaze 25, 27, 30, 36, 144, 178–179, 218, 256–257
genre label 228
gesture 164–165
"good taste" 203–205, 214, 219–222
grammar 54, 60

haul video 246–247, 250–251, 254, 257, 262, 268
hieroglyphics 69, 74
homing blogs 107, 111–112, 115, 117–118, 120, 124–126
hypermedial 246

icon/iconic signs 73–74
identity 250, 262–263
image-centricity 15, 189–195, 197–199
images 46, 54, 58–61
index/indexical signs 73
Instagram 203, 205–207, 209, 211, 215, 217, 219–220, 222

https://doi.org/10.1515/9781501510113-014

Index

interaction 95–96, 134, 136–138, 146, 151, 153–154, 160, 162
interpersonal media-selection 177–178
intimacy 153, 160, 176, 180

language 45–54, 56–58, 60–61
language endangerment 45–46, 50–54, 58–59, 61
language ideology 47, 52, 57–58
layout 10–12
Let's play 131–138, 141–143, 146–148
Listicle 1, 4, 6, 8–12, 14–15
logogram 70, 75–77

materiality 204, 211–214, 219–220
meaning 70–73, 77
media ideology 47–48, 53
"media manifold" 174, 182
mediality 189–195
mediated digital discourse 84, 100
message format 196–198
message size 196, 198
message transmission 196
metadiscourse 47
middle class 107, 109, 112, 117, 121, 125–126
modality 54, 58, 211, 214–220, 222
mode 11, 15, 45, 48, 54, 58, 191
modes 45, 48, 54, 58
moral panic 52, 57, 59
motherhood 107–110, 112, 117, 121, 123–126
multilingual 48, 52–53, 59
multimodality 1, 2, 4, 6–11, 15–16, 19–20, 48, 61, 151–152, 154, 158, 163, 265, 132, 136, 148, 189–200, 203, 222, 246
mutual elaboration 190

narrativity 11, 15
natural language processing 81, 100
network drawings 175
new/social media 195, 198–200
news discourse 45–62
non-verbal 84, 87
noticing 158, 164–165

old/print media 196
osmotic advertising 245, 262

paralinguistic 66, 87, 97, 99
parody 107, 117, 125, 126
participation structure 196, 198
participatory photo-elicitation 176
part-of-speech tagging 81, 88
pattern change 9, 12
pattern stability 6, 9, 10, 12
perception 138–139, 143–144, 146
photo-sharing 171–173, 175, 178–179
point of view (POV) 140, 142, 146
pointing 154, 160, 164–165
privacy settings 197–198
private 111–112, 165–166, 205–206
privilege 204, 206, 209, 219, 222
props 209, 211–214, 216
provenance 214
punctuation 91, 94–96, 100

questionnaire 81, 98–99

recontextualization 107–108, 124–126
referential function 81
relationship 153, 165–166
resemblance 68, 70–73, 75
revisualization 107–108, 124–125
right to look 20, 25, 36–37
ritualization 176–177

self-disclosure 197
selfies 24–25, 30
semiotic ideology 45, 48–49, 52–53, 58, 60
semiotic mode 189, 194, 197–198, 200, 203, 215
semiotic resources 2, 61, 218, 241, 246
shareability 190, 199
sharing 171–182
SMS 81, 88–89, 91, 93, 98–99
social class 110–112
social media 107, 109, 111, 117–118, 126
social networking site 1, 6–8
social relationships 171–174, 182
social semiotics 203, 206
"softeners" 81, 84, 86–87, 91, 97

space 152, 165
stance 153, 160
status 203, 205–206, 214, 219, 222
storicle 15–16, 232, 241
style 68–69, 107, 112, 115, 124–125
supermarkets 203, 205, 220
symbol scheme 72–73, 75
symbol/symbolic sign 75, 77
synchronicity 172, 196

text-image relations 189–195
textual data 84, 87–88
textual function 2, 6–10, 16
texture 203, 217, 219–220
token 71, 75
transgression 117

video game 131–132, 136, 140, 143, 147
videochat 151–154, 164–166

virality 4, 6–9, 14, 16
virtual tour 151–155, 158–160, 163–165
visual communication 45, 48, 58–59, 61
visual elicitation 175–176
visual interaction 171–172, 174–175, 181–182
visual resources 203, 247

watchability 131, 147
worthy-of-curation 7–8
writing/writing system 74
written language 46, 58

youth language 245, 256
YouTube 131–132, 134, 246, 250–251, 254, 261–262, 268

www.ingramcontent.com/pod-product-compliance
Lightning Source LLC
Chambersburg PA
CBHW061935220426
43662CB00012B/1915